War on the Waters

THE LITTLEFIELD HISTORY OF THE CIVIL WAR ERA
Gary W. Gallagher and T. Michael Parrish, editors

*Supported by the Littlefield Fund for Southern History,
University of Texas Libraries*

WAR
on the Waters

The Union and Confederate Navies, 1861–1865

James M. McPherson

UNIVERSITY OF NORTH CAROLINA PRESS *Chapel Hill*

Designed by Kimberly Bryant and set in Miller by Rebecca Evans.
Manufactured in the United States of America.

ISBN 978-0-8078-3588-3

Book Club Edition

To Annie,

who enjoys rocking the boat

Contents

Illustrations and Maps

MAPS

Introduction

In September 1864 Captain Charles Steedman of the U.S. Navy praised Rear Admiral David Glasgow Farragut for his decisive victory over Confederate forts and warships in the battle of Mobile Bay. "That little man," wrote Steedman of the wiry Farragut, who was just under medium height and clean shaven with a determined jaw, "has done more to put down the rebellion than any general except Grant and Sherman."[1]

Steedman's comment was not simply another example of naval boastfulness in the age-old interservice rivalry typical of the nation's armed forces. After many years of studying the American Civil War, I am convinced that Steedman was right. Farragut's victory at Mobile Bay and his even more spectacular achievement in the capture of New Orleans in April 1862, plus the part played by his fleet in the Mississippi River campaigns of 1862 and 1863, did indeed entitle him to equal status with Ulysses S. Grant and William T. Sherman in winning the war.

But Steedman was making a larger point, with which I also agree: the Union navy deserves more credit for Northern victory than it has traditionally received. General Grant made a similar point in his famous *Memoirs* when he praised the role of the navy's Mississippi River Squadron in Grant's most significant victory, the capture of Vicksburg in July 1863. "Without the navy's assistance," wrote Grant, "the campaign could not have been made."[2]

No less a personage than President Abraham Lincoln paid tribute to the contribution of the navy to the opening of the Mississippi and to other Union successes. "The Father of Waters again goes unvexed to the sea," said Lincoln in August 1863. After praising his armies for recent victories, the president added: "Nor must Uncle Sam's Web-feet be forgotten. At all the watery margins they have been present. Not only on the deep sea, the broad bay, and the rapid river, but also up the narrow muddy bayou, and wherever the ground was a little damp, they have been, and made their tracks."[3]

Jefferson Davis never wrote anything like this about the Confederate navy; Lincoln's style was *sui generis*. But the Confederate president might have praised "Uncle Jeff's Web-feet" for their technological innovations and notable achievements with limited resources. Unable to challenge the

Union navy in size and firepower, Southern mariners nevertheless developed ironclad technology, "torpedoes" (naval mines), and even a submarine that sank a Union warship. In the end, if Uncle Sam's Web-feet played a major role in Union victory, the Confederate navy helped to set back the Union cause on more than one occasion.

The four years of the Civil War can be divided into five overlapping parts in which naval clashes paralleled and in part produced a first wave of Union victories in 1861–62, successful Confederate resistance in 1862–63, a revival of Northern momentum in the latter half of 1863, Confederate resuscitation in early 1864, and final Union triumph from the second half of 1864 through the end of the war.

Two of the most important Union military successes in 1861 were accomplished almost entirely by the navy. On August 28–29 a fleet of seven warships battered the Confederate forts guarding Hatteras Inlet in North Carolina into submission without the army troops accompanying the flotilla firing a shot. This victory opened the interior seas of Pamlico and Albemarle Sounds to Union ships and shut down Confederate privateering operations from this sanctuary. Ten weeks later, on November 7, a large Union task force led by Flag Officer Samuel Francis Du Pont similarly pounded the enemy forts guarding Port Royal Bay into surrender, again without the help of the 12,000 soldiers accompanying the fleet. The troops took possession of the sea islands in this wealthy low-country rice and cotton region between Charleston and Savannah, while Du Pont established an extensive naval base for his South Atlantic Blockading Squadron at Port Royal, the largest natural harbor on the South Atlantic coast.

The Union navy's string of solo successes continued well into 1862. On February 6 the "Western Flotilla" of iron-armored river gunboats built by the army but operated by the navy captured Fort Henry on the Tennessee River. Wooden gunboats converted from river steamboats ranged all the way up the Tennessee River (southward) to Florence, Alabama, destroying railroad bridges and opening the way for Union army occupation of this resource-rich region. On April 24–25 Flag Officer Farragut's fleet of oceangoing warships fought its way up the Mississippi River past the forts and gunboats guarding the approaches to New Orleans and forced the surrender of the South's largest city and port. Once again, the Union army's only function was to occupy the prize captured by the navy.

Other Union successes in early 1862, however, were the result of combined operations in which both branches of the service played a cooperative role. On February 7–8 army troops commanded by Brigadier General

Ambrose E. Burnside waded ashore at Roanoke Island—controlling the passage between Pamlico and Albemarle Sounds—and captured its 2,600 defenders while the fleet of sixteen gunboats protected their flank and almost annihilated the flotilla of eight small Confederate vessels. A month later, Burnside's soldiers captured New Bern with crucial naval support, followed in April by similar combined operations that captured Beaufort and Fort Macon, leaving all North Carolina ports except Wilmington in Union hands.

Meanwhile, the brown-water navy on western rivers continued its offensive. Flag Officer Andrew Hull Foote followed his success against Fort Henry with an attack on the Cumberland River bastion of Fort Donelson on February 14, 1862. But this time, Confederate cannoneers gave Foote's armored gunboats a rude surprise, inflicting significant damage and driving them back. That repulse left it up to the army to compel the fort's unconditional surrender to Brigadier General Ulysses S. Grant on February 16. This achievement opened the way to Nashville, which was occupied by Union troops on February 25 with the support of gunboats that kept open the Cumberland River supply line for the rest of the war.

Foote moved most of his Western Flotilla to the Mississippi River, where on April 7 another combined army-navy task force captured Island No. 10, where the borders of Kentucky, Missouri, and Tennessee come together. Two months later, the river navy once again won a major victory all by itself when it sank or captured seven of the eight Confederate gunboats that tried to defend Memphis and raised the American flag over that city on June 6, 1862.

The Battle of Memphis was the Union navy's last unmixed success for some time. The small but intrepid Confederate navy, built from scratch, had already begun to fight back. It inaugurated the second phase of naval warfare, which coincided with Confederate counteroffensives on land that changed the conflict's momentum in 1862–63. Having captured the Norfolk Navy Yard when Virginia seceded in 1861, the Confederacy seized the partially destroyed steam frigate USS *Merrimack* and rebuilt it into the ironclad CSS *Virginia*. She steamed forth into Hampton Roads on March 8, 1862, sank two sailing frigates, and drove two steam frigates aground with the intention of finishing them off the next day. That night, however, the turreted ironclad USS *Monitor* arrived in time to fight the *Virginia* to a draw in an epochal duel on March 9.

Naval warfare would never again be the same after history's first battle between ironclads. Although the *Monitor* neutralized the *Virginia*'s threat to the Union fleet at Hampton Roads, the *Virginia* denied them access to the James River for two months, thereby delaying Union Major General George B. McClellan's campaign against Richmond. When the defending Confederate army pulled back toward its capital in May, Norfolk fell to Union forces and the Confederates had to blow up the *Virginia* because her draft was too deep to retreat up the James River. Union gunboats, including the *Monitor*, moved up the James to Drewry's Bluff only seven miles downriver from Richmond. Northern sailors were confident they could fight their way past enemy artillery on the bluff and force the surrender of Richmond with their big guns trained on the streets, as Farragut had done three weeks earlier at New Orleans. But a combination of obstructions in the river and accurate plunging fire from Confederate cannons stopped them cold on May 15.

Union momentum on the James River and along much of the South Atlantic coast came to a halt in the summer of 1862. The navy began to concentrate its efforts on the blockade, with only moderate success in preventing the growing traffic of blockade-runners into and out of ports like Wilmington, Charleston, and Mobile. The Confederate bastion at Vicksburg on the Mississippi River defied the combined efforts of the Union fleets that had captured New Orleans and Memphis. A Confederate ironclad built on the Yazoo River near Vicksburg, the CSS *Arkansas*, damaged several Union gunboats as it ran entirely through both Union fleets on July 15 to tie up under protection of the guns of Vicksburg. Rampant disease and the summer drop in the water level of the Mississippi forced both Union fleets to pull out, leaving the Confederates in control of the river from Vicksburg down to Port Hudson, which they also fortified.

In 1862 the Confederacy began to deploy on a large scale two naval weapons that achieved considerable success: commerce raiders against American merchant ships and "torpedoes" (mines) in Southern rivers, bays, and estuaries. The two most formidable commerce raiders, the CSS *Florida* and the CSS *Alabama*, came off the stocks at Birkenhead, England, in 1862 and roamed the seas for the next two years burning and ransoming American merchant ships and whalers—sixty-four plus one warship by the *Alabama* alone, and 225 altogether by a dozen raiders in addition to another twenty-seven taken by privateers, mostly early in the war. The exploits of the *Alabama* and the *Florida* drove most American-flagged ships into foreign registry. They also diverted dozens of Union warships from blockade duty to a fruitless effort to find and destroy these raiders on the high seas.

The Confederate Torpedo Bureau began experimenting with naval mines during 1861, but the devices became more sophisticated and their numbers grew exponentially as the war went on. The first Union warship sunk by one of these torpedoes was the USS *Cairo* in the Yazoo River near Vicksburg on December 12, 1862. Union sailors managed to fish up and disarm many of these mines, and others became inoperative because their powder was damp or they broke loose and drifted ashore. But enough detonated to sink or damage forty-three Union ships, making torpedoes the Confederacy's most lethal naval weapon. Their existence also caused a wariness among many Union ship captains that robbed them of the initiative and aggressiveness they had shown early in the war.

For almost a year, from the early summer of 1862 to the late spring of 1863, the Union navy achieved no major successes and suffered two significant failures—the loss of Galveston to a makeshift Confederate gunboat attack on New Year's Day 1863 and the repulse of the ironclad attack on Charleston on April 7. But then the tide began to turn once more. Acting Rear Admiral David D. Porter led several of his river gunboats (now designated the Mississippi Squadron) past the Vicksburg batteries on the night of April 16–17, 1863. They convoyed Grant's army across the river below Vicksburg to begin his campaign against this Confederate stronghold. Porter's gunboats and mortar scows bombarded Vicksburg day and night and sealed off its defenders from aid by water as tightly as Grant's troops did by land. The capitulation of Vicksburg on July 4, 1863, was a major turning point in the war. Admiral Farragut's blue-water warships had also ascended the Mississippi again to Port Hudson to help secure its surrender on July 9. President Lincoln's pronouncement that the Father of Waters again flowed unvexed to the sea was not quite accurate, because Confederate guerrillas continued to vex Union shipping on the Mississippi and its navigable tributaries. For the rest of the war, the main tasks of Porter's squadron were to patrol these rivers, suppress guerrillas, keep river supply lines open for Union armies, seize as much Southern cotton stored along the rivers as they could, and seal off the trans-Mississippi from the rest of the Confederacy—tasks they accomplished with considerable success.

Back in May 1861, U.S. General in Chief Winfield Scott had outlined his "Anaconda Plan" to bring the Confederacy to its knees by closing it off from the world with a blockade of the coast and control of the Mississippi River. By the latter half of 1863, the navy had done a great deal to make this plan a reality. While a trickle of supplies evaded Union naval patrols and crossed the river, and blockade-runners continued to slip in and out of several ports, both the blue-water blockaders and the brown-water gunboats continued to tighten their grip. After the failure of the attack on the forts guarding Charleston on April 7, 1863, the ironclad fleet, now commanded by Rear Admiral John A. Dahlgren, began a methodical, grinding joint operation with the army that never did succeed in capturing Charleston's defenses but virtually closed the port to blockade-runners. By the end of 1863, the Anaconda was forcing the Confederacy to gasp for breath.

In early 1864, however, Southern ingenuity threatened another reversal of fortunes. The submarine *H. L. Hunley* sank a Union blockade ship outside Charleston Harbor in February—the first such occurrence in history. In April the CSS *Albemarle*, an ironclad built on the edge of a cornfield far up the Roanoke River, aided the recapture of Plymouth, North Carolina, and sank a Union gunboat in a rare combined operation with a Confederate army division. In the same month, more than 1,000 miles to the west, a large-scale Union combined operation aimed at Shreveport, Louisiana, on the Red River resulted in a humiliating defeat for Major General Nathaniel P. Banks's Army of the Gulf and almost marooned much of Rear Admiral Porter's squadron in unusually low water at the rapids above Alexandria. A Wisconsin colonel with lumbering experience floating logs down rivers saved the fleet by building wing dams that floated the gunboats over the rapids.

These Confederate successes in the spring of 1864 seemed to presage a long, hot summer of discontent for the Union cause as Grant's overland campaign in Virginia bogged down with heavy casualties and Sherman appeared stymied before Atlanta. Once again, however, the Union navy won the first significant Northern victory in 1864, which turned out to be the beginning of the end for the Confederacy. On August 5, Rear Admiral Farragut damned the torpedoes and led his fleet into Mobile Bay. With the help of an army division, Farragut's sailors captured the forts guarding the bay and closed this port to blockade-runners. Sherman's capture of Atlanta in September and additional army victories in the Shenandoah Valley accelerated the momentum of Union success.

General Robert E. Lee's Army of Northern Virginia still held out, however, sustained in part by supplies brought into Wilmington, the last major Confederate port still available to blockade-runners. Since 1862 the Union navy had been trying to persuade the army to cooperate in joint operations to shut down this port. But General in Chief Henry W. Halleck said he

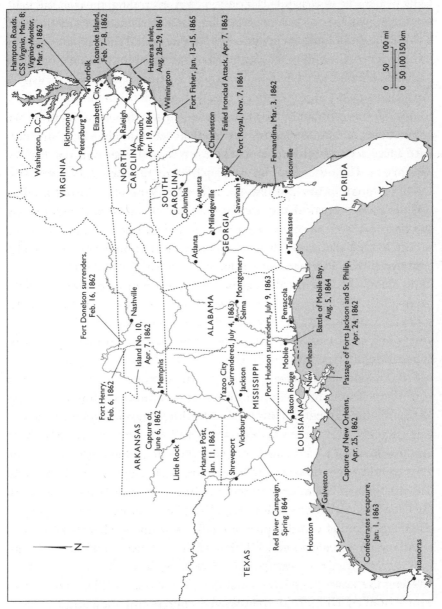

Key Naval Battles of the Civil War

could not spare the troops. Finally, in the fall of 1864, General Grant, Halleck's successor, gave the green light to the operation. Admiral Porter was transferred from the Mississippi Squadron to assemble the largest naval force of the war to attack Fort Fisher, which guarded one of the inlets to the Cape Fear River. On Christmas Eve the fleet began a two-day bombardment of the huge earthwork, but the hapless Major General Benjamin Butler commanding the assault troops decided that the naval gunfire had not softened the defenses enough for a successful attack. A furious Porter persuaded an exasperated Grant to petition Lincoln for Butler's removal from command. Lincoln complied; Grant appointed a new army commander, and on January 13 Porter's fleet renewed its attack, this time with more accurate fire control. The army's assault carried the fort on January 15. The other forts on the Cape Fear and Wilmington itself fell to Union forces in the next few weeks. Next to Vicksburg, this campaign was the most successful and decisive example of combined operations in the war.

The storied armies of the Civil War and the great battles they fought captured public attention during the war and have likewise attracted the lion's share of historical writing and popular memory ever since. This predominant focus on the land war is not unreasonable. The numbers of soldiers involved and the casualties they suffered dwarfed the size of the navies and their casualties. The sailors and marines in the Union navy constituted only 5 percent of all Union personnel, and the naval percentage of Confederate forces was considerably smaller.

Yet the Union navy's contribution to Northern victory was much greater than 5 percent. As this brief summary of naval actions during the war suggests, the Union navy was the dominant force by far in the war on the waters. In personnel and tonnage and firepower of ships, it was at least tenfold larger than the Confederate navy. The contrast with the relative strengths of Union and Confederate armies will strike any student of the Civil War. Although smaller in numbers and thinner in resources than its Union adversary, the Confederate army was able to fight its enemy on almost equal terms for most of the war. The two navies, however, were utterly asymmetrical in every respect—including the sources that have survived for the historian to tell their stories. The victories of Northern fleets contributed much more to the ultimate success of Union strategy than Confederate ships and torpedoes—effective as they sometimes were— did to Confederate strategy. Many actions carried out by the Union navy did not take place against enemy ships but against shore fortifications manned by the Confederate army. Although this book pays due attention to Confederate efforts, the main focus is necessarily on the Union navy.

Knowledge of the dramatic role played by the navies in the Civil War is essential to an understanding of its outcome. The pages that follow seek to convey both the knowledge and the drama.

chapter one

Mobilizing for War

n January 1861 the commandant of the Philadelphia Navy Yard, Captain Samuel Francis Du Pont, wrote an anguished letter to his longtime friend Commander Andrew Hull Foote, head of the Brooklyn Navy Yard. Fifty-seven and fifty-four years old, respectively, Du Pont and Foote had served in the U.S. Navy since they were teenagers. They were destined to become two of the first five admirals in American history a year and a half later. Descendant of a French royalist who had emigrated to America during the French Revolution, Du Pont was a tall and imposing figure with ramrod-straight posture and luxuriant mutton-chop whiskers. Although he resided in the slave state of Delaware, Du Pont had no time for secessionists who were at that moment taking seven states out of the Union and talking about uniting all fifteen slave states in a new nation. "What has made me most sick at heart," he wrote, "is to see the resignations from the Navy" of officers from Southern states. "If I feel sore at these resignations, what should a decent man feel at the doings in the Pensacola Navy Yard?" On January 12 Captain James Armstrong, commandant of the Pensacola Navy Yard, had surrendered this facility and Fort Barrancas to militia from Florida and Alabama without firing a shot. A native of Kentucky and one of the most senior captains in the navy with fifty-one years of service, Armstrong feared that an attempt to defend the navy yard might start a civil war. For this decision he was subsequently tried by court-martial and suspended for five years, ending his career in disgrace. His act brought contempt and shame to the navy, wrote Du Pont. "I stick by the flag and the national government," he declared, "whether my state do or not."[1]

There was no question where Foote's allegiance lay. A Connecticut Yankee, devout Christian, and temperance and antislavery advocate, he fervently believed that patriotism was next only to godliness. Concerning another high-ranking naval officer, however, there were initially some

Captain Samuel Francis Du Pont. This photograph probably dates
from the late 1850s. (Courtesy of the Library of Congress)

doubts. Captain David Glasgow Farragut had served fifty of his fifty-nine years in the U.S. Navy when the state he called home, Virginia, contemplated secession in 1861. Farragut had been born in Tennessee and was married to a Virginian. After his first wife died, he married another Virginia woman. He had a brother in New Orleans and a sister in Mississippi. "God forbid I should ever have to raise my hand against the South," he said to friends in Virginia as the sectional conflict heated up.[2]

Many of Farragut's acquaintances expected him to cast his lot with the new Confederate nation. But he had served at sea under the American flag in the War of 1812 and the Mexican-American War, and he was not about to abandon that flag in 1861. When the new president, Abraham Lincoln, called up the militia after the Confederates attacked Fort Sumter, Farragut expressed approval of his action. His Virginia friends told him that anyone holding this opinion could not live in Norfolk. "Well, then," Farragut replied, "I can live somewhere else." He decided to move to New York. "This act of mine may cause years of separation from your family," he told his wife, "so you must decide quickly whether you will go north or remain here." She resolved to go with him. As they prepared to leave, the thin-lipped captain offered a few parting words to his Virginia neighbors: "You fellows will catch the devil before you get through with this business." When Virginia seceded and its militia seized the Norfolk Navy Yard, Farragut told his brother: "I found things were growing worse . . . and told her [his wife] she must go at once. We all packed up in 2 hours & left on the evening steamer."[3] Farragut no doubt remembered this hurried departure when his victorious fleet steamed into New Orleans almost exactly a year later.

One of Farragut's Southern friends made the same choice he had made. Born in South Carolina, Percival Drayton was one of the most promising officers in the navy when his native state seceded on December 20, 1860. Although several of his numerous relatives fought for the Confederacy—including his older brother Thomas, a low-country planter and Confederate general—Percival never hesitated. "The whole conduct of the South has destroyed the little sympathy I once had for them," he wrote a month after South Carolinians fired on Fort Sumter. "A country can recover from anything except dismemberment. I hope this war will be carried on until any party advocating so suicidal a course is crushed out." Drayton became one of the best fighting captains in the Union navy, serving with Du Pont in the capture of Port Royal and the attack on Charleston and with Farragut as fleet captain at Mobile Bay. While commanding the steam sloop

USS *Pawnee* in operations along the South Carolina coast in November 1861, Drayton wrote to a friend in New York: "To think of my pitching in here right into such a nest of my relations . . . is very hard but I cannot exactly see the difference between their fighting against me and I against them except that their cause is as unholy a one as the world has ever seen and mine is just the reverse."[4]

Drayton's and Farragut's loyalty to the Union was not typical of officers from Confederate states. Some 259 of them resigned or were dismissed from the navy. Most went into the new Confederate navy. One hundred and forty of them had held the top three ranks in the U.S. Navy: thirteen captains, thirty-three commanders, and ninety-four lieutenants. Forty Southern officers of these ranks, mostly from border states that did not secede, remained in the Union navy.[5]

One of those who went South became the first—and, until almost the end of the war, the only—admiral in the Confederate navy: Franklin Buchanan of Maryland. He was a veteran of forty-five years in the U.S. Navy, the first superintendent of the Naval Academy when it was established in 1845, second in command of Matthew Perry's famous expedition to Japan (1852–54), and commandant of the Washington Navy Yard when the Civil War began. Three days after a secessionist mob in Baltimore attacked the 6th Massachusetts Militia on its way through the city to Washington on April 19, Buchanan entered the office of Secretary of the Navy Gideon Welles. The two men were a study in contrasts. Buchanan was smooth-shaven with a high forehead and receding hairline, thin lips turned down in a perpetual frown, and an imperious manner of command. Welles's naval experience was limited to a two-year stint as the civilian head of the Bureau of Provisions and Clothing during the Mexican-American War. A long career as a political journalist in Connecticut had given little promise of the resourceful administrative capacity he would demonstrate as wartime secretary of the navy. The wig he wore with brown curly hair down almost to his shoulders contrasted oddly with his long white beard, which caused President Lincoln to refer to him fondly as "Father Neptune." The president had announced a blockade of Confederate ports five days earlier, and Welles needed all the help he could get from experienced officers like Buchanan to make it work. But Buchanan had come to tender his resignation from the navy. The riot in Baltimore convinced him that Maryland would secede and join the Confederacy. It was his duty to go with his state. Welles expressed his regrets, but he did not try to talk Buchanan out of resigning. "Every man has to judge for himself," acknowledged the secretary.

Union Secretary of the Navy Gideon Welles. (Courtesy of the Library of Congress)

As the days went by and Maryland did not secede, Buchanan had second thoughts. Perhaps he had acted rashly. He tried to withdraw his resignation. But Welles wanted no sunshine patriots in his navy. Like Du Pont, he was angry at officers who had resigned to fight against their country. To Buchanan's request to retract his resignation, the secretary replied icily: "By direction of the president, your name has been stricken from the rolls of the Navy."[6]

Welles had been soured by an experience three weeks earlier concerning another senior Southern officer, Captain Samuel Barron of Virginia. As Welles sat eating dinner at the Willard Hotel on the evening of April 1 (his wife and family had not yet joined him in Washington), he was startled to receive a packet of papers from John Nicolay, one of Lincoln's private secretaries. Welles was even more astonished when he read a series of orders signed by the president that reassigned Captain Silas Stringham from his post as Welles's assistant to select officers for various commands and replaced him with Captain Barron. Welles rose quickly from his unfinished dinner and rushed to the White House. As Father Neptune burst into Lincoln's office brandishing the orders like a trident,

Commodore Franklin Buchanan of the Confederate navy. (Courtesy of the Library of Congress)

Lincoln looked up apprehensively. "What have I done wrong?" he asked. Welles showed him the orders, which Lincoln sheepishly admitted he had signed without reading carefully. They had been prepared under Secretary of State William H. Seward's supervision, he said, and the president was so distracted by a dozen other problems that he had mistakenly trusted Seward's recommendation.

This was not the first nor the last time Seward meddled with matters outside his department. Lincoln told Welles to ignore the orders. Both men recognized that this incident was part of Seward's effort to keep the Upper South states, especially Virginia, from seceding. Still under the erroneous impression that he was the "premier" of the administration, Seward naively believed that by giving Barron authority over personnel matters in the Navy Department, he would cement Barron's—and Virginia's—loyalty to the Union. Welles considered Barron a secessionist—the last man to be trusted with personnel assignments. He was right. Unknown to Lincoln or Welles at the time, Barron had already been appointed a captain in the Confederate navy—which as yet scarcely existed—and would soon resign to go South.[7]

Seward's fingerprints were all over another scheme to interfere with the navy as part of his increasingly desperate intrigues to conciliate the South by avoiding confrontation with the Confederacy at Fort Sumter. The situation at that potential tinderbox in Charleston Harbor had remained tense since South Carolina artillery in January had turned back the chartered ship *Star of the West*, which was carrying reinforcements to the fort. An uneasy truce likewise existed between the Florida militia that seized Pensacola and U.S. soldiers who continued to hold Fort Pickens across the entrance to Pensacola Bay. The first effort by the new Lincoln administration to reinforce Fort Pickens had foundered because the orders to the captain of the USS *Brooklyn* to land the troops were signed by the army's adjutant general and not by anyone in the Navy Department. Welles immediately signed and sent new orders, which were successfully carried out on April 14.[8]

In the meantime, however, Lincoln had also decided to resupply the U.S. garrison at Fort Sumter, even at the risk of provoking the Confederates to fire on the fort and supply ships. Seward opposed this decision. He continued to insist that a confrontation at Fort Sumter would start a war and drive the Upper South into secession. He also maintained that withdrawal of troops from the fort would encourage Unionists in the South (whose numbers he vastly overestimated) to regain influence there. Lincoln feared that withdrawal from Fort Sumter, which had become the master symbol of divided sovereignty, would undermine Southern Unionism by implicitly recognizing Confederate legitimacy.

Lincoln's Postmaster General, Montgomery Blair, thought so too. He introduced Lincoln to his brother-in-law Gustavus V. Fox, a former navy lieutenant, who suggested a way to run supplies and troops into Fort Sumter at night with shallow-draft tugboats. With his rotund figure and high, balding forehead, Fox did not look much like a dashing naval officer. But he had a can-do manner that convinced Lincoln—who was already weary of advisers who told him that something or other could *not* be done—that this thing *could* be done. He told Fox to work with Welles to assemble the supplies and warships to escort the troop transports and tugs to Charleston.[9]

Only three warships and the Treasury Department's revenue cutter *Harriet Lane* were available for the mission. The largest warship was the USS *Powhatan*, a 2,400-ton sidewheel steamer carrying ten big guns. It became the centerpiece of a monumental mix-up that illustrated the disarray of the Lincoln administration in the midst of this crisis. On April 1 Welles ordered the Brooklyn Navy Yard to ready the *Powhatan* for the Fort Sumter expedition. On the same date, Seward wrote his infamous memorandum to the president suggesting that he might reunite the nation by provoking a war with France or Spain and urging him to reinforce Fort Pickens as an assertion of authority but abandon Fort Sumter as a gesture of conciliation. Lincoln in effect gently slapped Seward's wrist for this effrontery. But on that day Seward also engineered the order placing Samuel Barron in charge of assigning naval personnel, which Welles got Lincoln to rescind. And Seward promulgated yet another dispatch on April 1 and got Lincoln to sign it; this one ordered the commander of the Brooklyn Navy Yard to prepare the *Powhatan* for an expedition to reinforce Fort Pickens. "She is bound on secret service," directed Seward, "and you will under no circumstances communicate to the Navy Department the fact that she is fitting out."[10]

Captain Foote, head of the navy yard, must have scratched his head when he received these two contradictory orders, the first signed by the secretary of the navy and the other by the president. Was one of them an April Fool's joke? Foote and Welles had been friends since their schoolboy days together in Connecticut forty years earlier. Despite the admonition to keep the second order secret from Welles, Foote sent a cryptic telegram questioning it.[11] On April 5 Welles finally realized what was going on. He confronted Seward, and both rushed to the White House. Although it was almost midnight, Lincoln was still awake. When he understood the nature of this messy contretemps, he ruefully admitted his responsibility and told Seward to send a wire to the navy yard to restore the *Powhatan* to the Fort Sumter expedition. Seward did so, but whether intentionally or not, he signed the telegram simply "Seward" without adding "By order of the President." When it reached Brooklyn, the *Powhatan* had already left under command of Lieutenant David D. Porter. A fast tug caught up with Porter before he reached the open sea, but when he read the telegram signed by Seward, he refused to obey it, claiming that the earlier order signed by Lincoln took precedence. The *Powhatan* continued to Fort Pickens, which had already been reinforced by the time it arrived.[12]

In the end, the *Powhatan*'s absence from the Fort Sumter expedition made no difference to the outcome. The nature of this operation had changed since Fox first suggested it. Lincoln realized that an effort to reinforce Sumter with 200 soldiers was likely to provoke shooting in which the North might appear to be the aggressor. So he decided to separate the issues of reinforcement and resupply and to notify the governor of South Carolina of his intentions. On April 6 he sent a messenger to tell Governor Francis Pickens to "expect an attempt will be made to supply Fort-Sumpter [a common misspelling] with provisions only; and if such attempt be not resisted, no effort to throw in men, arms, or ammunition, will be made, without further notice, or in case of an attack on the fort."[13] The governor forwarded this message to Brigadier General Pierre G. T. Beauregard, commander of the Confederate forces ringing Charleston Harbor. Beauregard immediately relayed it to President Jefferson Davis and his cabinet in Montgomery.

Lincoln had deftly put Davis on the spot. If he allowed the supplies to go in, the Federal presence at Fort Sumter would remain and the Confederate claim of sovereignty would lose credibility. But if Confederate guns made an unprovoked attack on the fort or on the boats bringing "food for hungry men," Davis would stand convicted of starting a war, which would unite the North and perhaps divide the Southern states. Davis did not hesitate. He ordered Beauregard to give notice and to open fire if Major Robert Anderson, commander of the eighty-odd soldiers in Fort Sumter, did not evacuate. Fox and his fleet were delayed and scattered by a storm; the tugs had to put into a shelter port and never arrived at all. By the time the rest of the fleet rendezvoused off the bar at the entrance to Charleston Harbor, Fort Sumter was under attack and the seas were too rough for the ships to get over the bar. The fort lowered the American flag in surrender on April 14. And the war came.

It came in such a way as to unite a previously divided Northern people in support of "putting down the rebellion." And Lincoln's call for militia to suppress the insurrection caused four more Upper South states to secede—but significantly, not the border slave states of Kentucky, Maryland, Missouri, and Delaware.

Fox was dejected by the failure of his mission and angry about the diversion of the *Powhatan*. Lincoln consoled him. "You and I both anticipated that the cause of the country would be advanced by making the attempt to provision Fort-Sumpter, even if it should fail," he wrote to Fox on May 1. "It is no small consolation now to feel that our anticipation is justified by the result." Lincoln assured Fox that "the qualities you developed in the effort, have greatly heightened you, in my estimation. For a daring and dangerous enterprise, of a similar character, you would, to-day, be the man, of all my acquaintances, whom I should select."[14]

A week later, Lincoln ordered Welles to cut any red tape that might prevent Fox's appointment as chief clerk of the Navy Department. "He is a live man," Lincoln wrote, "whose services we cannot well dispense with."[15] Welles appointed Fox that very day. In July Congress created the position of assistant secretary of the navy, and Lincoln promoted Fox to that job. In effect, Fox exercised the function of chief of naval operations for the next four years. Although his brusque manner and tendency to make snap judgments rubbed some naval officers the wrong way—Farragut once complained that he "assumes too much and presumes too much"— Fox and Welles worked well together and imparted great energy into an institution burdened with a lot of deadwood at the beginning of the war. In June 1862 Samuel F. Du Pont told his wife, who did not like Fox, that "all the past administrations of the Navy put together can in no manner compare with this last year in energy, development, and power." Fox could be irritating, acknowledged Du Pont: "I am often faulted by him in details, very provoking it is true, but these sink when I reflect that we have two hundred ships of war with rifle cannon now on the ocean—when in March [April] '61 we had not one within reach to save the Norfolk Navy Yard."[16]

WITHIN A WEEK OF THE attack on Fort Sumter, Presidents Davis and Lincoln issued proclamations that shaped significant elements of their respective naval strategies. On April 17 Davis offered letters of marque to private ships authorizing them to capture American-flagged merchant vessels. As the weaker naval power in two wars against Britain, the United States had commissioned swarms of privateers to prey on British ships and force the Royal Navy to divert its warships to commerce protection. Now the Confederacy proposed to pursue the same strategy against the United States. In a proclamation issued two days later announcing a blockade of Confederate ports, Lincoln declared that captured privateers would be tried for piracy.[17]

Lincoln's proclamation contained an internal inconsistency. The definition of privateers as pirates was grounded in the theory that the Confederacy was not a nation but an association of insurrectionists—"rebels" in the common terminology. At the same time, however, the declaration of a blockade seemed to recognize the legitimacy of the Confederacy, for blockades were an instrument of war between nations. For that reason, some Northerners—most notably Secretary of the Navy Welles—urged the president simply to announce a closure of ports in the rebellious states. To enforce such closure, however, would require warships stationed off these ports, which amounted to a blockade. The British government warned the United States that it would not respect a proclamation closing certain ports to international trade. The British minister to the United States, Lord Lyons, pointed out that a declaration closing Southern ports would cause foreign powers to recognize the Confederacy as controlling these ports *de jure*, as they already controlled them *de facto*, so they could trade freely with the Confederacy.[18] Having relied on blockades in their own numerous wars, however, Britain *would* respect a blockade imposed under international law. Lincoln took these points seriously and decided against the closure option. In effect, by imposing a blockade, the United States treated the Confederacy as a belligerent power but not as a nation.

That compromise was not forged immediately, however, and did not resolve the question of the status of privateers. Two dozen of them soon swooped out along the Atlantic coast and the Gulf of Mexico. They captured at least twenty-seven prizes, mainly in the spring and summer of 1861.[19] The most notorious and successful privateer was the brig *Jefferson Davis* (a former slave ship), which captured eight prizes in July and August. One of them was the schooner *S. J. Waring*, whose cook and steward was William Tillman, a free Negro. A prize crew of five men took the *S. J. Waring* toward the *Jefferson Davis*'s home port of Charleston. Tillman and two other crew members of the *Waring* remained on board. Certain that he would be sold into slavery when the *Waring* reached Charleston, Tillman killed the sleeping prize master and two sailors on the night of July 16–17. He released the two Yankee crewmen, and they sailed the recaptured prize back to New York, where Tillman was hailed as one of the war's first heroes. "To this colored man was the nation indebted for the first vindication of its honor at sea," declared the *New York Tribune*. "It goes far to console us for the sad reverse of our arms at Bull Run."[20]

The Union navy recaptured other prizes and also captured the crew of the privateer *Petrel* in July 1861. In a letter to Lincoln on July 16, President Jefferson Davis warned that he would order the execution of a Union prisoner of war for each member of a privateer crew executed for piracy.[21] The U.S. government nevertheless proceeded to try the *Petrel* crew in federal court in Philadelphia. Four of them were convicted. Several captured crewmen of the *Jefferson Davis* were also convicted. True to his word, President Davis ordered lots drawn by Union prisoners, with the losers (including a grandson of Paul Revere) to be hanged if the privateers suffered that fate. The Lincoln administration backed down in February 1862 and thereafter treated such captives as prisoners of war.[22]

By that time the privateers had virtually disappeared from the seas. Other nations refused to admit prizes to their ports, and the tightening Union blockade made it too difficult to bring them into Confederate ports. The future of Confederate commerce raiding belonged to naval cruisers, fast and well-armed steamers commanded by Confederate officers. They burned most of their captures rather than seizing them as prizes. Most of these cruisers were built or bought abroad, but the first one, the CSS *Sumter*, was a merchant ship purchased in New Orleans at the beginning of the war and converted into a warship. Like other seagoing steamers on both sides in the Civil War, the *Sumter* carried sails (a bark rig in her case) for long-distance cruising and fired up the boilers when needed for speed and maneuverability, or in adverse conditions of wind and weather.

The *Sumter*'s commander was Raphael Semmes, who became the most famous of all Confederate sea captains. A veteran of thirty-five years in the U.S. Navy, he resigned in 1861 when his home state of Alabama seceded. A handsome, dashing figure with a waxed handlebar mustache and small goatee, Semmes was unexcelled in seamanship in both the old navy and his new one. He was also a strong proslavery partisan. During his wartime cruises in the Caribbean and along the Brazilian coast, he often noted in his journal that the Confederacy was fighting not only for the defense of slavery in the South but also in Cuba and Brazil, the only other Western hemisphere societies where it still existed. To the governor of Martinique "I explained the true issue of the war, to wit, an abolition crusade against our slave property." He told the president of a Brazilian province in September 1861 that "this war was in fact a war as much in behalf of Brazil as ourselves; that we were fighting the first battle in favor of slavery, and that if we were beaten in this contest, Brazil would be the next one to be assailed by Yankee and English propagandists."[23]

In mid-June 1861 Semmes completed his preparations for the *Sumter*'s cruise to hunt Yankee merchantmen and dropped down the Mississippi to wait for a chance to evade the Union warships guarding each of the passes into the Gulf of Mexico. On June 30 he learned that the USS *Brooklyn* had gone off after a suspected blockade-runner. Semmes seized the opportunity and steamed into the Gulf at top speed. The returning *Brooklyn* took up the chase. The weight of her armament outgunned the *Sumter*'s by three to one. Black smoke poured from the funnels of both ships as they

Captain Raphael Semmes of the Confederate navy. (Courtesy of the Library of Congress)

built up maximum steam pressure. They also set all sails for greater speed. The *Sumter* could sail closer to the wind and soon left the larger *Brooklyn* behind.

Two days later, the *Sumter* captured her first prize, the sailing vessel *Golden Rocket*. She "made a beautiful bonfire," Semmes wrote, "and we did not enjoy the spectacle less because she was from the black Republican State of Maine."[24] During the next four days, the *Sumter* captured seven more American merchant vessels and tried to take them to Cuba as prizes. The Spanish government, having declared its neutrality in the American Civil War, interned them instead. Semmes departed in disgust and captured several more ships over the next few months. He burned them if both ship and cargo were American, and he bonded them (the value of the ship to be paid to the Confederacy after the war) if the ship's papers showed the cargo to belong to neutrals.

Semmes made effective use of a time-honored ruse in these captures. The *Sumter* flew the American flag as it approached similarly flagged merchant vessels. After ordering the ship hove to (they were all sailing vessels), Semmes ran up the Confederate flag as its guns bore on the hapless merchantman. By January 18, 1862, when the *Sumter* put into Gibraltar for repairs, she had captured eighteen ships altogether. Union warships blockaded the *Sumter* at Gibraltar. Semmes finally left her there and departed for England, from where he went on to perform even more destructive deeds as captain of the CSS *Alabama*. A Liverpool merchant bought the *Sumter* and turned her into a blockade-runner named *Gibraltar*.[25]

The Confederate strategy of diverting blockade ships into the pursuit of privateers and commerce raiders was working. From May 1861 onward, petitions poured into the Navy Department from shipping firms, bankers, and insurance companies demanding protection for merchant vessels. Newspaper editorials berated Welles for the navy's failure to catch the "pirates."[26] Welles was doing his best. Orders went out to a dozen or more navy captains to hunt down privateers and the *Sumter*. These instructions to Commander James S. Palmer of the USS *Iroquois* were typical of such orders: "You will continue in pursuit of the *Sumter* until you learn positively she has been captured or destroyed. You will then remain in the West Indies in search of other privateers and for the protection of American interests until further ordered."[27]

The ocean is a big place, however, and a single ship can be as hard to find as the proverbial needle in a haystack. Even the Gulf of Mexico and the Caribbean Sea cover thousands of square miles where as skillful a sailor as Semmes could evade his pursuers. American consuls in several countries tried to gain information about the *Sumter*'s location and pass it along to naval commanders. Union warships would go to where the raider was last reported and discover that she had left three days earlier for an unknown destination. The captain's clerk on the *Iroquois* expressed the frustration of that ship's crew: "We still keep going after the *Sumpter* and she still escapes us." On August 13, 1861, Lieutenant David D. Porter of the *Powhatan* reported to Welles that the *Sumter* was said to be short of coal, so Semmes "is in a position now where he can't escape, if properly looked after, at Porto Cabello." Porter kept up the futile pursuit, writing six weeks later that "I have chased her from point to point." At each place she was reported to have been, there was no sign of her. "I had to speculate on the course she would likely pursue," he admitted in frustration. "I can form no idea where the *Sumter* is at this time."[28]

IN THESE EARLY MONTHS of the war, Confederate efforts to wreak havoc on the American merchant marine and deflect blockade ships seemed more successful than the blockade itself. But the potential for a blockade to constrict the Confederate war effort was much greater than the raiders' potential to damage the Northern economy. As an agricultural society with little industry, the Confederacy was heavily dependent on imports of war matériel and export of cotton to pay for it. An effective blockade would do serious damage to this process.

The key word here, however, is "effective." After the secession of Virginia and the imminent departure of North Carolina, Lincoln extended the blockade to these states on April 27, 1861.[29] To patrol a coastline of 3,500 miles from Virginia to Texas with 189 harbors and coves where cargo could be landed was a herculean task. Only a dozen of these harbors had railroad connections to the interior, but imposing an effective blockade on just these ports would require large numbers of ships to cover the multiple channels and rivers and inland waterways radiating from or connecting several of them.

At the war's beginning, the Union navy did not have enough ships on hand to do more than show the flag at a few of these waterways. In April 1861 the navy had only a dozen warships in American waters, five of them sailing vessels that could perhaps catch other sailing ships trying to evade the blockade but were of little use against steamers. Twenty-six other warships—seventeen of them steam-powered—were scattered around the world from the Mediterranean Sea to the coasts of Africa and China. Of the navy's six new steam frigates and thirteen new steam sloops constructed since 1855 in a major naval buildup, only two of the sloops and none of the frigates were operational in home waters. Five of the six frigates, in fact, were laid up at navy yards for repairs.[30]

Orders went out to most of the ships in foreign waters to return home. Welles also embarked on a crash program to buy or charter as many merchant steamers, passenger steamers, and even New York ferryboats as he could that were capable of conversion into armed vessels for blockade duty. His purchasing agent for many of these ships was George D. Morgan, a New York businessman who also happened to be Welles's brother-in-law. They were embarrassed by charges of nepotism. But Morgan was an honest and savvy agent. Although he earned $70,000 in commissions for the eventual total of eighty-nine ships that he purchased, the navy got them for very reasonable prices. The department also bought eighty-seven other vessels from various sources in 1861. In addition, Welles contracted for the building of twenty-three new ships of about 500 tons each (the famous "ninety-day gunboats") plus fourteen screw sloops and twelve sidewheelers that began to come on line in the fall of 1861. The British minister to the United States, Lord Lyons, was impressed. He informed Foreign Secretary Lord Russell in May 1861 that "the greatest activity prevails in the United States Navy yards. Vessels are being fitted out with the utmost speed, and many have been purchased, with a view to establish the blockade effectively."[31]

The naval buildup included men as well as ships. On the eve of the war, the U.S. Navy numbered about 7,600 enlisted men and 1,200 officers of all ranks from ensign to captain. Welles persuaded Lincoln to authorize by executive order the recruitment of an additional 18,000 men for terms of one to three years. The president announced this action in a proclamation dated May 3, 1861. Many of these men would be drawn from the merchant marine and would enter the service as able seamen or ordinary seamen, depending on their level of skill and experience. Most, however, enlisted with little or no seafaring experience and were rated as landsmen or "boys" (seventeen or younger). Within two months, the Union navy had expanded to 13,000 men plus about 2,000 officers. By December 1862 the total number of naval personnel had grown to about 28,000 sailors and officers plus 12,000 mechanics and laborers in navy yards. In early 1865 the Union navy reached its maximum strength of 51,500 men and 16,880 mechanics and laborers. The total number of Union sailors and officers during the war as a whole was 101,207 because many sailors whose enlistment terms expired did not reenlist. The Confederate navy reached the peak of its strength at the end of 1864 with 4,966 enlisted men and officers. The Confederate total for the entire war is unknown, but because reenlistment was mandatory, that number probably exceeded the peak by only 1,000 or 2,000 men.[32]

Enlisted Union naval personnel differed in significant ways from volunteer soldiers: their average age was slightly older (twenty-six compared with twenty-five); they were more urban and working-class; 92 percent were from New England and mid-Atlantic states; and they were less literate, with a higher percentage of foreign-born (45 percent compared with 25 percent of soldiers) and of African Americans (about 17 percent compared with 9 percent in the army). Comparable data for Confederate sailors is not available, but nearly 20 percent of them were Irish-born—about four times the proportion of men in the Confederate army.[33]

While 97 percent of Union soldiers enlisted in the U.S. Volunteers rather than the Regular Army, there was no "volunteer" Union navy as such, so all sailors were part of the Regular U.S. Navy. But the officers who entered the navy from civilian life (almost all from the merchant marine) carried the designation of "acting" rather than a Regular rank: acting master, acting lieutenant, and so on. In December 1863 there were 1,977 "acting" officers from lieutenant (only sixty-eight of those) down to master's mate and 469 Regular navy officers from admiral down to ensign. Even though several acting officers commanded gunboats or ships, they held no higher rank than acting lieutenant initially, though by January 1865 thirteen of them had been promoted to acting lieutenant commander.[34] A much higher percentage of officers in the Union navy were long-term Regulars than in the army. They were also somewhat older and considerably more cosmopolitan, many having traveled all over the world in their decades of sea duty before 1861. Because there was no separate volunteer navy, and because of a greater social-class distance between officers and men in the navy than in the volunteer army regiments, the Union navy was more professional and disciplined than the army.

The Confederacy began the war with a substantial cadre of veteran officers who had resigned from the U.S. Navy, but it had almost no ships or enlisted men and only a tiny number of merchant mariners to draw on for experienced sailors. The South had important assets, however, in the high quality of many of its officers and in its secretary of the navy, Stephen R. Mallory. As a judge in Key West during the 1830s and 1840s, Mallory gained considerable maritime expertise while adjudicating the claims of shipowners and salvage wreckers in that notorious graveyard of ships. Elected to the U.S. Senate from Florida in 1851, he became chairman of the Naval Affairs Committee and helped steer through legislation to modernize the navy by the construction of powerful new steam frigates and sloops. A moderate who initially opposed secession, Mallory went with his state when Florida left the Union. A strong proponent of technological progress, he had informed himself about the new ironclad warships built by the British and French navies. He recognized that the fledgling Confederate navy could never match its enemy in quantity and firepower of traditional warships. From the outset, therefore, he focused on quality and innovation to challenge the Union blockade and to defend the Confederate coast.[35]

Mallory and his not-yet-existent navy got a huge windfall with the capture of the Gosport Navy Yard at Norfolk on April 20, 1861. Tensions had been building at the yard during the spring. Its commander, sixty-eight-year-old Commodore Charles S. McCauley, had been in the U.S. Navy since before Abraham Lincoln was born. McCauley was a native Phila-

Confederate Secretary of the Navy Stephen R. Mallory. (Courtesy of the Library of Congress)

delphian whose loyalty to the flag was undoubted, but he had achieved command of one of the navy's largest facilities more by seniority than by ability. Ten ships were laid up for repairs at the yard. Most of them were old sailing vessels. The exception was the forty-gun USS *Merrimack*, one of the proud new steam frigates, whose faulty engines were being rebuilt. On April 10 Welles ordered McCauley to make sure the *Merrimack* was ready to be moved to Philadelphia if Virginia secessionists threatened to take over the yard. But Welles added what turned out to be a fatal qualification: "It is desirable that there should be no steps taken to give needless alarm. . . . Exercise your own judgment."[36]

Most of McCauley's subordinate officers were Virginians. They convinced him that any signs of moving the *Merrimack* would provoke the trigger-happy militia gathering near the facility. Welles seemed to realize that McCauley would prove weak and indecisive in the face of this pressure. On April 11 he sent unequivocal orders to "have the *Merrimack* prepared" to depart and on the 12th to have her "removed to the Philadelphia Navy Yard with the utmost dispatch." McCauley replied that the engines would take four weeks to repair. Welles sent to Norfolk the navy's chief engineer, Benjamin F. Isherwood, who had the engines in shape to get up steam and depart on April 17.[37]

That day, the Virginia convention voted to secede, and a thousand militia headed for the yard. Welles dispatched Captain Hiram Paulding with the USS *Pawnee* to stiffen McCauley's backbone and get everything of value out of the yard that he could, including the *Merrimack*. But McCauley, now completely under the sway of younger officers—most of whom would soon resign and go over to the Confederacy—refused to let the *Merrimack* go. Instead, as the militia was poised to attack, he ordered all of the ships scuttled, "being satisfied," as he later explained to Welles, "that with the small force under my command the yard was no longer tenable." By the time Paulding arrived on the 20th the yard was ablaze and the ships scuttled except for the undamaged sailing frigate USS *Cumberland*, which Paulding had towed to safety. Finding the rest of the ships, including the *Merrimack*, beyond saving, Paulding ordered his men to finish the job in order to deny the rebels the dry dock, guns, ammunition, and anything else of value.[38]

They did not have time to carry out the destruction effectively. Virginians took over an undamaged dry dock, 1,200 cannon including fifty-two big Dahlgren smoothbores, the navy's most advanced weapon, and thousands of shot and shells. Many of the guns and much of the ammunition were soon on their way to every corner of the South, where they would be placed in the dozens of new and existing forts the Confederacy was building and upgrading to defend its coast and rivers. Coming so soon after the fall of Fort Sumter, the loss of the Gosport Navy Yard was a dispiriting disaster for the Union navy and a terrific boost of morale for the Confederacy. And the most important consequence was not yet known. Although burned to the waterline, the *Merrimack*'s hull and even its balky engines had survived intact, ready to be reincarnated as the CSS *Virginia*.

The conversion of the *Merrimack* into a powerful ironclad was a key part of Stephen Mallory's strategy of countering Northern naval superiority with Southern ingenuity. In June 1861 Mallory put one of the Confederacy's brightest young naval officers, Lieutenant John Mercer Brooke, in charge of this conversion. "There is but one way of successfully combating the North," wrote Brooke in an expression of his own as well as Mallory's position, and "that is to avail ourselves of the means we possess and build proper vessels superior to those of the enemy. This we can do as the vessels of the enemy must be built *for sea* whilst ours need only to navigate the southern bays rivers etc."[39]

It was true that Union blockading ships must have seagoing capability, and some of them were too large and deep-drafted to cross the bars and operate in Southern estuaries and rivers. But before the CSS *Virginia* and other new Confederate weapons could be ready, the traditional ships of the Union navy had scored major victories and Northern inventiveness had enabled new Union gunboats to dominate those Southern bays and rivers as well.

chapter two

Establishing the Blockade

The Union navy's primary task throughout the war was the blockade. In May 1861 Secretary Welles created the Atlantic Blockading Squadron to cover the South Atlantic coast from the Chesapeake Bay to the tip of Florida and the Gulf Blockading Squadron to patrol the Gulf Coast from Florida to Brownsville, Texas, on the border with Mexico. Welles appointed sixty-three-year-old Commodore Silas Stringham to command the Atlantic Squadron and seventy-year-old Captain William Mervine to command the Gulf Squadron. Each officer had been in the navy for fifty-two years. They were on the downward slope of honorable careers, but Welles was not yet ready to challenge the tradition of seniority for senior commands.

The base for the Atlantic Squadron was at Hampton Roads, where the army had retained control of Fort Monroe across four miles of water from Norfolk even as the Confederates seized the Gosport Navy Yard. Mervine's headquarters were in Key West. The distance in a *straight* line from each squadron's base to the far end of its blockade responsibilities was a thousand miles. Surely, the British minister Lord Lyons told Secretary of State Seward, the navy did not have a "force sufficient to establish an effective blockade of such a length of coast." But Seward blithely assured Lyons that "the whole would be blockaded, and blockaded effectively."[1]

Seward's assurance remained a hope rather than a reality for many months. In July Stringham reported sixteen ships on blockade duty in his squadron. But seven of them were at or near Hampton Roads, leaving only nine others for the rest of the South Atlantic coast. Of the sixteen vessels, four were slow sailing ships. At least they could be provisioned for several months at sea, while the steamers had to return every two or three weeks for coal and were vulnerable to breakdowns, so at any given time a substantial number of them were not on station. And three of Stringham's ships were the big steam frigates *Minnesota*, *Wabash*, and *Roanoke*—sister ships of the *Merrimack*—that carried powerful broadsides but were like an elephant chasing a gazelle when trying to catch a fast, nimble, shallow-drafted blockade-runner.[2]

New and faster gunboats would soon come on line, but in 1861 the blockade was a leaky sieve indeed. It is true that Union warships captured or destroyed a reported 153 runners that year, but this number constituted less than a tenth of all ships entering or leaving Confederate ports during that time.[3] "The blockade is a farce," wrote Acting Lieutenant John S. Barnes on the USS *Wabash* off Charleston in July 1861. "The sea is swarming with privateers, who have run the blockade under our very nose . . . and will continue to do so, until the government takes proper steps to put competent officers in command, and proper ships to do the work."[4] Barnes was something of a "croaker" (grumbler and complainer) in the argot of the time, but his words were echoed by an officer on the USS *Iroquois*, a fast six-gun screw sloop stationed off Savannah before it was sent to hunt for the CSS *Sumter*. "The blockade is a perfect farce," he wrote, "for we can see steamers run up and down the coast every day, and we are so far off that we are useless; before we can get underway they could be out of sight."[5]

With her thirteen-foot draft, the *Iroquois* could not get close enough to stop these shallow-draft vessels, some of which used the intracoastal waterways that snaked along the South Atlantic coast. Most of these coasters were not blockade-runners in the common understanding of the term, for they were carrying goods from one Southern port to another rather than bringing in war matériel and other freight from Nassau and Bermuda or running cotton out for export. From June to August 1861, for example, of 178 ships entering or clearing five major Southern ports, only eighteen were involved in foreign trade.[6] By the same token, most of the 153 runners captured or destroyed by the navy in 1861 were also engaged in this intra-Southern trade.

Many of those "swarming" privateers that Lieutenant Barnes complained of came out through Hatteras Inlet from Albemarle and Pamlico Sounds in North Carolina. Protected by a series of barrier islands (the Outer Banks), these sounds formed an inland sea that served as a back door to Richmond through the Dismal Swamp Canal—the front door having been closed by the Union navy's control of Hampton Roads. Hatteras Inlet was the main break in the Outer Banks, through which numerous small blockade-runners slipped during the war's early months. Privateers darted out through the inlet to snatch prizes off Cape Hatteras and re-treated into the sounds to escape pursuing warships that were kept at bay by two Confederate earthwork forts that guarded the narrow channel inside the shallow bar. "I now consider this inlet secure against any at-tempt of the enemy to enter it," wrote the chief engineer of the Confeder-ate coastal defenses on July 25, 1861.[7]

Secretary Welles and Commodore Stringham begged to differ. In Au-gust they organized a task force of seven warships carrying 141 guns plus two troop transports with 900 soldiers commanded by Major General Benjamin Butler. The forts mounted only nineteen guns, most of them old 32-pounders that were outranged by the Dahlgren guns on the larger ships (the *Wabash* and *Minnesota*) firing shot and shells weighing from 68 to 120 pounds. The old adage that one gun in a shore fortification was worth four on shipboard was about to be tested. All but one of the Union ships were steamers, and the sailing frigate USS *Cumberland* with its twenty-two 9-inch Dahlgrens was towed into action by the *Wabash*. On August 28 the transports began a clumsy landing of soldiers through the surf that destroyed most of their boats two miles up the beach from the forts. The main part of the fleet began pounding the forts while steaming in a circle to present a moving target, an innovative tactic made possible by steam power. The ships demolished the smaller Fort Clark and drove its men into Fort Hatteras before hauling off for the night.

Confederate reinforcements arrived overnight under none other than Commander Samuel Barron, the former U.S. navy officer whom Seward had once trusted to keep Virginia in the Union. The next day, the fleet returned and concentrated its fire on Fort Hatteras. The 10-inch forward pivot gun on the *Wabash* did much of the damage to the fort. The gun was commanded by Midshipman Roswell H. Lamson, who like his classmates had left the Naval Academy after his third year to go to war and was later commissioned lieutenant on shipboard. "It was terrible to watch the large shells as they came down in the fort bursting almost as soon as they struck, scatter sand and tents, dismounting guns and tearing everything but the bombproof covers to pieces," wrote Lamson to his cousin that evening. "For a long time we fired a shell every three minutes from the forward gun, and it was nothing but a continual bursting of shells around, over, and among them." At about noon, the fort ran up the white flag. Refus-ing to surrender to General Butler, whose troops had done virtually noth-ing, Barron declared that he would only "surrender to the men who had whipped him" and presented his sword to Commodore Stringham. Almost

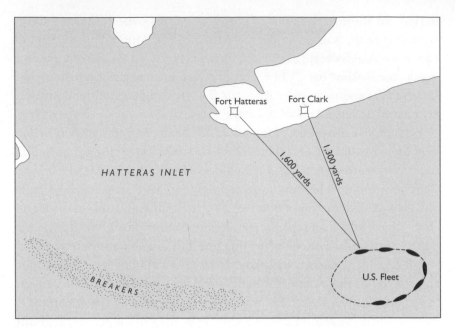

Fort Hatteras and Fort Clark, August 28–29, 1861

700 Confederates became prisoners of war, including Barron, who was exchanged eleven months later.[8]

This naval victory had important consequences. It gave a much-needed boost to Northern morale after the defeats at Bull Run and Wilson's Creek. It helped shut down Confederate privateering. In the two weeks after the capture of Fort Hatteras, navy ships seized six blockade-runners approaching the inlet whose captains had not learned that it was in Yankee hands. As far west as Kentucky, a Union officer enlisting recruits in that vital border state reported that "the Cape Hatteras business has alarmed the Confeds more than anything else that has yet been done. We have people continually coming from that direction . . . who tell us that the alarm of such an expedition is raising the devil in all their sea ports and distracts them very much."[9] The Union army was not yet prepared to follow up this naval success, but the achievement laid the groundwork for a campaign under General Ambrose E. Burnside that gained control of much of the North Carolina coast in early 1862.

As the *Wabash*'s shells were crashing into Fort Hatteras, a "Blockade Board" in Washington was putting the finishing touches on a series of remarkable reports that provided blueprints for naval operations during the next eight months. The attack on Hatteras Inlet had been one of this board's first recommendations. The board was the brainchild of Superintendent Alexander Bache of the U.S. Coast Survey. To carry on a successful blockade, the navy needed to amass all possible sources of information about the Southern coast, harbors, navigable estuaries and rivers, forts, and potential additional bases for blockade fleets. Assistant Secretary Gustavus Fox thought Bache's proposal was a great idea and asked Samuel F. Du Pont to chair the Blockade Board, Bache to provide the hydrographic and topographic information from the coast survey, Major John A. Barnard of the Army Engineers to supply data on coastal fortifications, and Commander Charles H. Davis to serve as secretary of the board.

Through the hot summer of 1861, these men worked long hours and submitted six detailed reports, or "memoirs." They recommended the acquisition of additional blockade bases on the South Atlantic coast and at Ship Island near the Mississippi coast halfway between Mobile and New Orleans. Once these objectives had been accomplished, the two existing blockade squadrons could be divided into four, thereby shortening the distance for ships returning to bases for supplies, coal, and repairs. When the new bases were established and enough ships and men became available, the capture of New Orleans should be the next strategic goal.[10]

While the Blockade Board was preparing its reports, Congress enacted legislation that authorized the army and navy to disregard the principle of seniority if it was "for the good of the service." Welles acted promptly to begin exercising this authority and to implement the recommendations of the board. In early September he replaced the septuagenarian William Mervine with Captain William W. McKean as commander of the Gulf Blockading Squadron. Mervine demanded a court of inquiry, but Welles refused, later writing in his diary that Mervine had "proved an utter failure. . . . He was long in getting out to his station, and accomplished nothing after he got there."[11] Two weeks later, Welles accepted the resignation of Silas Stringham as commander of the Atlantic Squadron. Despite Stringham's capture of Hatteras Inlet, he had shown little energy or imagination in enforcement of the blockade, and he felt aggrieved by Welles's apparent endorsement of newspaper criticism of him.[12]

Welles used the opportunity of Stringham's resignation to divide the squadron into the North Atlantic and South Atlantic Squadrons, with the North Carolina–South Carolina border as the dividing point. He appointed Captain Louis Goldsborough as the new commander of the North Atlantic Squadron and Samuel Francis Du Pont commander of the South Atlantic Squadron. To make these appointments, Welles ignored seniority by jumping Goldsborough over thirteen of his seniors on the captains' list and Du Pont over eighteen. When McKean replaced Mervine at the head of the Gulf Squadron, he had been number thirty-eight on the list (Mervine was number ten). "Things have taken an active turn," Du Pont informed his wife, "and this day is an epoch in naval history—seniority and rotation have seen their last day."[13]

One reason for the relief of Mervine was his failure to do anything about Ship Island, whose seizure from the Confederates the Blockade Board had pronounced "indispensable." It was "difficult to understand the reasons for the apparent inactivity and indifference that have governed in this matter," Welles told Mervine. "You have large ships, heavy batteries, and young and willing officers, with men sufficient to dispossess the insurgents from Ship Island."[14] A week after Welles replaced Mervine, one of those young and willing officers, fifty-one-year-old Commander Melancton Smith, shelled the half-built Confederate fort on the island with the 8-inch guns of the USS *Massachusetts*. The Confederates fled, and a landing party of U.S. marines and sailors took possession.[15]

Welles subsequently divided the Gulf Squadron into the East and West Gulf Squadrons. From its base at Key West, the East Squadron would patrol the Florida coast from Cape Canaveral (which was actually on the Atlantic) to a point just east of Pensacola, and the West Squadron would be responsible for the rest of the Confederacy's coast to the Mexican border. To command the West Gulf Squadron, Welles made one of his most inspired choices. On January 9, 1862, he named David Glasgow Farragut to the position. Thirty-seventh in seniority on the captain's list, Farragut was respected by many of his fellow officers but virtually unknown to the public. "Neither the President nor any member of the Cabinet knew him, or knew of him," Welles later wrote. "Members of Congress inquired who he was, and some of them remonstrated, and questioned whether I was not making a mistake for he was a Southern man and had a Southern wife." Welles knew of Farragut's expressions of Unionism when he moved from Norfolk to New York and was willing to gamble on his loyalty as well as ability. Rarely in the history of naval warfare has a gamble paid off so handsomely.[16]

FARRAGUT'S NAME would become a household word in 1862, but in November 1861 two other captains seized the limelight. As the new commander of the South Atlantic Squadron, Du Pont had the honor—and responsibility—of carrying out the first of his Blockade Board's recom-

David Glasgow Farragut, after he had been promoted to rear admiral. (Courtesy of the Library of Congress)

mendations to establish a navy base somewhere along the South Atlantic coast. The board initially considered several sites, but Du Pont finally settled on Port Royal Sound, about sixty miles south of Charleston and thirty-five miles north of Savannah. Du Pont knew that the entrance to Port Royal would be more heavily defended than other possible objectives. But it was also "the most desirable to have first and hold" because of its proximity to these two major Southern ports, its capacious anchorage, and the depth of water over its bar at high tide that would admit the larger Union warships.[17]

Du Pont put together the largest fleet in American history to that time: seventeen warships with 157 guns, twenty-five colliers and supply ships, and thirty-three troop transports carrying 12,000 soldiers and 600 marines. This armada was more impressive in numbers, however, than in the seagoing qualities of some of its vessels, which included several ferryboats and river steamers never intended for blue-water navigation. And the question of who would be in overall charge of the expedition was problematic. The army commander was Brigadier General Thomas West Sherman ("the other Sherman"). While Du Pont held the highest rank in the navy at that time as a captain, this was equivalent only to a colonel in the army. To prevent Du Pont from being outranked, Lincoln issued an order creating the rank of "Flag Officer" as equivalent to major general in the army, which meant that Du Pont now outranked Sherman. But neither officer could "assume any direct command, independent of consent, over an officer of the other service."[18]

This awkward arrangement could work only if Du Pont and Sherman displayed "the most cordial and effectual cooperation."[19] For the most part, they did, starting with a largely successful effort to keep the objective of the task force a secret from journalists and Confederate spies—and from their own subordinates. "Rumors rife" but no definite information about the fleet's destination, wrote a lieutenant in Du Pont's flagship *Wabash*. Commander Percival Drayton of the USS *Pocahontas* did not know where he was going and was glad for the secrecy, "which if it does nothing else, will have tended to keep our southern friends in a most unpleasant state of uncertainty."[20] Du Pont gave each ship captain sealed orders naming Port Royal as the objective, to be opened at sea only if the fleet became separated. It turned out to be a prescient precaution.

The armada departed from Hampton Roads on October 29. Two literary-minded officers on the *Wabash* waxed poetic in descriptions of their first night at sea. Captain Charles H. Davis, who had been secretary of the Blockade Board and was now Du Pont's fleet captain and chief of staff, wrote that "the sea is covered with lights at every point of the horizon. . . . I think of similar expeditions that have figured in history . . . and as I looked abroad on the ocean covered with our ships and transports . . . I participated in the glow and ardor and elation of heart inspired, no doubt, by the armada of Spain." A volunteer lieutenant and commander of a gun crew on the *Wabash* looked out "on either side of us, in line abreast, stretched for six miles the advanced guard of gunboats" followed by the transports. "Never did such a heterogeneous squadron venture upon the waters, nondescripts ad infinitum; vessels without shape before known to the maritime world. . . . Had some homeward bound vessel haplessly got within our lines, surely would the bewildered skipper have imagined that 'Great Birnam Wood to high Dunsinane' had come against him."[21]

These romantic images gave way to chaos and panic on November 1 as the fleet ran into what an officer on the *Wabash* described as "one of the severest gales I have ever experienced" off the North Carolina coast.[22] A steamer carrying 300 marines went down; the sailing frigate USS *Sabine* rescued all but seven of the men. Some vessels had to turn back, including small steamers for towing surfboats to land troops. Much of the army's ammunition was lost. On the morning of November 2, only eight other ships were in sight from the *Wabash*. By the time the flagship reached the bar off Port Royal on November 4, however, most of the fleet was reunited.[23] More vessels continued to arrive as the warships got over the bar on November 5 and prepared to attack the two Confederate earthwork forts mounting forty-three guns and situated three miles apart on either side of the wide channel.

This attack would be an all-navy show, for the loss of ammunition and surfboats made spectators of the army troops. "General Sherman says in my hearing that: 'These ships can't take the forts without cooperation with the troops,'" wrote a navy lieutenant on November 5. "I hope we will show him differently." Bad weather on November 6 postponed the attack, but the next day dawned clear and calm. In a letter home typical of sailors before they went into action, Roswell Lamson (still the commander of the *Wabash*'s forward pivot gun) wrote: "I have the greatest confidence in our men, and as I stand on the forecastle and see the stouthearted tars around me I feel a thrill I would not give for anything else in the world. . . . I pray God for strength and courage to perform [my] duty cheerfully, and if I fall I only hope it will be said, He did his duty and fell like an American Sailor."[24]

Du Pont adopted a tactical plan suggested by Flag Captain Davis for the ships to steam in an oval pattern between the two forts, pounding each in turn while presenting a moving target to the enemy. At 9:26 A.M. on November 7, fourteen warships led by the *Wabash* moved up midchannel between Fort Beauregard on the north and the stronger Fort Walker to the south, firing at both simultaneously. Du Pont placed five of his gunboats in a flanking position to protect the main fleet from the harassing fire of a small Confederate flotilla of converted tugs carrying one or two guns each. This "mosquito fleet" soon fled up the Beaufort River out of range of the heavier Yankee guns. Du Pont turned back and brought the fleet close under the guns of Fort Walker, then turned again for a second pass up midchannel.

Only the eighteen-gun sidewheeler USS *Susquehanna* followed the

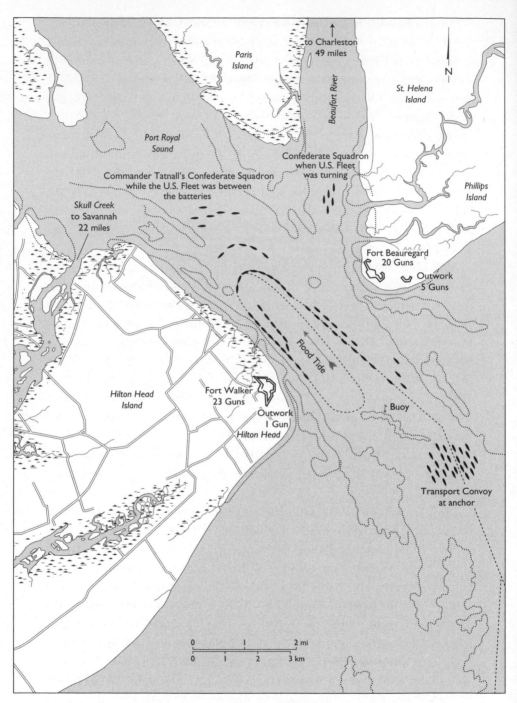

Union Assault on Port Royal, November 7, 1861

Wabash. The other ships in the main column stayed behind in an enfilading position off Fort Walker, perhaps from a misunderstanding of Du Pont's orders. The flagship repeatedly signaled them to join the *Wabash* and *Susquehanna* in a second pass near Fort Walker, but they did not move. "How is it that I can't get my signal obeyed, and my orders carried out?" an angry Du Pont expostulated. Noticing the problem, Commander Charles Steedman of the USS *Bienville*, an eight-gun sidewheeler from the flanking column, joined the *Wabash* and *Susquehanna* on the next circuit past Fort Walker. The USS *Pocahontas*, commanded by South Carolina native Percival Drayton, also arrived from its fierce battle with the storm and dashed in to add the weight of her five guns in the second attack on Fort Walker, commanded by his Confederate brother General Thomas Drayton.

This time, Du Pont brought the *Wabash* within 500 yards of the fort, causing the enemy to overshoot and cut up the rigging and smokestack but protecting the hull while the big frigate's broadside of 8-inch and 9-inch Dahlgren guns and the 100-pound Parrott pivot rifle tore up the fort and dismounted several guns. "The whistle and whiz and crash of shot and shell [was] literally incessant," wrote Roswell Lamson, who commanded the pivot gun. "Shell guns, Columbiads and rifled they cut us up in spars, rigging and hull pretty severely," but our guns "finally drove them out. . . . They fled in all directions leaving some of the guns loaded, their arms, tents &c." Another gun captain described his men "stripped to their waists and with brawny chests and arms exposed worked and hove at the guns like demons. . . . Our mainmast was shot through and through, and our after magazine flooded" but "the fire of the enemy gradually slackened and finally ceased as we drove them from their guns. . . . Going aloft, with my glass I could see them running for dear life, scattered in every direction."[25]

The *Wabash* landed its marines and fifty sailors to take possession of Fort Walker. Across the entrance to the bay, Confederates also evacuated Fort Beauregard before the ships could make another turn to drive them out. Union army troops came ashore and occupied both forts as well as the nearby town of Beaufort. The white residents fled to the mainland, leaving behind thousands of slaves on the rich long-staple cotton plantations. These "contrabands" thereby took their first tentative steps toward freedom. At the cost of only thirty-one casualties, Du Pont secured the finest natural harbor on the Southern coast. It was the North's most important victory in 1861 and provided a springboard for further advances along the coast as well as a large base for the blockade fleet.

Du Pont apparently reprimanded the senior commander of the gunboat division that failed to heed his signals to remain with the main column steaming in the elliptical pattern. But he said nothing about this dereliction in his official report, perhaps because their enfilade fire on Fort Walker helped drive out its garrison. But it was the big Dahlgren guns of the *Wabash* and *Susquehanna* that did the most damage. Du Pont wrote to Commander John A. Dahlgren, the navy's ordnance expert and inventor of the "soda bottle guns" with the bulbous breech, praising these guns for the "precision and destructive results" of their fire. "I never get *transporté*, as the French term it," wrote Du Pont, "but I will repeat, to the day of my death, that the second assault of this ship upon the forts, for rapidity, continuity, and precision of fire, has never been surpassed in naval warfare."[26]

The capture of Port Royal spread consternation and a belief in the invincibility of Yankee ships along the Carolina and Georgia coast. "Such a panic as seems to have existed through the low country can scarcely be described," wrote Percival Drayton, who had grown up there.[27] General Robert E. Lee shared the consternation, though not the panic. He arrived in Savannah as the newly appointed commander of South Atlantic coastal defenses one day after Du Pont's attack. Lee regarded this assignment as "another forlorn hope expedition—worse than West Virginia," where his failure to drive out the Yankees had caused some Southern newspapers to label him "Granny Lee." Sea power gave the enemy the ability to strike anywhere along the coast. "There are so many points to attack, and so little means to meet them on the water," Lee lamented, "that there is but little rest."[28]

Du Pont soon received some of the new ninety-day gunboats that were becoming available. With a draft of less than ten feet and a rated speed of ten knots, they were useful both for penetrating the maze of tidal inlets and rivers along the coast and for offshore blockading. Several of the ships that had been bought earlier by the Navy Department and converted to gunboats had proved equally useful. "Your purchased ships have turned out remarkably well," Du Pont wrote to Welles's brother-in-law George Morgan, while the ninety-day gunboats "are all I could desire."[29]

With these vessels, Du Pont soon confirmed Lee's worst fears. He sent them up some of the rivers as far as they could go, destroying bridges and convoying army troops to most of the sea islands. Gunboats occupied sounds and inlets from the North Edisto River just south of Charleston to

St. Mary's River on the Georgia-Florida border, closing these navigable inlets to blockade-runners. "It is my wish and purpose to hold every harbor, inlet, and sound on the coast of South Carolina," Du Pont declared.[30] He never did quite manage that, but his ubiquitous gunboats convinced Lee that attempts to defend low-country positions on navigable rivers were futile. "Wherever his fleet can be brought no opposition to his landing can be made except within range of our fixed batteries," wrote Lee on January 8, 1862. "We have nothing to oppose to its heavy guns, which sweep the low banks of this country with irresistable [*sic*] force." In late February, Lee ordered all Confederate units in the region to pull back to the mainland and establish new defensive positions beyond range of naval guns.[31]

When Du Pont led a fleet a few days later to attack Fernandina, Florida, a deepwater port with rail connections to Georgia and the Carolinas, he found its defenses abandoned and seized it almost without firing a shot. The only shots fired were by the USS *Ottawa* at a train trying to escape on tracks that ran along the Amelia River for more than a mile. The train got away, but a shell destroyed the drawbridge just after the last car got over it. "We took another train [and] five locomotives," Du Pont reported gleefully.[32] This affair must have been one of the only examples in history when a gunboat captured a train. The blue tide continued to sweep into Florida's principal Atlantic ports, occupying Jacksonville and St. Augustine in the second week of March 1862.[33]

The *Ottawa* proceeded up the St. John's River from Jacksonville and discovered the famous yacht *America*, which had won the 100-guinea cup in the race around the Isle of Wight in 1851 and given its name to the America's Cup that is today still the biggest prize in yacht racing. The Confederate government had purchased the *America* in 1861 but scuttled her to prevent capture when Union forces seized Jacksonville. The Union navy raised and repaired her, equipped her with three guns, and put her on blockade duty. The *America* actually captured a blockade-runner in October 1862 with the appropriate name of *David Crockett*.[34]

Du Pont's squadron capped its victories along the coast by occupying Tybee Island at the mouth of the Savannah River. Under the protection of gunboats, the army landed cannons and mortars on the island to bombard Fort Pulaski, a large brick edifice across the channel. At Du Pont's request, the army allowed naval gun crews to man one battery of rifled artillery, which played a key role in breaching the walls, threatening to blow up the powder magazine, and forcing the surrender of the fort on April 11. With the main channel now controlled by Union troops in the fort and the back channels of Wassaw and Ossabaw Sounds blocked by gunboats, Savannah was henceforth cut off from blockade-runners.

AS DU PONT sat in his commodious quarters in the *Wabash* on November 8, 1861, writing his report of the victory at Port Royal, the final act of another naval drama was taking place 700 miles to the south in the Old Bahama Channel off the coast of Cuba. The USS *San Jacinto* fired a shot across the bow of the British packet *Trent* and forced her to heave to in international waters. At the order of Captain Charles Wilkes, the executive officer boarded the *Trent* and seized James Mason and John Slidell, who had run the blockade at Charleston to Havana and were on their way to Europe as Confederate envoys to Britain and France.

Wilkes was something of a loose cannon in the American navy. Clean shaven with thin, severe facial features and cold, dark eyes, he had a bullying personality that demanded quick obedience from subordinates but often defied the orders of superiors. As a lieutenant, he had commanded a four-ship exploring-and-charting expedition in the South Pacific from 1838 to 1842 that had produced much valuable information, including confirmation of Antarctica's continental status. But his violent disciplinary measures earned the hatred of sailors and officers alike. He faced a court-martial upon his return to the United States but escaped conviction.

For the next two decades, Wilkes remained unpopular in the navy, and his career languished. The need for experienced officers when the war broke out, however, caused Welles to give him command of the *San Jacinto*, which was off the coast of Africa when Wilkes joined her in October 1861. Welles ordered him to join Du Pont's fleet for the attack on Port Royal, but Wilkes interpreted this order as a suggestion. He lingered in the eastern Atlantic for several weeks hoping (in vain) to catch a Confederate privateer, and then he headed for the Caribbean to hunt for the CSS *Sumter*. There he learned from the American consul in Havana that Mason and Slidell were about to embark on the *Trent*. Here, thought Wilkes, was a greater prize than the *Sumter*. He lay in wait for Mason and Slidell off the northern coast of Cuba. On November 8 the *Trent* steamed into sight, and Wilkes pounced.

Although the *Trent* was a ship of a neutral nation on its way from one neutral port to another, Wilkes informed Gideon Welles that he had looked into the books of international and maritime law on board the *San Jacinto* and learned that he had the right to capture enemy dispatches on board a neutral ship. As diplomats, he wrote, Mason and Slidell were "the embodiment of dispatches." Whether this novel interpretation of international law would have stood up in a prize court is impossible to know, because Wilkes did not send the *Trent* to a port with a prize court. He initially intended to do so but uncharacteristically allowed his executive officer to talk him out of it. He was already shorthanded, Wilkes explained to Welles, and to have put a prize crew on the *Trent* would have made him more so. The *Trent* was also carrying many passengers who would have been seriously inconvenienced by diversion to Key West. So he seized the Confederate diplomats and let the *Trent* go.[35]

The Northern press lionized Wilkes as a hero. He was fêted in Boston and lauded in Congress. Secretary of State Seward wrote that "the capture of Mason and Slidell created a sensation almost equal to the taking of Port Royal, and possibly great results may grow out of it." Secretary of the Navy Welles, in words he may later have regretted, congratulated Wilkes "on the great public service you have rendered. . . . Your conduct in seizing these public enemies was marked by intelligence, ability, decision, and firmness." Even Lincoln seemed to share the public mood of euphoria.[36]

But the president and other Cabinet members soon had second thoughts. Even before news of the British government's angry response reached Washington, Lincoln remarked to Attorney General Edward Bates: "I am not much of a prize lawyer, but it seems to me pretty clear that if Wilkes saw fit to make that capture on the high seas he had no right to turn his quarter-deck into a prize court."[37] Charles Sumner, chairman of the Senate Foreign Relations Committee, reminded Lincoln that the United States had declared war on Britain in 1812 for behavior similar to Wilkes's seizure of Mason and Slidell. The American minister to Britain, Charles Francis Adams, made the same point to Seward.

The jingo press in England clamored for revenge for this insult to the Union Jack. The Royal Navy strengthened its fleet in the western Atlantic and convoyed army reinforcements to Canada. The risk of war caused the American stock market to swoon. Government bonds found no buyers. The British Cabinet drafted an ultimatum to the United States demanding an apology and the release of Mason and Slidell. Queen Victoria's consort, Prince Albert, ill and soon to die, suggested language that softened the ultimatum, which Foreign Secretary Lord Russell accepted. Russell even suggested to Lord Lyons that if the Americans released Mason and Slidell, the British could be "rather easy about the apology."[38]

By mid-December the Lincoln administration recognized that it must give in. "To go to war with England now," said Attorney General Bates, who had initially supported Wilkes, "is to abandon all hope of suppressing the rebellion." While Lincoln knew that he must not have "two wars on his hands at a time," he also wanted to avoid the humiliation and political danger of appearing to give in to John Bull. Seward provided the solution. At Cabinet meetings on Christmas day and the following day, he presented a memorandum stating that Wilkes had acted without instructions and had erred in failing to bring the *Trent* into port for adjudication by a prize court. As a face-saving gesture, Seward added that the American government was gratified by Britain's recognition of the neutral rights for which the United States had always contended.[39]

Mason and Slidell made their way to London and Paris, where they spent three futile years trying to win the foreign recognition and intervention that might have occurred if they had remained imprisoned at Fort Warren in Boston Harbor. Wilkes was angry and bitter, but he got little sympathy from other naval officers. The administration suffered less political damage than Lincoln had feared, for most of the public had come to the same "one war at a time" conclusion as the president. And the reaction in Britain was surprisingly pro-American. "The first effect of the release of Messrs. Mason and Slidell has been extraordinary," wrote Charles Francis Adams from the American legation in London. "The current which ran against us with such extreme violence six weeks ago now seems to be going with equal fury in our direction."[40] That favorable current had crucial significance for the U.S. Navy, for the question of the blockade's legitimacy under international law was coming to a head.

IN 1856 THE LEADING maritime powers of Europe adopted the Declaration of Paris defining the international law of warfare at sea. A key part of this declaration stated: "Blockades, in order to be binding, must be effective; that is to say, maintained by a force sufficient really to prevent access to the coast of the enemy."[41] The United States had not signed the declaration because it also outlawed privateering, which had been a potent American naval weapon in the Revolution and the War of 1812. Now that the United States was a victim of Confederate privateering, however, Secretary of State Seward was eager to sign. But the complications of doing so in the midst of a civil war postponed the question until some future time. Nevertheless, the provisions of the Declaration of Paris remained in force for European powers. Confederate envoys (including Mason and Slidell when they finally reached Europe) presented long lists of ships they claimed had evaded the blockade to prove that it was a mere "paper blockade" and therefore illegal under international law. Jefferson Davis condemned the North's so-called blockade as a "monstrous pretension."[42]

Their contention that many vessels breached the blockade was quite true. In spite of Du Pont's success in sealing up various coves and inlets during the winter of 1861–62, he never had enough ships to seal them all or to stop small coasting vessels from using the labyrinth of inland waterways along the South Atlantic coast. "The lagoons of Venice are not more curious than these waters," he declared.[43] The same could be said of much of the Gulf coast. And captains of blockading ships could not control the weather, the clouds, or the moon. In clear weather, in the daytime, or on moonlit nights, the blockade-runners laid up, waiting for thick darkness or a storm. As Du Pont acknowledged in December 1861: "The vessels that lie in wait to run the blockade, having skillful pilots, and being desperate in their attempts, can not but sometimes succeed under favor of fog or darkness. . . . In the heavy easterly gales [our] steamers must run off or be wrecked on the enemy's coast, giving the opportunity to vessels to run *out*."[44]

Major ports like Charleston, Wilmington, and Mobile were difficult to blockade because of the multiple navigation channels separated by shoals and protected by Confederate forts that could keep blockade ships at a distance. The tricky currents and the bars at the entrance to channels into Charleston forced the blockaders to anchor or to patrol at a considerable distance from each other. A form of Catch-22 also plagued the blockade fleet. If they moved about while patrolling their stations, they needed to show lights to avoid collisions, but the lights served as a guide to enable runners to avoid them. Welles therefore ordered them to stay dark, which meant that they must remain at anchor or under way with just enough steerage to counter the currents and remain on station. Even if they kept up steam while at anchor and the lookout spotted a runner going in or out, the amount of time required to slip the anchor cable and get up to speed often enabled the runner to slip away in the darkness.

Blockade commanders gradually phased out sailing ships as more steamers became available. "I am painfully impressed with the worthlessness of Sailing vessels since I have got to work out here," wrote Du Pont in November 1861. But all squadron commanders continually complained to Welles that they did not have enough steamers to maintain a tight blockade, and those they did have needed constant repairs to broken machinery or leaking boilers. "One disease is chronic in all the ships: broken engines," said Du Pont. "The breaking downs break my heart."[45]

The problems of blockading Charleston prompted Gustavus Fox to come up with what he considered a brilliant solution: fill the hulks of old sailing vessels with stones and sink them in the channels. Du Pont and his captains were skeptical. On December 5, 1861, Du Pont wrote to his wife that the vessels of the "stone fleet" had arrived. "I hardly know what to do with them." Because of Fox's insistence on trying the experiment, however, Du Pont ordered his fleet captain Charles Davis to take charge of the sinking of the hulks. Davis was not happy with Fox's "pet idea." He professed "a special disgust for this business . . . the maggot, however, had got into Fox's brain."[46]

Davis managed to obstruct the main channel and part of Maffitt's channel. The Confederates complained loudly of this action, "so unworthy of any nation," in the words of Robert E. Lee, "the expression of the malice and revenge of a people."[47] Du Pont likened such complaints to crocodile tears. "I should probably not have recommended such a measure had I been consulted," he wrote, "but that we had not the *right* is simply absurd." The Confederates themselves had sunk obstructions inside Charleston Harbor, in the Savannah River, and elsewhere to block the advance of Union warships. "So it is all right for the rebels to obstruct, but it is dreadful for us. Then the idea of pretending to believe that these are *permanent* obstructions shows great ignorance of the nature of outside bars forced by the sea action." If the channels remained obstructed until the following spring, remarked Du Pont in December, "it will be worth all the trouble."[48] As matters turned out, two of the three channels remained open, and the action of tide and ocean currents opened new routes around the obstructions in the main channel well before spring.

For better or for worse, it would be up to the Union fleets at Charleston and elsewhere to demonstrate that the blockade was "effective" enough to be "binding" on other powers. "I am much pressed by the [Navy] Department on this subject," wrote Du Pont in words echoed by other squadron commanders, "for fear of foreign complications."[49] In November British Foreign Secretary Russell asked Lord Lyons for his opinion on the subject. Lyons confessed that he was "a good deal puzzled" about how to answer Russell's question. The blockade "is certainly by no means strict or vigorous along the immense extent of coast to which it is supposed to apply," he wrote. "On the other hand it is very far from being a mere Paper Blockade. A great many vessels are captured; it is a most serious interruption of

Trade; and if it were as ineffective as Mr. Jefferson Davis says in his message, he would not be so very anxious to get rid of it." When John Slidell presented to French officials yet another list of vessels that had run the blockade, they asked him "how it was that so little cotton had reached neutral ports." Slidell answered that most of the successful runners had small cargo capacity, and "the risk of capture was sufficiently great to deter those who had not an adventurous spirit from attempting it."[50]

Fatal admission! The true measure of the blockade's effectiveness was not how many ships got through or even how many were captured, but how many never tried. Lord Russell said as much in a statement on February 2, 1862, when in effect he announced a corollary to the Declaration of Paris: "Assuming . . . that a number of ships is stationed and remains at the entrance of a port, sufficient really to prevent access to it *or to create an evident danger of entering or leaving it* . . . the fact that various ships may have successfully escaped through it . . . will not of itself prevent the blockade from being an effective one by international law."[51]

The Russell corollary drove a stake into the heart of the Confederate effort to convince European governments of the blockade's illegitimacy. Blockade-running continued, of course, as sleeker and faster runners designed for the purpose became available to challenge the anaconda that was slowly tightening around the Confederacy. At the same time, however, more and better Union blockade ships came on line, and their commanders gained experience and devised improved tactics. The best way to shut down blockade-running, however, was to capture Confederate ports. In addition to Du Pont's achievements in this line along the South Atlantic coast, other Union forces enjoyed a great deal of success in this effort in the first half of 1862.

chapter three

We've Got New Orleans

While Du Pont's warships and General Thomas W. Sherman's soldiers consolidated their control of the South Atlantic coast, planning for two other large-scale combined operations went forward. At Hampton Roads the new commander of the North Atlantic Blockading Squadron, Louis M. Goldsborough, organized a flotilla of shallow-draft gunboats able to enter Pamlico Sound through Hatteras Inlet in North Carolina. In New England, Brigadier General Ambrose E. Burnside recruited several regiments of soldiers, many of whom were accustomed to working around water, for an amphibious force to accompany Goldsborough's flotilla into the sound. At the same time, General Benjamin Butler was recruiting soldiers from the same manpower pool for an expedition to the Gulf coast. Butler's new army would provide the ground troops to occupy New Orleans when it was captured by the naval force being put together in New York by the newly appointed commander of the West Gulf Blockading Squadron, David Glasgow Farragut.

The Burnside-Goldsborough expedition got off first. Although of contrasting personalities, the two men worked well together. Handsome, personable, with an impressive mustache that extended into cheek whiskers that gave a new word to the language with an inversion (sideburns) of his name, Burnside was popular with his men. Square-headed, dour, stocky in build (sailors called him "old Guts"), Goldsborough enjoyed no such popularity. But he demonstrated initiative and energy in organizing a flotilla of nineteen armed ferryboats, converted merchant vessels, and naval gunboats that rendezvoused at Hatteras Inlet in the first week of January.[1] The army transports arrived slowly, some of them scattered by fierce winter gales that wrecked three and delayed the entry of the rest into the sound. The navy ships got across the bar without trouble, but several of the army transports had too deep a draft to get over it without being unloaded and dragged across by powerful tugs. "My patience is well-nigh exhausted," Goldsborough told Welles, but by January 30 the army had managed, "*with our constant assistance*, in getting a large number of their vessels over the bulkhead." Goldsborough told Assistant Secretary Fox that he had learned one thing from this experience: "In case of another joint expedition, every thing concerning *all* the vessels should be arranged exclusively by the Navy, & kept under naval control."[2]

The objective of this operation was Roanoke Island, which commanded the passage between Pamlico Sound and Albemarle Sound to the north and was the key to control of the North Carolina coast from Cape Lookout to the Virginia border. North Carolina Confederates recognized the strategic importance of this region. They pleaded with Richmond for the return of some of the men and arms North Carolina had sent to Virginia. But Richmond seemed indifferent. On February 7 the Confederates on Roanoke Island prepared to defend it with fewer than 3,000 men and eight small gunboats mounting one or two guns each against Burnside's 9,000 troops and Goldsborough's motley but well-armed flotilla.

Union gunboats shelled Fort Bartow on the island for two days, finally forcing its evacuation, which enabled the Yankee sailors to clear away the pilings and sunken hulks the Confederates had planted across the entrance into Albemarle Sound. Goldsborough's ships drove the outgunned Confederate fleet away, sinking one of the enemy vessels. Meanwhile, other Union gunboats protected army transports and surfboats that landed on the beach along with six navy howitzers to support the army's attack the following day. By early afternoon on February 9, Burnside's soldiers had broken through the defenses on Roanoke Island and captured 2,675 Confederates at the cost of 264 casualties. The Union navy suffered only twenty-five casualties.

It was an important victory for combined arms. But the campaign was not over. Goldsborough ordered Commander Stephen C. Rowan, one of the navy's best officers, to take thirteen of the Union gunboats to go after the seven remaining Confederate vessels and "bag them all if possible."[3] Rowan very nearly did just that. He chased them up to Elizabeth City, the North Carolina terminus of the Dismal Swamp Canal. Finding the Confederate gunboats awaiting him there on February 10, Rowan hoisted a signal on his flagship USS *Delaware*: "Dash at the enemy." Dash they did, engaging the overmatched Southern gunboats in a free-for-all melee in which they sank or destroyed all but one.[4]

Over the next few weeks, Burnside and Goldsborough consolidated

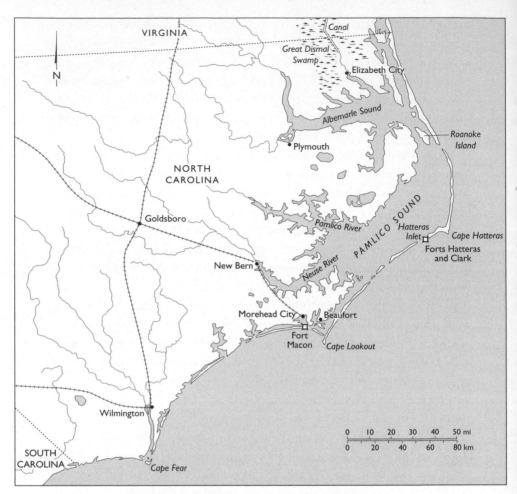

The Coast and Sounds of North Carolina

their control of the sounds and the estuaries of rivers flowing into them. Goldsborough was recalled to Hampton Roads after the CSS *Virginia*'s attack on the Union fleet there and its duel with the USS *Monitor*. Rowan took command of the flotilla in the sounds and planned with Burnside for an attack on New Bern, North Carolina's colonial capital and an important port on the Neuse River with rail connections to the interior. On March 13 Rowan's gunboats convoyed transports carrying 12,000 soldiers and marines to a landing several miles south of the city. In tandem with the marching troops, the gunboats steamed upriver, enfilading and shelling each of five Confederate forts as they moved along. Rowan ordered his gunners to lay down a blanket of fire just ahead of advancing Union

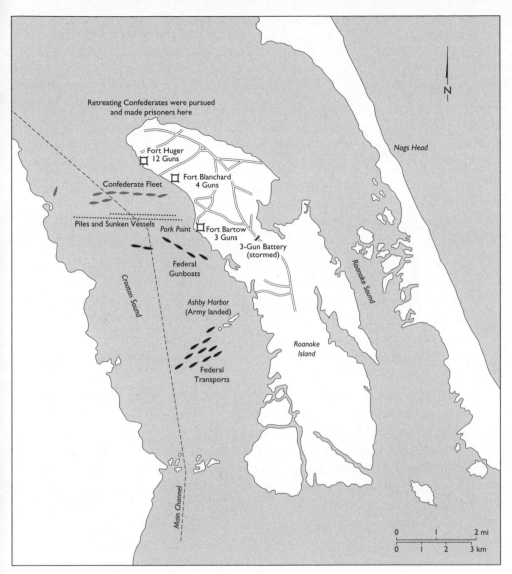

Union Operations against Roanoke Island, February 7–8, 1862

troops. "I commenced throwing 5, 10, 15 second shells inshore," he wrote in his after-action report, "and notwithstanding the risk, I determined to continue till the general sent me word. I know the persuasive power of a 9-inch [shell], and thought it better to kill a Union man or two than to lose the effect of my moral suasion."[5]

No friendly-fire casualties occurred, and the gunboats also managed to avoid torpedoes that the Confederates had planted in the river. Fort Thompson five miles south of New Bern anchored the river flank of the main Confederate defenses. Rowan's gunboats shelled the fort while attacking Union soldiers broke the enemy line and captured the city, but most of its 4,000 defenders escaped.

Burnside's cooperation with the navy continued. Their next target was the port and rail terminus at the twin cities of Beaufort and Morehead City thirty-five miles south of New Bern. These towns fell easily to the army on March 23, but Fort Macon, protecting the entrance to Beaufort Harbor, proved more difficult. On April 25, however, a combined bombardment by four gunboats and army artillery in which the naval gunfire functioned mainly as a diversion finally forced the fort's capitulation.[6] The navy quickly built up a large coaling and supply base for the North Atlantic Squadron at Beaufort.

This North Carolina campaign from January to April 1862 was the most successful example of combined army-navy operations in the war along the Atlantic coast. Apart from closing all ports in the state except Wilmington to blockade-runners, however, its strategic consequences were limited. Wilmington was a major port and grew more significant over time. The original Union plan to drive sixty miles inland from New Bern along the Neuse River to cut the important Confederate rail junction at Goldsboro was abandoned. The Neuse River was not navigable beyond Kinston (and not even that far in low water), so the navy could not support an advance to Goldsboro. Half of Burnside's troops, including the general himself, were called to Virginia in July 1862 to reinforce the Army of the Potomac, leaving barely enough Union soldiers to garrison the coastal enclaves. Much of the burden of protecting these precarious footholds on the North Carolina mainland fell to navy gunboats. By 1863 the commander of the North Atlantic Squadron was convinced that "the occupation of so many points in the sounds" was "expensive, insecure, and subjecting us to attack in detail."[7] Northern preoccupation with the Virginia theater precluded the commitment of sufficient troops for further large-scale offensive operations in North Carolina until 1865.

THE STORY WAS DIFFERENT with the second major naval campaign that began in early 1862. New Orleans was the largest city and port
in the Confederacy. It was also the most difficult to blockade. A hundred
miles below the city, the Mississippi River debouches into the Gulf through
four passes. The water over the bars of at least two of them was deep
enough most of the year for the oceangoing ships of that era. Recognizing
the difficulty of blockading multiple entrances, Welles ordered William
Mervine, then the commander of the Gulf Squadron, to establish a battery
at Head of the Passes, where the river divided into its separate channels
toward the Gulf. Mervine reported that the ground was too swampy for
a land battery. After his removal from command, his successor, William
McKean, decided instead to station four ships (two of them sailing vessels) with a total of forty-three guns at the Head of the Passes to block all
entrance and egress.[8] But as the Blockade Board reported, the Mississippi
River was not the only access by water to New Orleans. Blockade-runners
of small enough draft could go via Lake Pontchartrain or Lake Borne to
Mississippi Sound, or by Barataria Bay or Berwick on the Atchafalaya
River. Stopping up all of these holes might be impossible; the best solution was to capture New Orleans itself.[9]

Confederate leaders had long anticipated such a possibility. Even before
the war began, the provisional Confederate Congress appointed a committee of naval experts to recommend measures to defend coastal cities, including New Orleans. On February 21, 1861, the committee recommended
strengthening Forts Jackson and St. Philip seventy miles downriver from
the city and stretching a heavy chain and raft barrier across the river just
below the forts.[10] Once the war began, Louisiana Confederates bought
several steamboats for conversion to gunboats and started construction
of two large ironclads.

Long before these two vessels were completed (indeed, they never
were), the Confederates converted a Mississippi River towboat into what
amounted to the war's first ironclad, the CSS *Manassas*, by sheathing it in
one-inch plates of cylindrical shape with the apex only two and a half feet
above the water so that it looked like a huge turtle shell. At 3:00 A.M. on
October 12, 1861, the *Manassas* led four other gunboats down the river for
a surprise attack on the Union warships at the Head of the Passes. With
her cast-iron prow, the Manassas rammed the USS *Richmond* and stove
in its wooden hull below the waterline. The other Confederate gunboats
opened fire and loosed three fire rafts, which created panic in the Union
fleet. All four Union ships fled downriver.

The sailing ship USS *Vincennes* ran aground and her captain, Commander Robert Handy, misread the flagship *Richmond*'s signal to "cross the bar" as "abandon ship." He did so and then tried to set her afire, but he failed. Captain John Pope of the *Richmond* (not to be confused with the Union general of the same name) reported that Handy was "a laughing-stock of all and everyone. . . . [He] is not fit to command a ship." Squadron commander McKean agreed. Branding the affair "disgraceful" to the U.S. Navy, he relieved Handy but also accepted Pope's request to be relieved "for reasons of health." Neither Pope nor Handy got another command.[11]

This scrimmage turned out to be the last Confederate victory in the lower Mississippi valley for many months. With the appointment of Farragut as commander of the West Gulf Squadron, the Union navy began to organize a fleet of twenty-two blue-water steam sloops and gunboats to ascend the river and attack Forts Jackson and St. Philip. This armada also included twenty schooners purchased by the Navy Department and specially adapted to mount 13-inch mortars to bombard the forts with their 216-pound shells.[12]

Welles named Commander David Dixon Porter to take charge of these mortar schooners. The son of Captain David Porter, one of the American heroes in the War of 1812, David D. Porter was forty-eight years old in 1862 and a veteran of thirty-one years in the U.S. Navy. He was ambitious, able, and energetic but also cocky, self-seeking, and careless with the truth. He had recommended his foster brother Farragut for appointment as commander of the squadron. But Porter soon went behind Farragut's back in private letters to Assistant Secretary Fox in which he seemed to be intriguing to get the command for himself. Referring to delays in assembling the fleet and difficulties in getting its larger ships over the bar at Southwest Pass, Porter told Fox on March 28 that "too much time has been lost in getting these ships ready. . . . This matter throughout has not been well managed. . . . It is very difficult for a man of his age [Farragut was twelve years older than Porter] finding himself commanding so large a force for the first time in his life. . . . Men of his age in a seafaring life are not fit for the command of important enterprises, they lack the vigor of youth."[13]

Porter could not have been more wrong, as events would soon prove. Farragut was in fact full of energy and very much in charge. "Success is the only thing listened to in this war," he wrote to his wife, "and I know I must sink or swim by that rule. . . . As to being prepared for defeat, I certainly am not. Any man who is prepared for defeat would be half defeated before he commenced."[14] In fairness to Porter, it should be noted that he contributed his skills and energy to the effort to get the larger ships over the bar, using his gunboats (designated to tow the mortar schooners) to pull them through the mud and loyally carrying out Farragut's orders.[15]

By early April, Farragut had gotten the ships over the bar and was preparing to attack the two brick forts mounting 126 guns blocking his way to New Orleans. The ships stripped for action. Commander Samuel Phillips Lee of the USS *Oneida* described how "we have *housed* topmasts, *slung* gaffs, *racked* or *snaked* everything that may fall from aloft, secured spare spars over the sides, & made other arrangements for the coming trial." The larger steam sloops, including Farragut's flagship USS *Hartford*, bighted their chain cables up and down their sides abreast the engine and piled sandbags on the bow deck.[16]

Although General Benjamin Butler and an army of 15,000 men were part of this campaign, the Navy Department—and the Northern people— seemed to expect them to play the subordinate role of occupying New Orleans after the navy captured it. "You will . . . proceed up the Mississippi River and reduce the defences which guard the approaches to New Orleans," stipulated Welles's official orders to Farragut, "and take possession of it under the guns of your squadron."[17] Iowa senator James Grimes, a member of the Senate Committee on Naval Affairs, told Fox that "the country looks to the Navy. . . . Don't wait for the Army; take [New Orleans] & hold it until the Army comes up."[18] And that is exactly how it happened.

The Confederates prepared to meet the coming onslaught with as much firepower on the water and in the forts as they could muster. Shortages of iron and skilled workers delayed completion of two formidable ironclads, the CSS *Louisiana* and the CSS *Mississippi*, designed to carry sixteen and eighteen guns, respectively. The *Louisiana*, still without her engines in working order, was towed down to the forts to add her firepower as a floating battery. Meanwhile, Major General Mansfield Lovell, in charge of the defense of New Orleans, had purchased fourteen river steamboats, armed them and equipped several with reinforced bows for ramming, and manned them with steamboat crews. This force, in the words of the Confederate secretary of war, "is a peculiar one. It is not to be part of the Navy, for it is intended for service on the rivers." Lovell had little confidence in the fighting power of this makeshift flotilla. "The river pilots who are the head of the fleet," he wrote, "are men of limited ideas, no system, and no administrative capacity whatever. . . . There is little or no discipline or subordination—too much 'steamboat' and too little of the 'man-of-war' to be very effective."[19]

Lovell was ordered to send eight of these gunboats up the Mississippi to deal with Union threats to Island No. 10 near the Tennessee-Kentucky line, leaving him with six vessels and two others outfitted by the state of Louisiana plus the turtle-shell ironclad *Manassas*. After Grant's capture of Fort Donelson in February 1862, Lovell also had to send 5,000 army soldiers to Tennessee, leaving him with only 3,000 militia to defend New Orleans.[20]

On April 18 Porter's mortar boats opened their bombardment of the forts from a distance of 3,000 to 3,500 yards. Most of the schooners were concealed behind a grove of trees on a bend of the river, with fully leafed tree branches lashed to their masts for camouflage. After a pause during the first night to evaluate effectiveness, the mortars kept up their fire night and day. A sailor on the *Hartford* watched this after-dark pyrotechnic display with awe. "As the shells left the gun the track of [their burning fuses] through the air was distinctly visible, and the shots were quite accurate," he wrote in his diary. The mortar crews fired "so fast that six to seven shells could be seen coursing through the air at once."[21] The stronger of the two works, Fort Jackson on the west bank, was the main target. The commander of Confederate defenses, Brigadier General Johnson K. Duncan, reported that "the mortar fire was accurate and terrible, many of the shells falling everywhere within the fort." Several guns in Fort Jackson were disabled, but the others kept firing and inflicted considerable damage on the fleet. A captured Confederate naval officer later told Samuel Phillips Lee of the *Oneida* that Porter's mortar bombardment "had not produced any military results (though so many shells had fallen in the forts) as the dismounted guns were immediately replaced; and that every gun was in place the morning we passed the forts."[22]

Farragut had never been very confident that the mortars, even in concert with the firepower of the big Dahlgren guns of his fleet, could knock out the forts. As time went by and with the mortars averaging 3,000 rounds each day, his skepticism seemed confirmed, despite Porter's assurances that just one or two days more would do the job. Farragut resolved to run past the forts at night and steam upriver to New Orleans, leaving the forts isolated and ripe for plucking by Butler's troops. On the "wild night" of April 20, "dark, rainy, with half a gale of wind blowing down the river," two gunboats under the command of Lieutenant Charles H. B.

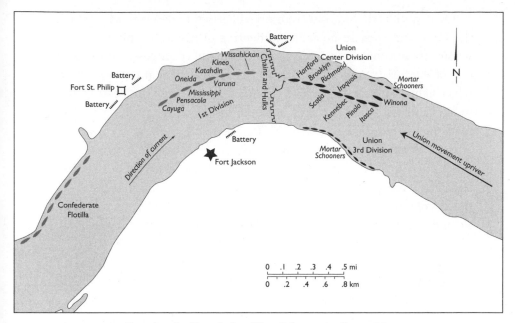

Running the Forts below New Orleans, April 24, 1862

Caldwell and Commander Henry H. Bell steamed quietly up to the heavy chain that was shackled to anchored hulks stretched across the river as an impassable obstruction. Spotted from the forts, which opened fire, Bell intrepidly unshackled the chain from one of the hulks. Caldwell took his gunboat upriver through the opening, turned around under fire, and with a full head of steam aided by the four-knot current smashed through another length of chain, opening a gap wide enough for Farragut's ships to steam through it.[23]

But this action also opened an opportunity for the Confederates to send more fire rafts piled with kindling and logs doused with oil down upon the warships and mortar schooners. The fleet surgeon on the *Hartford* described one fire-raft attack preceded by a flag of truce as a ruse. "A large rebel steamer is coming down *with a white flag of truce*," he recorded in his diary. "Orders are given for a steamer to go and meet her, but the traitor steamer set fire to three fire-rafts she had in tow, hoisted the enemy colors and ran up the river! Such is the use they make of flags of truce. As she turned back the forts opened all their guns upon our fleet. Their rifled cannon, fired with great precision, are troubling us much."[24] Picket boats equipped with grapnels clamped on to the fire rafts and towed them harmlessly to shore, as they had done before.

Incidents like this one only reinforced Farragut's determination to pass the forts. On April 22 he called a meeting of his ship captains, among whom "there is but little or no sanguine feeling of success," according to one of them.[25] In military annals it was proverbial that councils of war never fight. But this one proved an exception, despite the pessimism of many captains. After Farragut outlined his plans for running past the forts, he invited their responses. "The prevailing opinion seemed to be adverse to making the attempt to pass the forts at that time," wrote one of the participants, "that it was premature; that the forts had not yet been sufficiently reduced by the fire of the mortar vessels, and that the risk of the loss of too many vessels was too great to be run." But Farragut said that the mortars would soon exhaust their ammunition and that it was now or never: "I believe in celerity."[26]

The commanders returned to their ships to prepare for what many still thought of as a doomed enterprise. Many followed the tradition of writing what might be their last letter home. "Our people view this conflict as most desperate," wrote the executive officer of the USS *Pensacola*, Lieutenant Francis Roe. "These may be the last lines I will ever write. But I have an unflinching trust in God that we shall plant the Union flag upon the enemy's forts by noon tomorrow. . . . If I fall, I leave my darlings to the care of my country."[27]

At 2:00 A.M. on April 24, seventeen ships carrying 154 guns weighed anchor and proceeded toward the forts in three divisions, with the *Hartford* and the other larger ships in the middle division. The mortar fleet and the five steamers that towed them opened a furious bombardment to keep down the fire of the forts. Captain Theodorus Bailey was commander of the first division, leading the van in the USS *Cayuga*, one of the ninety-day gunboats just commissioned in February. As he approached the forts, wrote Bailey in his official report, "we were struck from stem to stern. At length we were close up with St. Philip, when we opened with grape and canister. Scarcely were we above the line of fire when we found ourselves attacked by the rebel fleet of gunboats; this was hot, but more congenial work." Three of them converged on the *Cayuga* hoping to ram and board her. Her 11-inch Dahlgren fired on one of them at thirty yards distance. "The effect was very destructive. He immediately sheered inshore, ran aground, and burned himself up." Two other gunboats in Bailey's division, the USS *Oneida* and USS *Varuna*, emerged from the smoke and darkness to help, as more of the Confederate River Defense gunboats swarmed around the three Union ships. "The enemy were so thick," said Bailey,

The sinking of the USS *Varuna* by the Confederate gunboats *J. C. Breckinridge* and *Governor Moore*, April 24, 1862. The *Breckinridge* on the left rams the *Varuna* while the *Moore* on the right prepares to ram her other side. (From *Frank Leslie's Illustrated History of the Civil War*)

"that it was like duck shooting; what missed one rebel hit another. With their aid we cleared the kitchen"—but not before two of the Confederate ships rammed and sank the *Varuna*.[28]

Samuel Phillips Lee of the *Oneida* took up the account. After passing the forts with minimal damage, "the smoke had now become so thick that it was very difficult for me to pilot the ship even from the Forecastle. . . . We were soon among the rebel gunboats but the smoke and darkness made it impossible to distinguish friends from foes." The enemy gunboats showed lights, however, which gave the *Oneida* a target. "The two rebel gunboats which had run into the Varuna . . . and stove her, finding it impossible to escape the Oneida ran ashore and set fire to their vessels." The *Oneida* also saved the *Cayuga* from the fate of the *Varuna*. "The Brave Lee," wrote Captain Bailey, "came to my relief in the nick of time. I had more rebel steamers engaging me than I could attend to without support when Lee . . . came dashing up delivering a refreshing fire." David D. Porter wrote to Assistant Secretary Fox that "I never saw a ship more beautifully fought and managed" than the *Oneida*. Lee "was under fire more than anyone else. . . . His ship was a good deal cut up. He had much more than his share of killed and wounded and said less about it than those who did not take the bull so closely by the horns."[29]

After this melee, the *Cayuga* continued upriver and at dawn spotted an encampment of five companies of Louisiana militia on shore beyond the levee. High water enabled the ship's guns to fire over the levee. The *Cayuga* loosed several rounds at the camp. The executive officer "shouted to them to come on board and deliver up their arms, or we would blow them to pieces," as the officer described it in a letter to his family in New Hampshire. "It seemed rather odd for a regiment on shore to be surrendering to a ship," he acknowledged. But as the Confederate colonel later explained to a court of inquiry, "after losing some thirty men killed and wounded, with no possibility of escape or rescue . . . I thought it my duty to surrender."[30]

Just behind the *Cayuga* came the *Pensacola*. Lieutenant Roe did live to see the American flag wave over the forts and to hug his children again— though his uniform was half torn off by shrapnel. The *Pensacola* fought the forts and enemy gunboats simultaneously. "The guns' crews, right under me, were decimated," Roe reported four days later. "The groans, shrieks, and wails of the dying and wounded were so horrible that I shudder now at the recollection of it."[31]

On the *Hartford*, Farragut climbed the port mizzen ratline to get above the roiling smoke from the guns and fire rafts for a better view of what was happening. Holding on to the shrouds, he "stood there as cool as if leaning against a mantel in his own home," according to a sailor. Farragut's signal officer pleaded with him to come down. "We can't afford to lose you, Flag Officer," he said. "They'll get you up there, sure." Farragut finally came down, and as he reached the deck, a shell exploded where he had been standing on the ratline.[32]

On deck of the *Hartford* during much of the action was the fleet surgeon, who made notes in real time to write up in his journal. "I can not and will not attempt a description of this awful, dreadful, trying scene," he wrote—but then he proceeded to do so. "The din, the roar, the crash, the whistling of balls, the bursting of shells, the crashing of masts and timbers, the shrieks of the wounded and dying . . . was a scene which has never been surpassed. A magazine in Fort Jackson was exploded. The river was filled with burning fire-rafts."[33]

Veering to evade one of these rafts, the *Hartford* ran aground under the guns of Fort St. Philip. A Confederate tug pushed the raft against her port quarter. Flames climbed up the side of the hull and shot halfway up the mast. "I thought it was all up with us," wrote Farragut later that morning to Porter, who had stayed behind with the mortar boats. But after a few

Part of Farragut's fleet passing Fort St. Philip, April 24, 1862. The guns on the parapet of the fort (in the background) fire on the Union ships, including Farragut's flagship, the USS *Hartford* (partly obscured by the smoke of a Confederate gunboat in the foreground), while the turtle-backed ironclad CSS *Manassas* moves in to attack. the Union ships. (From *Frank Leslie's Illustrated History of the Civil War*)

seconds of confusion, the crew went to fire stations and began playing hoses on the burning ship. The quick-thinking signal officer—the same man who had talked Farragut down from the rigging—rolled three 20-pound shells to the side of the deck, uncapped them, and pushed them over the side onto the blazing raft, blowing it into fragments. The hoses finally doused the fire on the ship, the engineers applied all power to back the *Hartford* off the mud, and she proceeded upriver.[34]

After treating some wounded men below, the surgeon again came on deck, where "I saw a big river steamboat coming straight for us. Her decks were black with armed men who evidently hoped to board our ship." The forecastle gun manned by marines "immediately planted a shell in the advancing steamboat. It must have gone straight to her boiler or magazine, for there was a terrific explosion and the entire vessel, with her swarming human freight disappeared."[35]

Fourteen of Farragut's seventeen ships made it past the forts and the ironclad CSS *Louisiana*, moored as a floating battery. The last three gunboats in the third division got tangled in the chain of the obstructions as dawn was breaking and the forts concentrated all their fire on them. They finally escaped downriver.[36] The most feared Confederate vessel was the ironclad ram *Manassas*. In a letter to his wife, Farragut described what happened to that enemy ship. "After we had passed the forts," he wrote, "I saw the ram coming up. I hailed Melancton Smith," commander of the big sidewheeler USS *Mississippi*, "and told him to run her down. Smith turned his ship, head down stream, and they ran at each other. We all looked on with intense anxiety. When within fifty yards, the enemy's heart failed him, and he turned to the right and ran on shore. Smith poured in a broadside, which riddled her. She floated down stream, on fire from her own furnaces," and soon sank. Conning the *Mississippi* in this confrontation was twenty-four-year-old Lieutenant George Dewey, who would sail into Manila Bay with guns blazing thirty-six years later.[37]

At midmorning of April 24, thirteen vessels of Farragut's fleet rendezvoused at Quarantine Station seven miles above the forts. Only the *Varuna* had been lost. All of the other ships were more or less seriously damaged but still operational. Casualties were thirty-seven killed and 147 wounded. The captain's clerk on the USS *Iroquois* seemed more upset by the damage and casualties than by success in passing the forts. "My poor ship is knocked almost to pieces," he lamented. "Fore and aft our bulwarks are torn to kindling wood. . . . All our men were killed in the same way, torn to pieces. The head of a powder boy was blown away and never found." On the other hand, Captain Thomas Craven of the USS *Brooklyn*, a sister ship of the *Hartford*, had been one of the officers who had counseled delay in trying to pass the forts. But now he judged the battle "the most brilliant thing in the way of a naval fight ever performed. . . . I had always looked upon it as a most desperate undertaking, and thought that but few of our number would be left to witness our most terrible disaster. But the Lord of Hosts was with us."[38]

Although Confederate casualties in the forts were light, their gunboats lost an unknown but large number killed. Seven of the eight vessels in the Southern River Defense fleet plus the *Manassas* were destroyed and the other one eventually captured. In truth, these rebel mariners had not performed very well, several of their steamers having been sunk while trying to flee. In a report to the Confederate War Department, General Mansfield Lovell offered a scathing indictment of their civilian captains and crews. "Unwilling to govern themselves, and unwilling to be governed by others, their total want of system, vigilance, and discipline rendered them useless and helpless when the enemy finally dashed upon them suddenly in a dark night."[39]

Cut off and isolated, with Butler's troops finally approaching the forts, the garrison at Fort Jackson mutinied, and both forts surrendered to Porter and the navy on April 28. The Confederates blew up their big ironclads *Louisiana* and *Mississippi* to prevent their capture. Meanwhile, Farragut had taken his battered but victorious vessels upriver to New Orleans on April 25. The remaining militia fled and the city was virtually defenseless, except for two earthworks with fourteen guns flanking the river at Chalmette three miles downstream from New Orleans, where Andrew Jackson had stopped the British in 1815. But nothing would stop Farragut. His screw sloops *Hartford*, *Brooklyn*, and *Pensacola*, plus the gunboats *Oneida* and *Cayuga*, came on firing, first with their bow guns and then veering left or right to fire crushing broadsides into the works. In twenty minutes the Confederate guns were silenced and "those who could run," as Farragut reported to Welles, "were running in every direction."[40]

Rumors of the Federal advance had preceded their actual arrival by twenty-four hours. Panic overtook the city. Some 30,000 bales of cotton were stored there; most of them were soon in flames and floating down the river. Hogsheads of tobacco and barrels of sugar, corn, and rice were broken open and poured into the river or looted by opportunists who flocked to the levee, which became "one general conflagration of everything that could be of use to the enemy," wrote a local matron.[41] The orgy of conflagration was not confined to New Orleans. At Baton Rouge eighty miles up the river, the smoke from burning cotton suffused the atmosphere. "Wagons and drays, and everything that could be driven, or rolled along were to be seen in every direction loaded with the bales," wrote a nineteen-year-old Baton Rouge woman. "Up and down the levee, as far as we could see, negroes were rolling it down to the brink of the river, where they would set the [bales] afire, and push them in, to float burning down the river." Cotton was not the only thing destroyed. "Every grog shop has been emptied, and gutters and pavements flowing with liquors of all kinds, so that if the Yankees are fond of strong drink, I fear they will fare ill."[42]

Union sailors were amazed by this saturnalia of destruction. As their ships approached New Orleans, "over a thousand bales of [burning] cotton passed us floating down the river," wrote the captain of the *Richmond*. "We passed over twenty large ships on fire before we came in sight of New Orleans, and there a horrible sight met our eyes. They had set fire to all the ships and steamers for miles along the wharves."[43] Farragut shook his head sadly. "Such vandalism I have never witnessed," he wrote to his wife. His fleet surgeon noted on April 25 that "the gunboats were busy all evening towing burning ships and fire-rafts and fire-ships free of the fleet."[44]

There followed four days of confusion and violence in the streets of New Orleans that threatened to break into full-scale urban warfare. "The rebels committed before our eyes the most atrocious act that ever was heard of," recorded the keeper of the *Richmond*'s log. As the band of another warship struck up "The Star-Spangled Banner," a crowd gathered and waved handkerchiefs apparently in support of their old flag. "At the same moment," wrote the log-keeper, "a troop of horsemen came riding up one of the streets and fired a volley into the men, women, and children. If it had not been for the innocent people that would have been destroyed we would have fired a whole broadside of grape into them."[45]

Most of the people who gathered on the streets cursed the Yankees and yelled blood-curdling threats. After a few marines raised the American flag on the U.S. mint, several men tore it down and ripped it to shreds. The future Southern author George Washington Cable, then seventeen years old, witnessed the fury of the mob. "The crowds on the levee howled and screamed with rage," he recalled. "The swarming decks answered never a word; but one old tar on the *Hartford*, standing with lanyard in hand beside a great pivot-gun, so plain to view that you could see him smile, silently patted its big black breech and blandly grinned."[46]

In a tragicomedy of "negotiations" for surrender of the city, the mayor refused to do anything while the mobs grew more vitriolic. Tiring of the farce, Farragut on April 29 sent in the marines. The *Hartford*'s surgeon described the scene in his diary. April 29: "Our ships were placed in position to bombard the city. At noon one hundred and twenty marines . . . and fifty sailors with two howitzers . . . landed and marched to City Hall and hauled down the flag of Louisiana. . . . They hoisted the U.S. colors over the custom-house and mint. . . . New Orleans silent and sullen, citizens insolent and abusive and our marines on shore guarding colors." May 1: "General Butler arrived with three regiments . . . with colors flying and bands playing *Yankee Doodle* and *The Star-Spangled Banner*."[47]

The capture of New Orleans had a greater public impact in both North and South—and abroad—than any other event of the war thus far. If those dark hours before the dawn of April 24 when Farragut's fleet passed the forts do not quite merit the dramatic words of one book title, *The Night the War Was Lost*, the hyperbole can be forgiven. "New Orleans falling seems to have made a stampede in 'Secessia,'" wrote David D. Porter to Gustavus

Fox. "You may put the rebellion down as 'spavined,' 'broken-backed' and 'wind-galled.'"[48] Southern newspapers bemoaned the "Great Disaster and Humiliation . . . sudden shock . . . unexpected and heavy blow . . . deplorable calamity . . . by far the most serious reverse of the war." The fire-eating secessionist Edmund Ruffin, who proudly claimed to have fired the first shot at Fort Sumter, lamented "the recent disaster at New Orleans. . . . I cannot help admitting . . . the possibility of the subjugation of the southern states."[49]

Northern elation mirrored Southern dejection. From Washington, Elizabeth Blair Lee, whose brother Montgomery was in Lincoln's Cabinet, wrote to her husband, who had commanded the *Oneida* in the capture of New Orleans, that "our people are in a frenzy of exultation" over this achievement.[50] Far away in London, young Henry Adams returned to the American legation from a springtime walk in Hyde Park to find his normally austere father dancing across the floor and shouting, "We've got New Orleans." "The effect of this news here," added Henry, "has been greater than anything yet." The Confederate envoy James Mason also wrote from London that "the fall of New Orleans will certainly exercise a depressing influence here for intervention."[51] It was the climactic event in the series of Union victories that winter and spring that dampened even Emperor Napoleon III's pre-Confederate sympathies. "There is little more said just now," wrote the American minister to France, about "the propriety of an early recognition of the south."[52]

Most of those victories had been won wholly or in part by the navy. But Farragut did not intend to rest on his laurels. His original orders instructed him after capturing New Orleans to "take advantage of the panic to push a strong force up river to take all their defenses in the rear. You will also reduce the fortifications which defend Mobile Bay and turn them over to the army to hold."[53] This was a tall order indeed, as events would demonstrate. In the spring of 1862, however, many people in the North—and in the South also for that matter—considered the Union navy invincible.

Farragut would have preferred to attack Mobile before going up the Mississippi. He was a blue-water sailor, never very happy confined by river banks with mud or sandbars uncomfortably close under his keel. From New Orleans on the day that marines raised the flag over public buildings, Farragut wrote to the Navy Department: "As soon as I see General Butler safely in possession of this place I will sail for Mobile with the fleet. . . . Depend upon it, we will keep up the stampede upon them."[54]

But Farragut evidently looked again at his orders, which specified priority for opening the river before attacking Mobile. A week later he informed Welles that he had sent seven gunboats "up the river to keep up the panic as far as possible. The large ships, I fear, will not be able to go higher than Baton Rouge [they did go higher], while I have sent the smaller vessels, under Commander [Samuel Phillips] Lee, as high as Vicksburg." Reports of the Yankees' approach caused another round of cotton burning hundreds of miles up the river. "From every plantation rises the smoke of burning cotton," wrote Kate Stone at her family's Louisiana plantation north of Vicksburg. "Mama has $420,000 worth burning on the gin ridge now."[55] Lee's gunboats compelled the surrender of Baton Rouge and Natchez on the way up. But when Lee reached Vicksburg on May 18 and demanded its capitulation, the Confederate military governor sent a cheeky reply: "Mississippians don't know, and refuse to learn, how to surrender to any enemy. If Commodore Farragut or Brigadier-General Butler can teach them, let them come and try."[56]

Farragut would soon come and try. His initial message to the Navy Department stating his intention to take the fleet to Mobile had set off alarm bells in Washington. "The opening of the Mississippi is of more importance than Mobile," Fox wrote to him. "Carry out your instructions of January 20 about ascending the Mississippi River, as it is of the utmost importance. . . . Mobile, Pensacola, and in fact the whole coast sinks into insignificance compared to this."[57]

Farragut found these communications awaiting him when he returned to New Orleans from Vicksburg, where he had gone personally with some of his vessels for a reconnaissance. In letters to his wife, he complained of the Navy Department's pressure on him and ignorance of the difficulties he faced. "They will keep us in this river until the vessels break down, and all the little reputation we have made has evaporated," he wrote. "The Government appear to think we can do anything. They expect me to navigate the Mississippi nine hundred miles in the face of batteries, iron-clad rams, etc. . . . But fighting is nothing to the evils of the river—getting on shore, running afoul of one another, losing anchors, etc. . . . I was threatened with an attack of nervous fever . . . owing to the loss of rest when my ship was aground. I thought she was gone." To Secretary Welles, Farragut reported that "the elements of destruction to the Navy in this river are beyond anything I have ever encountered. . . . More anchors have been lost and vessels ruined than I have seen in a lifetime, and those vessels that do not run into others are themselves run into and crushed in such a manner as to render them unseaworthy."[58]

Welles's reaction to this letter is unknown. He was aware that Farragut would soon be named the first rear admiral in the history of the U.S. Navy. In effect, Welles and Fox told Farragut: We know that the job of capturing Vicksburg will be challenging, but we also know that you can do anything, and are now an admiral, so go do it. By June 11, Farragut was on his way back up the river to Vicksburg, this time in his beloved flagship, *Hartford.* "[W]hen I will go down again God only knows," he wrote to Captain Theodorus Bailey. "It appears the Department is under the impression that it is easier for me, with my dilapidated vessels, to encounter the difficulties of the Mississippi and ascend a thousand miles against a strong current, than it is for Foote and Davis, with vessels peculiarly constructed for the river, to come down the stream."[59]

The Western Flotilla, commanded first by Andrew H. Foote and then by Charles H. Davis, had fought its way down the river, earning them promotions to become the fourth and fifth rear admirals in the navy's history. The Flotilla's rendezvous with Farragut's fleet at Vicksburg in July 1862 climaxed a story that began a year earlier in St. Louis.

chapter four

The River War in 1861–1862

James B. Eads of St. Louis knew the Mississippi River better than any man alive. Forty-one years old in 1861, he had invented a diving bell attached to a surface vessel for salvaging wrecked steamboats from the bottom of the river. He had also developed machinery to remove the snags (submerged trees) that caused many of those wrecks. With the support of fellow Missourian Edward Bates, the U.S. attorney general, Eads proposed to convert some of his vessels to river gunboats with casemates and other vital parts protected by two-to-three-inch iron plates. He obtained a contract with the War Department for two such gunboats. Why the War Department rather than Navy Department? The government considered inland operations, even on rivers, to be the responsibility of the army, "to which the subject more properly belongs," in the words of Secretary of the Navy Gideon Welles.[1]

Indeed, Welles was at first quite adamant in his insistence that "the gunboats on the Mississippi and Western rivers are under the control and direction of the War Department, with which the Navy has no connection either in building or fitting up of boats or officering them."[2] In May 1861 Welles had sent Commander John Rodgers (whose father of the same name had achieved fame as a navy captain in the War of 1812) to advise the army in the purchase of riverboats for conversion to gunboats. Instead, Rodgers bought three on his own authority and arranged for their conversion by lowering the boilers into the hold, strengthening the decks to support the weight of guns, and adding five inches of oak backing to the bulwarks. These first "timberclads"—the USS *Conestoga*, the USS *Lexington*, and the USS *Tyler*—would become famous in the annals of riverine warfare. But in June 1861, Welles did not know that yet, and he chastised Rodgers for going beyond his orders. "The Department can not recognize or sanction any contract for boats," he told Rodgers, "nor with our limited

The USS *St. Louis*, one of the Eads ironclad "Pook's Turtles." (Courtesy of the National Archives)

number of officers can we spare any such number as are proposed for interior operations. . . . The movement in that quarter pertains to the Army and not the Navy."[3]

Welles would eventually change his tune on this matter. And the contretemps did not hurt Rodgers' career, for he went on to command several vessels in two theaters and was ultimately promoted to rear admiral. In 1861 the quartermaster general of the army, Montgomery Meigs, paid for the timberclads and also for the two snag boats from Eads. In addition, the army contracted with Eads in August 1861 for the construction of seven new gunboats designed by Eads with modifications by Rodgers and by naval constructor Samuel Pook. Flat-bottomed and wide-beamed to give them a shallow draft of only six feet, with the sloping casemates sheathed in two and a half inches of iron protecting the machinery, paddle wheels, and crew quarters, and carrying thirteen guns, these ironclads named after river cities were called "Pook's Turtles" because the casemate designed by the naval constructor resembled the shell of that aquatic reptile.

Despite continuing confusion and contention over which service would supply and pay the officers (the navy) and crew (the army), and provide the ordnance and fittings for the boats (both), this hybrid fleet soon achieved an extraordinary record on the western rivers. This success was owing mainly to the personalities and leadership qualities of two men: Andrew H. Foote and Ulysses S. Grant.

In September 1861 Welles named Foote as commander of what became known as the Western Flotilla. With a long and distinguished antebellum career of service on two oceans and the Mediterranean and Caribbean Seas, Foote would have preferred a blue-water assignment in the Civil War. But his old schoolmate and boyhood friend Welles wanted him for tougher and more important duty: creating the new brown-water army/ navy, which Welles now recognized as both a challenge and an opportunity for the navy. Foote's correspondence during the months when he organized, outfitted, and crewed his new flotilla sometimes reads like the story of Sisyphus trying to roll the stone uphill. "Weary days are my lot," he wrote to his wife in December. "If I could be fitted out at a navy yard, I would not care; but this fitting out of vessels where no one knows anything is discouraging."[4] Several weeks later he declared that "if I could have been at once placed under the Navy Dept all would have gone well, but between Army & Navy, I have had more work and mental suffering than I ever expected."[5]

Foote's biggest headache was finding enough crewmen for his twelve boats. He scraped several barrels to come up with the men: soldiers detailed from the army, volunteer riverboat men, civilian steamboat pilots and engineers, and a few seamen recruited from the saltwater navy. But he never had enough men and had to cannibalize crewmen from some boats left out of the initial operations in order to provide minimal crews for vessels that went into action in February 1862. This whole experience, he wrote in March, had added "ten years prematurely . . . to my age."[6]

If Foote had one comfort during those months, it was his good relationship with Grant. By tradition and law, neither commander could give orders to the other's branch of the service. But both Grant and Foote were free from the overweening egotism that seemed to infect so many other officers, and they were therefore able to work well together. They also agreed on the right strategy for their campaigns on land and water. They established their base at Cairo, Illinois, at or near the junction of four major navigable rivers: the Ohio, the Mississippi, the Tennessee, and the Cumberland. The last three of these rivers pointed like arrows deep into the heartland of the Confederacy. The Mississippi ran for hundreds of miles through the best cotton land in the world, while the Tennessee and Cumberland Rivers flowed through some of the principal grain-growing, mule- and horse-breeding, and iron-producing areas of the South. Union conquest and control of these regions would strike a crippling blow to the Confederacy. As they became available in late 1861 and early 1862, Foote's timberclads and ironclads gave Grant's troops the mobility and additional firepower that made this conquest possible.

Confederates were well aware of the strategic importance of this river network. They too began to convert steamboats into gunboats and to begin construction of ironclads in this theater to counter potential Union thrusts. They knew that the industrial North could always outproduce them, however, so they relied mainly on fixed fortifications at key points along the rivers to defend their heartland. Farragut would demonstrate the defects of this strategy, but that demonstration was several months in the future as Southern engineers began to construct their river forts in 1861. They built most of them on high bluffs or other points with clear fields of fire along the Mississippi River from Columbus, Kentucky, down to Grand Gulf, Mississippi. They were particularly proud of the elaborate fortifications and 140 guns at Columbus, which someone labeled the "Gibraltar of the West." Because of this focus on the Mississippi, however, Confederates devoted less effort to the Tennessee and Cumberland Rivers. It was their bad luck that this was the way the Yankees decided to come.

At first, however, the Federals seemed as fixated on the Mississippi as the Confederates. On November 7 the timberclads *Lexington* and *Tyler* escorted army transports carrying five of Grant's regiments for an attack on a Confederate camp at Belmont, Missouri, across the river from Columbus. After overrunning the camp, Grant's troops were eventually driven back by the reinforced enemy. The timberclads exchanged shells with the Columbus batteries and the counterattacking Confederate infantry, holding them off long enough to get Grant's men safely reembarked.

Both Foote and Grant considered this expedition and a subsequent feint against Columbus as preliminary to a real attack on the Gibraltar of the West. So did Major General Leonidas Polk, Confederate commander at Columbus, who called on Richmond for "strong reinforcements."[7] On the day after Christmas, Gustavus Fox wrote to Foote: "I hope we shall soon hear of your success at Columbus, the key of the West; when that falls down goes everything there." President Lincoln got into the act, urging the completion of mortar rafts to "rain the rebels out" of Columbus with "a refreshing shower of sulphur and brimstone."[8]

As matters turned out, the mortar rafts were not completed in time, and Foote's flotilla never did attack Columbus. Instead, the Confederates evacuated their Gibraltar in late February because of dramatic events on the Tennessee and Cumberland Rivers. The energetic Lieutenant Seth L. Phelps, commander of the timberclad *Conestoga*, had been carrying out reconnaissances on these rivers since October, keeping track of the Confederate construction of Fort Henry on the Tennessee and Fort Donelson on the Cumberland just south of the Kentucky-Tennessee border where the two rivers were only twelve miles apart. By capturing these forts and pushing up both rivers (southward), Phelps told Foote, Union forces would get into the rear of Polk at Columbus and General Albert Sidney Johnston's main Confederate army centered at Bowling Green, Kentucky. Phelps convinced Foote and Grant, who urged Major General Henry W. Halleck, commander of army forces in that theater, to turn Grant and his 15,000 men loose for an attack on Fort Henry supported by Foote's ironclads and timberclads.[9]

Halleck finally did so on February 1. Foote and Grant moved immediately. Despite continued deficiencies in manpower, Foote cobbled together enough crews to man the three timberclads and four of the nine ironclads. The timberclads under Lieutenant Phelps fished up eight "torpedoes" that the Confederates had planted downriver from Fort Henry. Moored just under the surface, each sheet-metal cylinder contained seventy-five pounds of powder with the percussion cap to explode it when touched by a vessel's hull. These "infernal machines" and other types of mines (then called torpedoes) turned out to be the Confederacy's most deadly naval weapon. But not this time, for Phelps seems to have found and disarmed all of the torpedoes that the river current had not already torn loose.

Convoyed by the gunboats, army transports landed Grant's troops three miles below the fort on February 4 and 5. The plan was for the gunboats to shell the fort while the infantry marched to attack it from the rear and prevent the garrison from escaping. In the event, heavy rain and bottomless muddy roads delayed the troops. Confederate Brigadier General Lloyd Tilghman sent most of his 2,500 men to Fort Donelson, retaining just enough at Fort Henry to man the twelve guns bearing on the river. The fort was not situated on high ground, and its lower tier was flooded by the rising river after the heavy rains of the last few days. (Fort Heiman on high ground across the river was uncompleted and did not figure in the battle.)

On February 6 the four ironclads steamed line abreast toward Fort Henry, their bow guns blazing away while the three timberclads stayed to the rear and added their less-effective long-range fire to the attack. The outgunned rebel cannoneers kept up a courageous fire, scoring some

Attack by the Union Western Flotilla on Fort Henry, February 6, 1862.
The four ironclads steamed close to the fort in the left distance while the three
timberclads (on the right) stayed in the rear and fired over the ironclads.
(From *Frank Leslie's Illustrated History of the Civil War*)

eighty hits on the ironclads, one of them blowing up the boiler of the converted snagboat USS *Essex* and scalding twenty men to death. Nevertheless, Foote kept the other three ironclads going upriver toward the fort, closing to within 300 yards when the garrison, most of their guns disabled and half of the men dead or wounded, raised the white flag. Union troops were nowhere in sight, so Tilghman surrendered to Foote.[10]

The timberclads went upriver under the ubiquitous Seth Phelps to destroy or capture any Confederate vessels they found. They wrecked the railroad bridge over the Tennessee River twenty-five miles above Fort Henry, thus severing the connection between the two parts of Johnston's army at Bowling Green and Columbus. Phelps continued another 150 miles upriver to the rapids at Muscle Shoals near Florence, Alabama. Along the way, his little flotilla burned seven steamboats loaded with supplies and brought back two others, including the powerful *Eastport*, which the Confederates were converting into an ironclad. Phelps reported that they also captured "250,000 feet of the best quality of ship and building lumber, and the iron, machinery, spikes, plating-nails, etc. belonging to the rebel gun-boats."[11]

Coming at the same time as the capture of Roanoke Island, the victory at Fort Henry caused elation in the North and consternation in Confederate circles. A naval lieutenant in the Bureau of Ordnance and Hydrography in Washington reported to Foote that "we all went wild over your

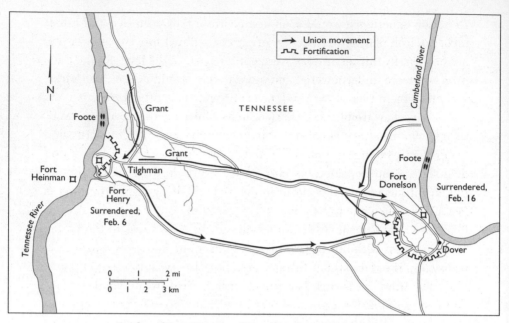

Battles of Fort Henry and Fort Donelson, February 1862

success. . . . Uncle Abe was joyful, and said everything of the navy boys and spoke of you—in his plain, sensible appreciation of merit and skill."[12]

Grant and Foote wasted no time in celebration. Grant wired Halleck on February 6: "I shall take and destroy Fort Donelson on the 8th."[13] Foote took his battered ironclads downriver to Cairo, where he arranged to make quick repairs on two of them and bring these two plus two others that had not fought at Fort Henry up the Cumberland River to Fort Donelson. Grant had only twelve miles to march overland, while Foote had more than 150 miles to go by water. Grant was slowed by bad weather and problems of resupply, so neither the troops nor gunboats arrived until February 12 and 13.

Everyone except Foote seemed to expect that his "invincible" ironclads could repeat their performance at Fort Henry. Foote wanted more time to prepare his vessels and to bring up two more that were still undergoing repairs. He also recognized that the twelve guns in Fort Donelson's two batteries situated forty feet above water level could direct a plunging fire against weak points on his ironclads. The casemates sloped at a thirty-five-degree angle and worked well to deflect fire from enemy vessels and from guns at water level as at Fort Henry, but they were vulnerable to plunging fire. Some parts of these vessels were not protected by armor, and the Fort

Donelson experience would soon demonstrate that even two and a half inches of iron plating were not proof against a direct hit. The answer was not necessarily thicker armor covering more parts of the boat, for the Eads ironclads were underpowered and more weight would deepen their draft and make them even slower and more unwieldy in swift currents.

Foote was aware of these shortcomings. But he acquiesced to Grant's request that he attack Fort Donelson on February 14 while Grant's 25,000 troops encircled the land side of the fort to prevent the escape of its 14,000 defenders. Foote repeated his Fort Henry tactics in the attack, bringing the four ironclads steadily closer to the fort and firing their bow guns as fast as possible while two timberclads fired from a safer distance. A Confederate private in the 49th Tennessee was an eyewitness to the battle. "The gunboats with full Determination to take our Battrey by Storme . . . pressed up the river stidley firing on us," he wrote with unique orthography. "The Bum shells were bursting in the air threatening sudden death and distrucktion. Stil tha came on . . . within Three Hundred yards of the Batterys and tha turned loosed their guns with grap shot to run our gunners away from thear Guns but tha finding our men to hard and brave for them, tha concluded to givit up and tha turned down the River while the Iron and Wood was flying from them upin the air tha sneaked down behind the bend badly tore to peasis."[14]

This private did not exaggerate by much. Foote admitted that he had brought his ironclads too close to the enemy batteries, thereby increasing the angle of their plunging fire. "I will not go so close again, although at Fort Henry I produced an effect by it," he told his wife.[15] Confederate shots riddled the gunboats' smokestacks, shot away tiller ropes, cracked armor, and smashed through pilot houses into the bowels of the vessels. One by one, they drifted back downriver out of the fight. Each ironclad was hit at least forty times; eleven sailors were killed and forty-one wounded, while not a single gun or gunner in the fort was lost. One of the wounded was Foote, who suffered a painful injury to his ankle by a shot that entered the pilothouse of his flagship USS *St. Louis* and killed the pilot standing next to him.[16]

The navy had suffered a very bloody nose and the Confederate defenders enjoyed a great boost in morale. It did them little good, however, for when the garrison tried a breakout attack the next day while Grant was absent downriver to consult with Foote, the Union general returned and organized a counterattack that closed the gate and forced the surrender of the fort and 12,500 prisoners on February 16. Even though the victory was almost entirely an army affair this time, Foote and his flotilla shared in the credit and in the adulation heaped on the victors. Now that the Cumberland River was open all the way to Nashville, that city fell on February 25. To avoid being cut off and captured, General Leonidas Polk evacuated Columbus. Almost all of Kentucky and much of middle and west Tennessee came under Union control, as Johnston concentrated his remaining troops at Corinth in northeast Mississippi.

Leaving the timberclads *Tyler* and *Lexington* to support further army operations in the Tennessee and Cumberland valleys, Foote took the rest of his flotilla to begin the push down the Mississippi. When the Confederates abandoned Columbus, they established their next line of defense on the big river at Island No. 10 (so named because it was the tenth island down from the confluence of the Ohio and Mississippi Rivers at Cairo). Situated in the middle of a reverse S-curve in the river near the borders of Kentucky, Tennessee, and Missouri, Confederate batteries on the island and on the Tennessee shore had clear fields of fire against any vessels trying to pass down the river. General Polk considered Island No. 10 an even stronger bastion than Columbus. It "can be held by a much smaller force. . . . I do not think the enemy's gunboats can pass the island." A powerful floating battery was part of the Confederate defenses there. Its commander was confident of "a victory if the enemy attack this place with his gunboats. I do not believe it possible for him to run a part of his boats by in the night."[17]

Foote shared this belief. He was not the same bold leader on the Mississippi that he had been on the Tennessee and Cumberland Rivers. The damage suffered by his ironclads at Fort Donelson had given him pause. Because his boats would be fighting downstream on the Mississippi, they would drift toward the enemy if disabled rather than fall back out of range as they had at Fort Donelson. Foote's wound did not heal but grew worse as the weeks went by. He needed to be on crutches much of the time. As he came under increasing pressure to attack Island No. 10, the weight of responsibility and expectations festered in his mind as his wound festered in his ankle. In mid-March he learned that his thirteen-year-old son had died at home in New Haven. The courageous captain of whom it was said that "you 'pray like a saint and fight like a devil'" continued to pray but seemed reluctant to fight.[18] In letters to his wife, Foote complained of "pressure which would crush most men . . . the vast responsibility of this river, which, if disaster occur to my boats, the rebels could retake Columbus, capture St. Louis, and command the Mississippi River." Foote told

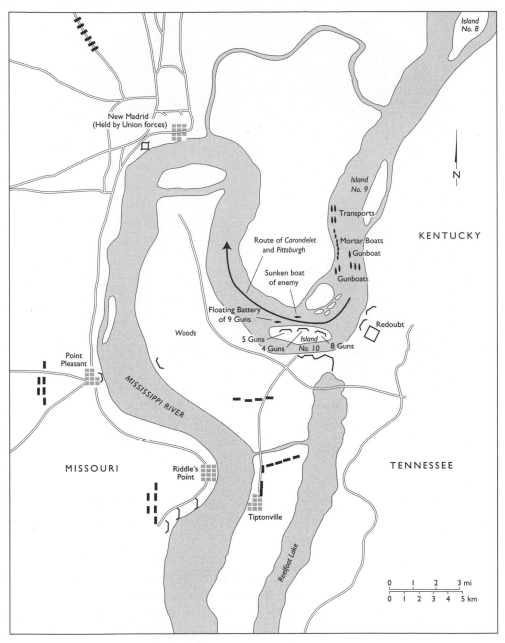

Island
No. 8

New Madrid
(Held by Union forces)

Island
No. 9

Transports

Mortar Boats

Gunboat

KENTUCKY

Route of *Carondelet*
and *Pittsburgh*

Gunboats

Sunken boat
of enemy

Floating Battery
of 9 Guns

Redoubt

Woods

5 Guns

Island
No. 10

8 Guns

4 Guns

Point
Pleasant

N

MISSISSIPPI RIVER

TENNESSEE

MISSOURI

Riddle's
Point

Tiptonville

Reelfoot Lake

0   1   2   3 mi
0   1   2   3   4   5 km

The Campaign against Island No. 10

Mortar raft firing on Island No. 10 at night, March 18. 1862.
(From *Frank Leslie's Illustrated History of the Civil War*)

Welles that "I shall be very cautious, as I appreciate the vast responsibility of keeping our flotilla from falling into the rebels' hands, as it would turn the whole tide of affairs against us."[19]

Foote's army partner was no longer Grant, who remained on the Tennessee River with his army at Pittsburg Landing near a church called Shiloh. Foote was now working with Brigadier General John Pope, who commanded 18,000 men of the Army of the Mississippi. In mid-March Pope's troops and Foote's flotilla approached Island No. 10, where fifty-two big guns on the island and shore formed interlocking positions of great strength. Several dozen more guns were spaced along the Tennessee bank. Foote's seven ironclads were accompanied by ten mortar rafts, unwieldy makeshift vessels that, like David D. Porter's mortar schooners far to the south, fired a 13-inch shell in a high arc to explode over or among enemy batteries. On March 17 the mortars and ironclads opened a furious fire that did some damage to enemy fortifications but did not knock the guns out of action. In keeping with Foote's promise of caution to Welles, he did not risk his boats by going too close. For the rest of the month, the mortars and gunboats kept up a long-range desultory bombardment.

General Pope repeatedly urged Foote to run two or three of his ironclads past Island No. 10 at night to join him at New Madrid. From there, he said, they could silence the Confederate shore batteries and convoy his troop transports across the river to close the Confederate garrison's sole escape route to the south and capture all 7,000 of them. Foote balked, believing that trying to run past the island "would result in the almost certain destruction of the boats which should attempt to pass the six forts with fifty guns bearing upon the vessels."[20] Pope grew impatient with what he considered Foote's timidity. "As Commodore Foote is unable to reduce and unwilling to run his gunboats past" the enemy batteries, Pope wrote to General Halleck, "I would ask, as they belong to the United States, that he be directed to remove his crews from two of them and turn over the boats to me. I will bring them here."[21]

It did not come to that. Commander Henry Walke, skipper of the USS *Carondelet* and Foote's best fighting captain, was eager to run the batteries. On March 30 Foote finally authorized him to try it on the first dark and stormy night. Walke prepared carefully. He placed hay bales, lumber, coal sacks, and chain cables to protect vulnerable parts of the deck and pilot house and lashed a loaded coal barge to the port side to absorb enemy shots. On the night of April 4, the *Carondelet* steamed quietly down the river in a thunderstorm while flashes of lightning provided the only light for the pilot. Suddenly the soot in the *Carondelet*'s chimney (smokestack) caught fire and sent flames belching skyward, lighting the vessel for enemy gunners. But most of the Confederate guns in both the shore and island batteries could not be depressed enough to hit the swiftly moving vessel, and she got through having been hit only twice—once in the coal barge and once in a hay bale.

Despite this success, Foote initially resisted Pope's request for a second ironclad. "There is so much hazard in running the blockade," he wrote, "and the rebels being so much on the alert, I consider it injudicious to hazard another boat."[22] But with what must have been a sigh of exasperation, he gave in and allowed the USS *Pittsburgh* to try it during another thunderstorm on the night of April 6–7. She also got through safely. The accurate firepower of these two gunboats, especially the *Carondelet*, silenced enemy batteries on the Tennessee shore below New Madrid. Pope crossed his troops, barred the enemy's retreat route, and bagged all but a few hundred of them on April 8. He also captured three Confederate generals, seven colonels, more than a hundred heavy guns, and several Confederate transports, one of which the navy fitted out as the famous hospital boat *Red Rover*. In his report to General Halleck, Pope praised the "prompt, gallant, and cheerful" Commander Walke—but he said nothing about Foote.[23]

This striking achievement won Pope promotion to major general and eventually a top command in Virginia, where he came to grief in the Second Battle of Bull Run at the end of August. It also won new fame for the river navy and plaudits for Foote—whether or not he deserved them in this case. Praise for the Western Flotilla extended to the orphaned timberclads *Tyler* and *Lexington*, which had been left in the Tennessee River. They convoyed the transports that carried Grant's troops to Pittsburg Landing. During the battle of Shiloh, they helped stop the Confederate assault on Grant's left flank on the afternoon of April 6, enfilading the Confederate line at Dill's Branch with shells from their 8-inch Dahlgren guns. "In this repulse," Grant acknowledged in his report, "much is due to the presence of the gunboats *Tyler* and *Lexington*." All night long on April 6–7, the gunboats lobbed shells into Confederate camps, "therefore," as General Pierre G. T. Beauregard reported, "on the following morning the troops under my command were not in condition to cope with an equal force . . . [aided] by such an auxiliary as the enemy's gunboats."[24]

AFTER THE BATTLE OF SHILOH, General Halleck came personally to Pittsburg Landing to command an overland advance on the Confederate rail junction of Corinth, Mississippi. At the same time, Foote's flotilla and Pope's troops moved downriver fifty miles to the next Confederate bastion on the Mississippi, Fort Pillow. With forty guns dug into the sides and top of a bluff, this fort was not as strong as Columbus or Island No. 10. But now the Confederates had a navy of their own to support the fort: eight fast steamboats converted into rams and named the River Defense Fleet. Originally intended to be part of the defense of New Orleans, these gunboats had been ordered upriver in late March 1862. At that time, the danger to New Orleans from above appeared more imminent than from Farragut's fleet, which was still detained below Forts Jackson and St. Philip. Commanded by Flag Officer James E. Montgomery, these rebel rams carried only one gun each but were armored with cotton bales

Flag Officer Andrew Hull Foote in 1862. (Courtesy of the National Archives)

pressed between double oak bulwarks and iron an inch thick to protect the engines. The reinforced bows were solid twelve-inch timber sheathed with four-inch oak planks and iron bands bent around the bow to create a powerful ram.[25]

The presence of this Confederate fleet increased the caution Foote had shown at Island No. 10. The initial Union plan called for Pope to disembark his troops and attack Fort Pillow from the land side while Foote's ironclads and mortar rafts bombarded it from the river. But on April 15 General Halleck ordered Pope to bring all but two of his regiments to join Halleck's army in the campaign against Corinth. That ended the possibility of joint operations against Fort Pillow, so the mortar rafts began an intermittent shelling of the fort while Foote tried to decide what to do next. After a week of this activity, an Alabama soldier stationed in the fort reported that the shelling "so far has done little injury, save in killing some mules, dogs, & one man." After another week, however, he told his wife that "it was more dreadful than you can imagine. One shell will blow a hole into the ground large as half your room. Yesterday a shell struck a fellow & litterally [*sic*] tore him into fragments, and you could find pieces of him scattered all around."[26]

Foote grew discouraged. His wound was so painful that he could scarcely sleep, and he seemed unable to make any plans. "We are much weaker as gun-boats than the rebels or our people suppose, therefore I dare not run great risks," Foote wrote to Welles after two weeks in front of Fort Pillow. "I will do the best I can; but do not expect, as the country does, too much of us, for really our means are not adequate to the work assigned us."[27]

Welles recognized that it was his old friend from schoolboy days who was no longer adequate to the task. Foote had been requesting a leave to recover from his wound; Welles now granted it and named Captain Charles H. Davis as temporary commander of the Western Flotilla. When Davis arrived to take over, he found Foote "very reduced in strength, fallen off in flesh, and depressed in spirits . . . and his mind is exhausted by incessant labor, strain, and responsibility."[28]

Foote's wound continued to bother him, and though he was promoted to rear admiral in July 1862, he never did return to the flotilla. A decade later, Welles told Foote's biographer that the flag officer's most important contribution to Union victory was not the battles he won but the creation of a river navy without any precedent to guide him. "His battles gave him renown," said Welles, "but his patient and herculean labors in procuring and organizing the flotilla with which these battles were fought was less known but almost incredible."[29]

With his high, balding forehead, luxurious mustache, and scholarly mien, Charles Davis looked more like a college professor than a dashing naval officer. And in fact he had graduated from Harvard with a degree in mathematics in 1841 while on leave from the navy as a lieutenant. A noted hydrographer, he was more at home studying astronomy and the geology of the seas than barking orders from the quarterdeck of a ship. He had performed well as Samuel Francis Du Pont's fleet captain in the Port Royal campaign, however, and he was Foote's own choice to take his place in the Western Flotilla.

The morning after Davis raised his flag in the USS *Benton* on May 9, he received a baptism of fire in river warfare. On May 10 the Eads iron-clad USS *Cincinnati* escorted one of the mortar boats down to Craigshead Point two miles above Fort Pillow to commence the daily shelling of the fort. This normal routine suddenly became anything but normal. Black smoke from around the bend soon revealed the eight vessels of the Con-federate River Defense Fleet steaming upriver at top speed. They headed directly for the *Cincinnati*, which cast loose and fired a salvo from her three bow guns. Before the gunners could reload, the CSS *General Bragg* rammed her starboard quarter just abaft the armor plate, leaving a large hole. Then the CSS *General Price* plowed into the port side and the CSS *General Sumter* rammed the *Cincinnati*'s stern at full speed. She limped to the bank and went down in twelve feet of water.

As the other Union ironclads desperately got up steam to attack the audacious rebels, the CSS *General Van Dorn* headed for the USS *Mound City*. An ensign on that vessel described the action in a letter to his fiancée. The *Van Dorn*

> was now coming on our starboard (right) side as fast as she could travel, notwithstanding we were pouring broadside after broadside into her, and ran into us, striking about four feet from the bow. This turned us clear around . . . and she passed close in front of us, receiv-ing the contents of our three bow guns. . . . Though every one of our shot and shell struck her, strange to say she got off without sinking, [while] our boat began to go down as soon as the "Van Dorn" struck us, for she [tore] away nearly half of our forecastle [and] opened an awful hole in our bows.

The *Mound City* had to run herself aground on a sandbar to prevent sinking.[30]

By this time, the rest of the Union flotilla was bearing down on the scene, so the commander of the Confederate rams decided to quit while he was ahead. His River Defense Fleet used their superior speed to escape downriver without further damage. In fact, despite Charles Davis's exag-gerated claims of having driven off the enemy with considerable loss, the Confederate vessels had suffered surprisingly little harm.[31] Although both the *Cincinnati* and *Mound City* were raised and repaired, this Battle of Plum Point Bend was a definite Confederate victory. Southern Flag Officer James Montgomery proudly proclaimed that the Union gunboats would "never penetrate farther down the Mississippi."[32]

He should never have said never. Davis was about to get some rams of his own, though at first he was dubious about their value. "They are not good for much in reality," he wrote to his wife, "but they are so formidable in appearance that they would strike terror to the soul of Killard"— whoever he was.[33] Davis would soon be compelled to change his mind, but not until after conflicts of authority almost poisoned his relations with the commander of the ram fleet.

That personage was Charles Ellet Jr., one of those eccentric geniuses that wars often thrust forth. Fifty-two years old, small and frail in build, and wizened in appearance, Ellet was a giant in energy and ambition. A civil engineer by profession, he had designed some of the country's first suspension bridges. His hobby, however, was the study of the tactics of ramming in naval history. The advent of steam power, he argued, made possible the revival of this ancient technique eclipsed for centuries by the broadside firepower of frigates and ships of the line powered by sails. For several years before the Civil War, Ellet had tried without success to interest the Navy Department in his ideas. Nor did Gideon Welles pay much attention to him in 1861. The sinking of the USS *Cumberland* by the ram of the CSS *Virginia* in March 1862 finally got Ellet a hearing—with Secretary of War Edwin M. Stanton. The normally dour Stanton was impressed. Ellet "has more ingenuity, more personal courage, and more enterprise than anybody else I have seen," he declared.[34]

In March 1862 Stanton appointed Ellet a colonel in the army and authorized him to buy seven strong river steamboats and convert them into rams. Ellet traveled to Pittsburgh, Cincinnati, and New Albany, Indiana, and purchased the seven boats.[35] Within weeks he had them converted and their crews filled, including volunteers from the 59th and 63rd Illinois Regiments. Charles Ellet's brother Alfred, a captain in the 59th, recruited many of these crew members. Stanton appointed Alfred Ellet a lieutenant colonel and second in command to his brother. Twelve other family members—sons, nephews, cousins, and in-laws—also became officers and crewmen on what were soon known as the Ellet Rams.

To turn these four sidewheelers and three sternwheelers into weapons of war, Ellet had carpenters bolt three oak beams twelve to sixteen inches thick from stem to stern, the middle one directly over the keelson. They bound these beams together crosswise with iron rods and screwbolts fastened to the hull so that the whole weight of the boat (400 tons) would add its momentum to that of the central bulkhead at the moment of impact. The boilers and engines were held steady by iron stays and shielded by two-foot-thick oak timbers bolted together. At fifteen miles an hour downstream, these lethal weapons "will assuredly make their way through the hull of any transport or gunboat they may chance to hit fairly," wrote Charles Ellet. He had the boats painted black to give them an even more fearsome appearance.[36]

Flag Officer Davis's initial skepticism about Ellet's fleet was compounded by questions of command and control. Ellet was an army colonel and reported to the secretary of war. In theory, of course, all of the Western Flotilla was an army enterprise, but in practice by this time the navy had taken it over, a reality ratified by congressional legislation in July formally turning the flotilla over to the navy—except Ellet's ram fleet. From the day he joined the flotilla on May 24, Ellet insisted on his independence from Davis's authority, and Davis insisted on the opposite. On May 25 Ellet proposed to lead six rams supported by one of the ironclads to run past Fort Pillow and attack the Confederate fleet below. But Davis expressed an "unwillingness to assume any risk at this time," as Ellet reported to Stanton.[37] And when Davis did decide to move, he informed Ellet that "the rams under your command should follow in the rear and on the wings of my squadron. . . . It will be most expedient and proper that the gunboats should take the front rank. . . . The rams, coming up in the rear, should watch for an opportunity" to "take the enemy in the flank, to assault any straggler," but otherwise they should stay out of the way.[38]

Ellet was having none of that. He told Davis that he intended to move against the enemy at dawn on June 3, with or without the gunboats. In words that Davis surely construed as an insult, Ellet requested volunteers from the gunboats to come aboard the rams to take part "for the sake of the example alone which all connected with the Navy are sure to offer whenever the opportunity is presented to them to engage in a daring and patriotic enterprise." Davis icily refused and added: "I would thank you to inform me how far you consider yourself under my authority; and I shall esteem it a favor to receive from you a copy of the orders under which you are acting."[39]

Ellet produced his orders from the War Department and told Davis he intended to attack. He would send his dispatch boat as bait toward an enemy boat lying under the protection of Fort Pillow's guns and then ram any Confederate vessels that came to its support with his own *Queen of the West* and his brother Alfred's *Monarch*. "An exaggerated view of the powers of these rebel rams has spread among my fleet from the gunboats," he told Stanton, "and I feel the necessity of doing something to check the extension of the contagion." They moved to the attack on June 4. The enemy ram retreated, and the Ellets discovered that Fort Pillow was being evacuated. The garrison's commander had learned that General Beauregard had abandoned Corinth on May 30, thus exposing Fort Pillow to capture from the rear, and he decided to pull out. Alfred Ellet went ashore on June 5 and raised the American flag over Fort Pillow. In his report to the Navy Department, Flag Officer Davis did not mention this incident.[40]

The next Union objective on the river was Memphis. The city was not fortified, but because of its importance, the Confederates decided to defend it with their eight rams. Just in case they might lose, however, they sent one of the two uncompleted ironclads they were building in Memphis, the CSS *Arkansas*, down to the Yazoo River. They destroyed the other one on the stocks, the CSS *Tennessee*, to prevent its possible capture by the Yankees. Those Yankees came on with five of Davis's ironclads and four of Ellet's rams and faced the rebel fleet at dawn on June 6. Captain James Montgomery invited the citizens of Memphis to "come down at sunrise" to watch him "sink the Yankee fleet." "I have come here," he told them, "that you may see Lincoln's gunboats sent to the bottom by the fleet which you have built and manned."[41]

Thousands of Memphis residents did line the bluffs to watch the battle. Davis placed his gunboats five abreast across the river and began exchanging long-range fire with the Confederate fleet. Behind the ironclads, Charles Ellet took the *Queen of the West* over to his brother's *Monarch* and shouted to Alfred: "Round out and follow me! Now is our chance!" Getting up a full head of steam, they dashed between the gunboats and headed for the enemy rams at thirteen knots. The *Queen* smashed into the *Colonel Lovell* and almost cut her in two. She went down with sixty-eight of her eighty-six crewmen. Two other Confederate rams, the *General Price* and the *General Beauregard*, converged on the *Monarch* from opposite sides. She slipped between them and they collided with each other. The *Price* sank in shallow water while the *Monarch* circled around and rammed the *Beauregard* with a blow that started her sinking when a shot from one of the Union ironclads now arriving on the scene hit the *Beauregard* and burst her boilers.

The five remaining rebel rams tried to escape downriver. In a running fight for ten miles, the Union gunboats and rams sank or captured four of them. Only the *General Van Dorn* escaped. Watching from the shore, Confederate Brigadier General M. Jeff Thompson (for whom one of the rams was named) reported that "the enemy's rams did most of the execution and were handled more adroitly than ours."[42] The Federals were able to raise and repair four of the Confederate rams and add them to their own fleet.

The only casualty in the Union flotilla was Charles Ellet, wounded in the leg by a pistol shot while maneuvering against one of the enemy vessels. His son, nineteen-year-old Charles Rivers Ellet, landed at Memphis and with three crew members from the *Monarch* walked calmly through the cursing crowd to raise the American flag over the post office. Davis generously gave credit to Ellet's "bold and successful attack on the enemy rams," describing him as "conspicuous for his gallantry."[43] Ellet's wound did not at first seem serious, but infection soon laid him low and he died of blood poisoning two weeks later. His brother Alfred became commander of the ram fleet and worked out a compatible relationship with Davis and the navy.[44]

THE ELLET RAMS preceded the gunboats down to Vicksburg, where on July 1 they made contact with the oceangoing fleet that Farragut had brought up from New Orleans. Upstream from Vicksburg, the Mississippi River first looped north and then back south again to pass the 200-foot bluff on the east bank where the city was located. The Confederates had emplaced numerous batteries of big guns at several levels both above and below the city. Farragut had arrived during the last week of June with three sloops of war and eight gunboats plus sixteen of David D. Porter's mortar schooners. Farragut had come, he explained to his wife, "by a peremptory order of the [Navy] Department and the President of the United States 'to clear the river through'" by capturing Vicksburg.[45]

Deciding to test Vicksburg's defenses, Farragut repeated his tactics at Forts Jackson and St. Philip by running upriver past the batteries with broadsides blazing while Porter's mortars stayed behind to pound the enemy positions. The river was too difficult to navigate at night, so they had to begin this maneuver at dawn on June 28. "The whole fleet moved up to the attack," wrote a diary-keeping sailor on Farragut's flagship *Hartford*. "The shells from the mortars were being hurled right over our heads, and as [enemy] battery after battery was unmasked from every conceivable position, the ridge of the bluff was one sheet of fire. The big ships sent in their broadsides, the mortars scores of shells, and all combined to make up a grand display and terrible conflict."[46]

All but three of Farragut's ships made it past the batteries, at the cost of about ten men killed in the fleet. Farragut was again lucky that he was

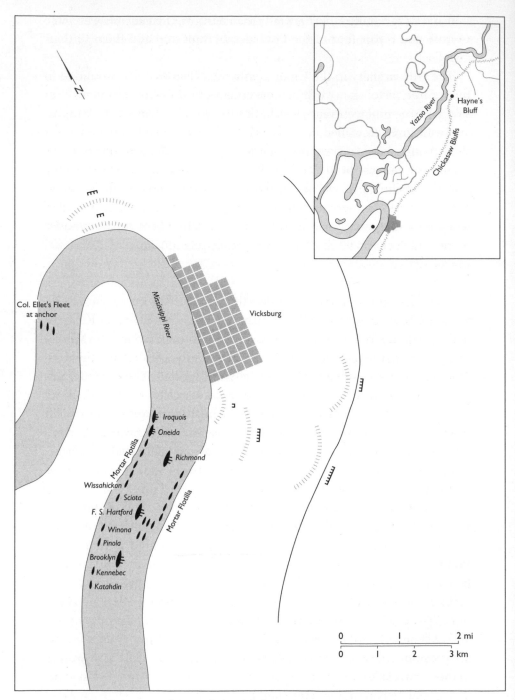

The Attack on Vicksburg, June 28, 1862

not one of them, for the *Hartford* was "riddled from stem to stern." Farragut had just climbed down from his favorite spot in the mizzen rigging when an enemy shot cut the rigging just above his head. "The same shot cut the halyard that hoisted my flag, which dropped to half-mast without being perceived by us," Farragut laconically informed his wife. "This circumstance caused the other vessels to think that I was killed."[47]

This experience convinced Farragut that while the fleet could pass the batteries and drive the gunners from their weapons, they "return to them as soon as we have passed and rake us." Naval guns and mortars could not knock out all of the enemy's dug-in batteries, nor could they capture the town and hold it against Confederate infantry, 15,000 of whom under Major General Earl Van Dorn were in the area. "I am satisfied," Farragut wrote to Welles, "that it is not possible for us to take Vicksburg without an army force of twelve to fifteen thousand men."[48]

General Benjamin Butler had sent 3,000 soldiers with the fleet, but they were far too few to do anything except to start digging a canal across the peninsula between the loops in the river in the vain hope that it would create a new channel beyond range of Confederate batteries. Farragut wrote to General Halleck, whose 110,000 men had recently occupied Corinth, and asked for enough troops to capture Vicksburg in a combined operation. Not for the first or last time would Halleck prove himself to be General "Can't-Be-Done" in response to such requests. "The scattered and weakened condition of my forces," he replied to Farragut on July 3, "renders it impossible for me to detach any troops to cooperate with you at Vicksburg."[49]

While waiting for a reply from Halleck and for the arrival of Charles Davis's ironclads from Memphis, Farragut asked Alfred Ellet to take two of his rams on a scout up the Yazoo River to learn what they could about the CSS *Arkansas*. Rumors had reached the Federals that this ironclad was almost completed at Yazoo City and ready to come down and attack Farragut's wooden ships. For once the rumors were accurate. Lieutenant Isaac Newton Brown was preparing this formidable vessel for action. A native of Kentucky who had cast his lot with the Confederacy after twenty-seven years in the U.S. Navy, Brown was determined to do all the damage he could to Farragut's fleet. "I will hit them hard when ready," he promised.[50]

But Alfred Ellet was as intrepid as his older brother Charles had been, and he intended to ram the *Arkansas* if he found her. The two Union rams encountered obstructions and a shore battery sixty-five miles up the Yazoo River and could go no farther. Just below the obstructions were three Confederate gunboats, including the *General Van Dorn*, the only vessel of the River Defense Fleet to escape from Memphis. Ellet prepared to ram her when, to his astonishment, the Confederates set the three vessels on fire and cut them loose in the narrow channel. Ellet took evasive action and escaped, while three more of the enemy's increasingly scarce gunboats burned up.[51]

The arrival of Davis's flotilla from Memphis in early July increased Union firepower but did not compensate for the lack of ground troops. For the next two weeks, the combined fleets carried on a desultory shelling of Vicksburg. The only result, according to Commander Samuel Phillips Lee of the USS *Oneida*, was to give "the enemy confidence in his means of defence & in his ability to obstruct the navigation of the river by permanent batteries." Farragut became alarmed by the dropping level of the river in the summer drought, which threatened to trap his warships hundreds of miles from blue water. Intense heat sapped the morale of unacclimated Northern soldiers and sailors. Scores fell ill and several died each day from malaria, dysentery, or typhoid. Lee reported all but two officers on the *Oneida* down with fevers, "& they don't seem to recruit again."[52] The commander of the USS *Richmond* was depressed by the prospect of staying in the river all summer "smitten with insects, heat intolerable, fevers, chills, and dysentery, and inglorious inactivity, losing all that the fleet has won in honor and reputation." An ensign on the timberclad USS *Tyler* wrote to his future wife that "the boat is actually alive with roaches and rats, mosquitoes and flies, knats [*sic*] and bugs. . . . While I am writing, the roaches are running all over my patent desk."[53]

On July 15 the inactivity and boredom came to an end, but not in a way that pleased the Federals. Early that morning, the *Queen of the West*, the *Tyler,* and the *Carondelet* went up the Yazoo River on a reconnaissance. They encountered the *Arkansas* bearing down on them firing as many of its ten guns as would bear. Unfortunately for the Union fleet, the *Queen* was commanded that day by a former lieutenant in the 63rd Illinois. None of the Ellets was aboard to force him to ram the *Arkansas*, which they surely would have done even at the risk of destroying their own vessel. Instead, the *Queen* turned tail and fled. The other two Union gunboats gave a better account of themselves, damaging the *Arkansas* and inflicting several casualties but at the cost of sixteen dead, thirty-six wounded, and eight missing and probably drowned on the two Union vessels.

The *Arkansas* continued down into the Mississippi, where she found both Union fleets anchored with fires banked and steam down to save scarce coal. As the *Arkansas* passed through the Union fleets, the inert warships fired heavy broadsides at her, cracking some armor and riddling her smokestack, but they could not stop her. In return, as Commander Isaac Brown later wrote, the *Arkansas* fired back "to every point of the circumference, without the fear of hitting a friend or missing an enemy."[54] She finally reached the protection of Vicksburg batteries below the Union fleet. It was an impressive achievement, but a costly one. In the fights on the Yazoo and Mississippi, the *Arkansas* lost twenty-five men killed and twenty-eight wounded. "The scene around the gun deck upon our arrival was ghastly in the extreme," wrote a master's mate on the *Arkansas*. "Blood and brains bespattered everything, whilst arms, legs, and several headless trunks were strewn about."[55]

If the *Arkansas*'s feat was not quite "the most brilliant ever recorded in naval annals," in the words of General Earl Van Dorn, it boosted Southern morale and was acutely embarrassing to the combined Union fleets. "Caught with our breeches down!" admitted the fleet surgeon on the *Hartford*.[56] Farragut reported the incident to Welles with "deep mortification." He was determined upon retaliation: "I shall leave no stone unturned to destroy her." That very evening, Farragut led his own fleet downriver past Vicksburg hoping to blow the crippled *Arkansas* out of the water, but he could not find her in the gathering darkness. This failure only whetted Farragut's wrath. He intended to "try to destroy her until my squadron is destroyed or she is. . . . There is no rest for the wicked until she is destroyed."[57]

Farragut urged Davis to cooperate with him in a joint attack, "taking the fire of the batteries and looking only to the destruction of the ram, regardless of the consequences to ourselves." After all, he told the commander of the Western Flotilla, "as you have the ironclad boats the country will expect you to cope with the ram better than my wooden vessels . . . but I desire to do my part and full share in this matter." Davis did not like this proposition any better than he had earlier liked Charles Ellet's proposal to attack the River Defense Fleet at Fort Pillow. He considered Farragut, like Ellet, no better than "an excited, hot-headed boy."[58] Like General George B. McClellan, Davis feared risk more than he welcomed opportunity. "I should be unwilling to put in jeopardy all the great triumphs and interests which are placed in my keeping," he told Farragut. "It would be an inexcusable sacrifice of the greatest interests of the country to abandon the possession of the upper Mississippi, and that this would be the unavoidable consequence of an attack such as you propose." But like

General Ulysses S. Grant, Farragut embraced opportunity more than he feared risk. With or without Davis's support, he said on July 19, he would "go in for the attack."[59]

Farragut had just been promoted to rear admiral, and though that did not give him authority over Davis's flotilla, the cautious commander of the ironclad gunboats reluctantly agreed to an attack with limited risk. While both fleets engaged the Vicksburg batteries, the *Queen of the West*, under Alfred Ellet, and the USS *Essex*, commanded by William D. "Dirty Bill" Porter, would ram the *Arkansas* at the levee. Porter was David D. Porter's older brother. He was even more of a blowhard than David but also bold and courageous. He had supervised the rebuilding of the converted snag-boat *Essex* into a more powerful ironclad after the shot through her boiler at Fort Henry. On July 22 Porter and Ellet headed toward the *Arkansas*, taking heavy fire from the Vicksburg batteries as they came. Both hit the *Arkansas* with glancing blows, and the *Essex* fired a broadside from point-blank range. But the attack at first appeared to do little damage. The shock of the hit by the *Queen*, however, apparently cracked the engines' connecting rods, potentially deranging the *Arkansas*'s weak and unreliable engines. Two weeks later, the rods broke as the *Arkansas* was approaching Baton Rouge to support an ultimately unsuccessful attack by Confederate infantry on the Union garrison there. As the *Essex* and two Union gunboats confronted the crippled Confederate ironclad, her captain ordered the vessel abandoned and blown up. The spectacular but brief career of the *Arkansas* was over.[60]

The *Arkansas* had been able to get as far downriver as Baton Rouge because Welles had finally ordered Farragut, to his great relief, to take his ships back to the Gulf before the dropping river level left them stranded. "We don't know where we will be next," Farragut informed his wife, "but just so that we are on salt water, I shall be satisfied & hope not to grumble at the fates that will take me out of a fresh water river."[61]

With Farragut's fleet went the 3,000 army troops, three-quarters of whom were on the sick list. One-fourth of Farragut's sailors were also sick.[62] Left alone with his ironclads and Ellet's rams, Davis suddenly discovered that 40 percent of his men were also down with various afflictions. He decided to pull back to a new base at Helena, Arkansas, 160 miles north of Vicksburg. "There is no knowing . . . how this move of mine may be taken" in Washington, Davis wrote in his campaign diary. "But it seems to me that the only course now to be pursued is to yield to the climate and postpone any further action at Vicksburg till the fever season is over." He explained to Welles that guerrillas and mobile artillery lined the river to his rear, "thus my supplies, as well as mails, were cut off, unless sent under convoy." So "I determined to leave Vicksburg, where my own force, un-aided and very much encumbered, could be of no further service; to close up my lines, now too extended; to open again the sources of communication and supply."[63]

Welles did not record his opinion of this explanation. But David D. Porter wrote to Fox that "there was one flag officer too many" at Vicksburg. "I saw enough to convince me that Davis should not have been one of them, he deserves to lose his command." Welles evidently agreed. In August he appointed Davis as chief of the Bureau of Navigation in Washington.[64]

Until these retreats from Vicksburg, the Federals had controlled the entire Mississippi River except Vicksburg itself, at least nominally. Now the Confederates controlled 400 miles of it from below Helena to Port Hudson (just north of Baton Rouge), where they built strong fortifications. The momentum of Union victories on the western rivers from Fort Henry in February to Memphis in June came to a halt. Union momentum along the Atlantic coast also stalled in the spring and summer of 1862 as the Confederacy stormed back on both land and water.

chapter five

The Confederacy Strikes Back

The CSS *Virginia* was not the first ironclad warship in history, nor in the Civil War, nor even in the Confederacy. The U.S. Congress had appropriated funds for an armored steam vessel in 1842, which became known as the "Stevens Battery" after its designer Robert Stevens, but it was never completed. The French had experimented with armored floating batteries in the Crimean War. Both Britain and France had operational ironclad warships by 1861. The cigar-shaped CSS *Manassas* with its one inch of iron sheathing attacked the USS *Richmond* downriver from New Orleans on October 12, 1861. The city class of ironclad river gunboats built by James B. Eads in 1861 first went into action at Fort Henry a month before the *Virginia* made its rendezvous with destiny at Hampton Roads on March 8, 1862. But the *Virginia* was the most famous of the Confederate ironclads. Its unique design became the prototype for twenty subsequent ironclads built or begun by the Confederacy. And its clash with the USS *Monitor* became the iconic naval battle of the war.

Stephen R. Mallory was the godfather of the Confederate ironclad program. "I regard the possession of an iron-plated ship as a matter of the first necessity," he told the chairman of the Naval Affairs Committee in the provisional Confederate Congress in May 1861. Such a ship could "traverse the entire coast of the United States," said Mallory, "prevent all blockades, and encounter, with a fair prospect of success, their entire navy. If to cope with them upon the sea we follow their example and build wooden ships, [we can never match them,] but inequality of numbers may be compensated by invulnerability."[1]

Recognizing the Confederacy's slender industrial capacity, Mallory initially hoped to buy or contract for the construction of ironclads in Europe. He sent Lieutenant James H. North to France and Britain for this purpose. Mallory embraced the fantasy that France might sell to the Confederacy the new ironclad *Gloire*, pride of its fleet. North was soon compelled to disabuse him of this expectation and to report that no ironclads were for sale in Europe.[2] North later contracted for the building of an ironclad in a Glasgow shipyard, and other Confederate agents signed contracts for the construction of such vessels in England and France. But the long lead time to complete such ships meant that, even if the Confederacy could get them out of Europe, they might arrive too late to accomplish their purpose. And as things turned out, they never arrived at all, for the British and French governments decided to enforce their neutrality by preventing them from leaving.

The Confederacy was thus forced to rely on its own resources to construct ironclads. To build them from scratch would take a long time, and the Union navy was unlikely to wait. Lieutenant John M. Brooke, Naval Constructor John L. Porter, and Chief Engineer William P. Williamson came up with a solution. On June 23, 1861, they met with Mallory in Richmond and decided to build their ironclad on the hull of the USS *Merrimack*, burned to the waterline by the Federals when they had evacuated Norfolk in April. "This is our only chance," said Brooke, "to get a suitable vessel in a short time."[3]

Brooke provided the basic design, Porter supervised construction (the two men later quarreled publicly over which deserved the main credit), and Williamson rebuilt the faulty engines, whose defects were the reason the *Merrimack* was in for repairs when Norfolk fell. Work began in July but proceeded slowly and encountered frustrating delays because of shortages of iron, congestion on the railroads hauling materials, and the necessity of retooling at the Tredegar Iron Works to roll two layers of two-inch plates to cover the hull and casemate. Bolted onto the 263-foot hull, the casemate was 170 feet long and sloped at an angle of 36 degrees, which tests by Brooke showed was the best inflection to deflect shots fired by enemy warships. In these tests, Brooke also experimented with tallow and other kinds of grease on the iron plates to augment deflection. The casemate was pierced for three 9-inch Dahlgren smoothbore naval guns in each broadside plus two 7-inch rifles forward and two 6.4-inch rifles aft designed by Brooke. A seven-foot iron ram was bolted to the prow below the waterline. The Confederates christened their powerful though ungainly new warship the CSS *Virginia*. But Northerners and even many Southerners continued to call it the *Merrimack* (often spelled *Merrimac*).

There was no shortage of Union intelligence about the progress (or lack thereof) of the *Virginia*, despite efforts by Richmond newspapers to publish false information.[4] Although the Confederates had gotten a head start, the Union navy soon embarked on its own saltwater ironclad program. At the request of Gideon Welles, in August 1861 the U.S. Congress appropriated funds to build three experimental ironclads. Welles created a three-man Ironclad Board of senior captains to choose the best designs. Would-be inventors submitted sixteen proposals. The board selected only two of them, one for a six-gun, 950-ton corvette with tumblehome sides protected by two and a half inches of interlocking iron plates that became the USS *Galena* and the other a 4,120-ton screw frigate of conventional design and twenty guns, sheathed with varying thicknesses of iron plating that became the USS *New Ironsides*.

The board expressed some doubts about the buoyancy of these vessels, however, so the prospective builder of the *Galena*, Cornelius Bushnell, decided to consult an expert on ship construction named John Ericsson. A Swedish-born naturalized citizen, Ericsson had invented the screw propeller and designed the first American screw frigate, the USS *Princeton*. When a cannon on the *Princeton* burst during trials in 1844, killing the secretaries of state and navy, some of the blame attached to Ericsson even though he had nothing to do with designing the gun. This experience soured him on the navy. For the next seventeen years, Ericsson designed commercial vessels and patented other innovations. In 1861 he did not submit a proposal to the Ironclad Board.

Ericsson assured Bushnell that the *Galena* would float and then asked if he would like to see an ironclad model that Ericsson himself had built. Bushnell was impressed by the unique features of the model. He persuaded Ericsson to let him show it to Welles and then to President Lincoln. Both were intrigued. Technological innovations fascinated Lincoln, who held a patent on a device to lift riverboats over shoals. At a meeting with the Ironclad Board on September 13, when members expressed skepticism about Ericsson's design, Lincoln characteristically commented: "All I have to say is what the girl said when she put her foot in the stocking: 'It strikes me there is something in it.'"[5] But Captain Charles H. Davis upheld his reputation for conservatism in naval technology by ridiculing Ericsson's model. In a parody of Exodus 20:4, he told Bushnell: "You may take the little thing home and worship it; it would not be idolatry, since it was made in the image of nothing that is in heaven above, or that is in earth beneath, or that is in the water under the earth."[6]

Bushnell was taken aback, but he decided to try a white lie to win Ericsson a contract for the third ironclad. He returned to New York and told

Ericsson that two of the three members of the board were favorable, but that Davis had some technical questions. Ericsson immediately agreed to go to Washington and answer the questions. In a bravura performance, he won them over, including Davis. They gave him a contract but specified that the ship must be built in ninety days and prove to be a "complete success" (without defining the criteria for success) or the builders must refund the $275,000 the government agreed to pay for it.

Ericsson got started at once. He subcontracted several parts of the vessel while maintaining close supervision of the building of the hull and turret. He named his ship the *Monitor* to signal its purpose to admonish and punish the South for its wrongdoing. A flat-bottomed hull housed all the machinery and was topped by a rotating turret protected with eight inches of plating and containing two 11-inch Dahlgren smoothbore guns that could fire a 170-pound shot or 136-pound shell in any direction except straight ahead, where the pilot house sheathed in nine inches of armor was located.

The novel features of the *Monitor* caused some observers—including naval traditionalists—to mock it as "Ericsson's folly," a cheesebox on a raft, or a tin can on a shingle. Admitting that "this vessel is an experiment," the seventy-one-year-old chairman of the Ironclad Board, Commodore Joseph Smith, named forty-three-year-old Lieutenant John Worden to command it. "I believe you are the right sort of officer to put in command of her," he told Worden. The crew were all volunteers. One of them wrote that "we heard every kind of derisive epithet applied to our vessel . . . an 'iron coffin for her crew' & we were styled fool hardy for daring to make the trip in her, & this too by naval men."[7]

The *Monitor*'s almost-submerged hull presented a small target to enemy fire. But would it float with all that iron? Doubters were proved wrong when it came down the ways in Brooklyn on January 30, 1862, and floated with exactly the eleven-foot draft Ericsson had predicted. Two weeks later, the *Virginia* was launched in Norfolk, where she remained upright and buoyant with a twenty-two-foot draft when fully loaded with coal and ammunition. Mallory appointed Franklin Buchanan as her captain. "The *Virginia* is a novelty in naval construction, is untried, and her powers unknown," he acknowledged to Buchanan; nevertheless, "the opportunity and the means of striking a blow for our Navy are now for the first time presented."[8]

Both ships went into action after very little in the way of sea trials to work out the flaws and train the crews. On March 8 Buchanan took the

The CSS *Virginia* sinking the USS *Cumberland*, March 8, 1862. In the background are the *Virginia*'s two gunboat consorts, the CSS *Yorktown* and the CSS *Jamestown*, adding their firepower to the attack on the *Cumberland*. (From *Frank Leslie's Illustrated History of the Civil War*)

Virginia down the Elizabeth River on what the crew thought was a trial run. Not until they emerged into Hampton Roads did he tell them that this was the real thing. Accompanied by two gunboat consorts, the *Virginia* headed toward Newport News, where two sailing frigates were anchored: the fifty-gun USS *Congress* and the twenty-four-gun USS *Cumberland*. Firing a broadside at the *Congress* as he passed, Buchanan steamed toward the *Cumberland* as the *Virginia*'s powerful 7-inch Brooke rifles riddled the helpless frigate, whose shots in return "struck and glanced off," in the words of one Northern witness, "having no more effect than peas from a pop-gun."[9] Following up on Brooke's experiments with tallow grease, Buchanan had the ship coated with it "to increase the tendency of the projectiles to glance."[10] The *Virginia* plowed straight into the starboard side of the *Cumberland* and sent her to the bottom. *Virginia*'s ram stuck in the *Cumberland* and almost took her down with the Union frigate until the ram broke off and freed the Confederate ironclad. The guns of the *Cumberland* kept firing until the water closed over them.

The Virginia went next for the *Congress*, whose captain had grounded her to prevent the enemy from coming close enough to ram. But the ironclad's guns did so much damage and killed so many of the crew that the *Congress* struck her colors. The commander of the *Congress*, Lieutenant Joseph Smith Jr., was the son and namesake of the chairman of the

Ironclad Board. When Lieutenant Smith's father learned that the *Congress* had surrendered, he said simply: "Then Joe is dead." And indeed he was.[11] As the *Virginia*'s consorts approached the *Congress* to take off the wounded, Union infantry on shore—who maintained that *they* had not surrendered—opened fire on them with small arms. Incensed, Buchanan recalled the boats and opened fire again on the *Congress* with hot shot and incendiary shells, setting her afire.

Meanwhile, the screw frigate USS *Minnesota* had steamed up from her anchorage off Fort Monroe to get into the fray. But she ran aground, and her 9-inch Dahlgrens seemed to make no more impression on the *Virginia* than had those of the *Cumberland*. Before the *Virginia* could attack the *Minnesota*, the falling tide compelled her to return home. But no one doubted that she would be back on the morrow. She left behind 121 dead on the *Cumberland* and 240 on the *Congress*, which blew up that night when the fire reached her magazine. It was the most lethal day in the history of the U.S. Navy until December 7, 1941.

The *Virginia* did not get off scot-free. Although none of the ninety-eight shots that struck her penetrated the armor, they did knock out two of her guns, shot away all of her deck fittings and part of her smokestack (reducing its draft), and killed two of the crew and wounded several others. One of the latter was Captain Buchanan, shot through the thigh when he came on deck in a fury carrying a musket to fire at Yankee infantry on shore who had refused to recognize the *Congress*'s surrender. The executive officer, Lieutenant Catesby ap R. Jones, took over and prepared to finish off the *Minnesota* and perhaps other ships the next day. But when Jones brought the *Virginia* out on the morning of March 9, he spotted a strange craft next to the *Minnesota*. "We thought at first it was a raft on which one of the *Minnesota*'s boilers was being taken to the shore for repairs," wrote a midshipman on the *Virginia*. But the "boiler" ran out a gun and fired. The *Monitor* had arrived.[12]

It was not an easy trip, and she almost did not make it. On the second day out from New York, a storm came up and the waves washed over the decks, pouring down the blower pipes and stretching the belts that drove the ventilating fans so that they stopped working. Smoke and gases accumulated in the engine room and caused several firemen and engineers to pass out. The paymaster, William Keeler, who had some mechanical experience, helped pull out one of the unconscious engineers, "though by this time almost suffocated myself." He then "succeeded finally in getting the ventilators started once more & the blowers going."[13]

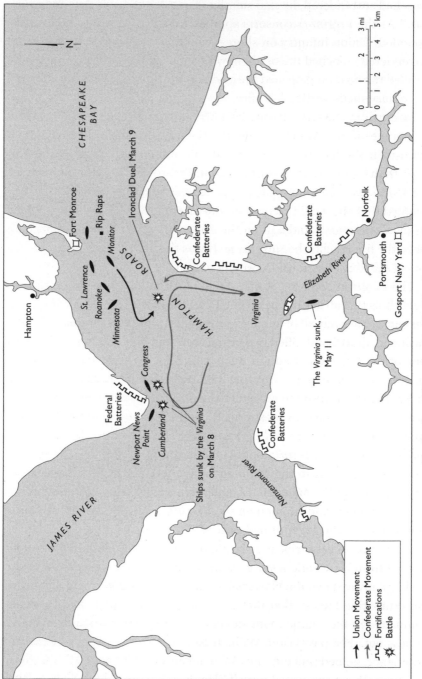

The Battles of Hampton Roads, March 8–9, 1862

The *Monitor* moved closer to the coastline where the water was smoother and finally made it to Hampton Roads after dark on March 8. There the crew learned of the momentous events of that day. They got a dramatic demonstration of those events just after midnight when the *Congress* blew up. Paymaster Keeler was on deck watching the burning frigate "when suddenly a volcano seemed to open instantaneously, almost beneath our feet & a vast column of flame & fire shot forth until it seemed to pierce the skies," as he described the scene in a letter to his wife. "Pieces of burning timbers, exploding shells, huge fragments of the wreck, grenades & rockets filled the air and fell sparkling & hissing in all directions."[14]

Because of their battle with the storm, none of the *Monitor*'s crewmen had gotten more than a few hour's sleep in the past three days. Lieutenant Dana Greene, the *Monitor*'s twenty-two-year-old executive officer, had not slept for fifty-one hours when, as commander of the guns, he ordered the first shot fired at 8:30 A.M. But as the adrenalin started pumping, "we forgot all fatigue, hard work, and everything else," he informed his family, "& went to work fighting as hard as men ever fought. We loaded and fired the guns as fast as we could—I pointed and fired the guns myself. . . . My men & myself were perfectly black with smoke, and powder." The gunners "stripped themselves to their waists," wrote Paymaster Keeler, "the perspiration falling from them like rain."[15] The same frantic action took place on the *Virginia*, while on the *Minnesota* a mile or so away from the action, the gunners also stripped to the waist to fire at the *Virginia*. At least two of their shots hit the *Monitor* instead as the two ironclads came to close quarters and sometimes fired their guns almost muzzle to muzzle.

Loading and firing those big guns took several minutes each on both vessels. During a battle of four hours, with several pauses, the *Monitor* fired only forty-one shots, scoring twenty hits, while the *Virginia* hit the *Monitor* twenty-three times out of an unrecorded number of shots. Nearly a hundred feet shorter in length and with only its turret and pilothouse more than one foot above the surface, the *Monitor* presented a fraction of the *Virginia*'s target area. Although the *Monitor*'s 170-pound shots cracked a few plates on the *Virginia* and the latter's shells made dents in the *Monitor*'s turret, neither vessel seriously damaged the other. It could have been different. Expecting to attack the still-grounded *Minnesota* and other wooden ships on March 9, the *Virginia* carried only explosive shells in its magazine. They shattered and exploded when they hit the *Monitor* but did not have the penetrating power of a solid iron bolt or shot. The *Monitor*'s cartridges were charged with only fifteen pounds of powder each because there had been no time to test or "proof" the guns and their recoil inside the turret with heavier charges before they went into action. Later tests of the *Monitor*'s guns showed them capable of firing safely with forty-five pounds of powder. Even the thirty pounds normally used in 11-inch Dahlgrens probably would have done significant damage to the *Virginia*.

One of the *Virginia*'s shells did cause serious problems on the *Monitor*. It exploded against the pilothouse when Lieutenant Worden was peering through the slit and temporarily blinded him. Lieutenant Greene took over, but during the confusion after Worden's wounding, the *Monitor* had moved away into shallower water. Thinking her disengaging, Lieutenant Jones decided to return to Norfolk with another victory to the *Virginia*'s credit. Watching the *Virginia* depart, the *Monitor*'s crew celebrated what they considered *their* victory. Immediately after returning to the north side of Hampton Roads, the chief engineer of the *Monitor*, Alban Stimers, wrote a note to Ericsson congratulating him on the "great success" of his invention. "Thousands have this day blessed you," Stimers told him. "I have heard whole crews cheer you. Every man feels you have saved this place to the nation by furnishing us with the means to whip an ironclad frigate that was, until our arrival, having it all her own way with our most powerful vessels."[16]

Stimers was hardly impartial, but even one of the senior lieutenants in the Confederate navy, George T. Sinclair, who watched the battle from the shore, wrote that the *Virginia* "met much more than a match in the Erickson [*sic*] from the fact that she is much faster, more easily managed, runs with either end first, and is invulnerable to any gun or guns I ever saw. . . . The Virginia is cut up a good deal, almost entirely by the Erickson, the projectiles from the other guns [i.e. of the *Minnesota*] having done her apparently little harm."[17]

Whether the *Virginia* or *Monitor* won this particular showdown was less important, perhaps, than the symbolism of the battle as a victory of the future over the past. The graceful frigates and powerful line-of-battle ships with their towering masts and sturdy oak timbers would gradually fade into history and legend. March 9, 1862, witnessed a giant step in the revolution in naval warfare begun a generation earlier by the application of steam power to warships. Many contemporaries recognized as much, including the captain of the USS *Minnesota*, who had watched with growing astonishment as the little *Monitor*, with its two guns, saved his forty-gun frigate. "Gun after gun was fired by the *Monitor*," he wrote in his official report, "which was returned with whole broadsides by th[e] with no more effect, apparently, than so many pebblestones thr[own by a] child . . . clearly establishing that wooden vessels cannot contend [success-] fully with ironclad ones; for never before was anything like it drea[med] by the greatest enthusiast in maritime warfare."[18]

One of the Confederacy's foremost nautical scientists, Matthew Fontaine Maury, had previously advocated the construction of a fleet of small steam gunboats to swarm like bees to sting large Union warships to death. Several of these had been built or begun by early 1862. But the *Virginia-Monitor* clash pretty much ended that program. "As to the wooden gunboats we are building," wrote Lieutenant Sinclair on March 11, "they are not worth a cent. The death knell of the wooden ships for war purposes was sounded last Saturday." Maury himself ecstatically proclaimed that the *Virginia* "at a single dash, overturned the 'wooden walls' of Old England and rendered effete the navies of the world."[19]

So dramatic was the impact of this event that both sides embarked on large-scale programs to build ironclads, most of them on the models of the *Virginia* and *Monitor*. In subsequent experience, however, these vessels turned out to have significant shortcomings. They were underpowered, slow, unseaworthy, and insufferably hot and humid in warm weather. The engines on Confederate ironclads were unreliable and prone to breakdowns; the rate of fire on *Monitor*-class vessels was agonizingly slow. But in the euphoric aftermath of the Battle of Hampton Roads, they seemed like war-changing superships.

As for the question of who "won" that battle, the tactical victory must be awarded to the *Monitor*. Its mission was to protect the wooden warships at Hampton Roads, and that mission it accomplished. But the *Virginia* won a strategic victory by infecting many Union naval officers with "ram fever" that inhibited their aggressiveness whenever Confederate ironclads were in the vicinity—or were suspected to be. That strategic impact began with the *Virginia*'s continuing presence at Norfolk, which neutralized much of the Union fleet and impeded its ability—or willingness—to provide naval support for General George B. McClellan's efforts to capture Yorktown at the beginning of his ultimately unsuccessful Peninsula Campaign.

FLAG OFFICER Louis M. Goldsborough of the Union's North Atlantic Blockading Squadron was in North Carolina waters with the gunboats supporting General Burnside's campaign when the *Monitor-Virginia* battle took place. He hurried back to Hampton Roads and was

Part of the crew of the USS *Monitor* relaxing on deck after their fight with the *Virginia* (note the dents in the turret). (Courtesy of the Library of Congress)

greeted by an order from Secretary of the Navy Welles: "It is directed by the President that the *Monitor* be not too much exposed; that in no event should any attempt be made to proceed with her unattended to Norfolk," where the *Virginia* was undergoing repairs.[20]

This constraint did not sit well with the *Monitor*'s crew, which wanted another chance at their antagonist. "If they would only let us go up the [Elizabeth] river & get at the rat in his hole it would suit us exactly," wrote an officer on the *Monitor*. But "they fear to have us attack her for fear we may be used up" and then "the consequences would be terrible" by again exposing the fleet to the rampages of the *Virginia*, "so here we are compelled to remain inactive. . . . The fact is the Government is getting to regard the *Monitor* in pretty much the same light as an over careful house wife regards her ancient china set—too valuable to use . . . yet anxious that all shall know what she owns & that she can use it when the occasion demands."[21]

The Union navy rushed several ships to Hampton Roads with reinforced iron-plated bows to ram the *Virginia* if she came out. One of them was the *Vanderbilt*, a gift to the government by the millionaire Cornelius

Vanderbilt. This large sidewheeler was the fastest ship in the navy at the time. When the *Virginia* was repaired, she came down the Elizabeth River into Hampton Roads, but not far enough for the *Vanderbilt* to build up a full head of steam to ram her. Meanwhile, the Confederates devised a plan to lure the *Monitor* within reach of several small gunboats by feinting a foray by the *Virginia*. Men from the gunboats would then board and capture the *Monitor*. The latter refused the bait, however, causing newspapers in Norfolk to mock Yankee cowardice. Several crew members on the *Monitor* were stung by this charge. "All we want is a chance to . . . teach them who is Cowards," they declared in a petition to their old commander, John Worden, who was still recovering from the wound to his eyes.[22]

This cat-and-mouse game between the two ironclads continued even after McClellan's Army of the Potomac arrived in early April at the tip of the peninsula formed by the York and James Rivers. The navy had convoyed McClellan's huge armada of troop transports down the Potomac River and Chesapeake Bay without serious mishap, and the general counted on naval support to help him break the Confederate line across the peninsula anchored at Yorktown. Gustavus Fox urged Goldsborough to cooperate with McClellan, "bearing in mind that your first duty [is] to take care of the Merrimack. . . . At the same time I do not like to have the Army say that the Navy could not help them, so we are ordering everything we can raise to report to you."[23]

Goldsborough told Commander John S. Missroon to proceed with three gunboats to assist McClellan's attack on the batteries at Yorktown and Gloucester flanking the York River. Missroon took one look at the Confederate defenses there and reported that they had fifty big guns sited on the narrows in the river that could blow him out of the water. "All the gunboats of the Navy would fail to take it, but would be destroyed in the attempt," he told McClellan. "To attack the works on the river front several heavy frigates or vessels of much endurance would be necessary."[24] McClellan complained to Fox and urged Missroon's replacement by a more aggressive commander. "I fear friend Missroon is not the man for the place," wrote McClellan. "He is a little too careful of his vessels, & has yet done us no good—not even annoyed the enemy."[25] Here was a classic example of the pot calling the kettle black. Just a few days earlier, McClellan had refused to attack the weak Confederate lines on the Warwick River despite overwhelming numerical superiority.

McClellan's complaints brought orders from Welles instructing Goldsborough to "actively and earnestly cooperate" with the general. "It is important and absolutely essential" that the navy should give him "all the assistance he may require . . . consistently with your other duties." The last phrase gave Goldsborough an out; his "other duties" included above all making sure the *Virginia* remained neutralized. "You know my position here," Goldsborough reminded McClellan. "I dare not leave the *Merrimack* and consorts unguarded. Were she out of the way everything I have here should be at work in your behalf; but as things now stand you must not count upon my sending any more vessels."[26]

Relations between McClellan and Missroon continued to deteriorate. On April 23 Missroon asked to be relieved then changed his mind and withdrew the request the same day. It was too late; a few days later, he was relieved and sent home, never again to hold an important command. Fox came down from Washington to check on the situation at Hampton Roads. When the Confederates evacuated their Yorktown line on May 3 just as McClellan was ready to open on them with his siege artillery, Fox inspected the batteries on the York River that had so intimidated Missroon. He claimed to find them much less formidable than reported. By this time in the war, Farragut's fleet had passed Forts Jackson and St. Philip and two of Foote's gunboats had run past Island No. 10 — stronger works than those at Yorktown. "If Missroon had pushed by [at night] with a couple of gunboats," Fox declared, "the Navy would have had the credit of driving the army of the rebels out, besides immortality to himself. . . . The water batteries on both sides were insignificant, and, according to all our naval conflicts thus far, could have been passed with impunity" and the batteries taken in reverse, because none of the guns pointed upstream.[27]

Fox was not the only high official who visited Hampton Roads and made observations that were critical of the navy's operations there. None other than President Lincoln, along with Secretary of War Stanton and Secretary of the Treasury Salmon P. Chase, came down in early May. Their purpose was to prod McClellan into action. But the general was at Williamsburg organizing the pursuit of retreating Confederates, so they prodded Goldsborough instead. At the president's bidding, Goldsborough organized several gunboats and the *Monitor* to shell Confederate batteries at Sewell's Point. In a spirited action, they drove the enemy away, causing Lincoln to wonder why Goldsborough had not done so earlier. The president also ordered General John Wool, commander of the Fort Monroe garrison, to land troops on the south side of Hampton Roads to take Norfolk. They accomplished this goal without opposition because the

Confederates were evacuating the city after destroying the navy yard far more thoroughly than the Federals had done when they abandoned it a year earlier.

Although the Confederates would have abandoned Norfolk anyway after the main Southern army on the peninsula had retreated from the Yorktown line, the flurry of activity prompted by the president helped end two months of stalemate at Hampton Roads. Nothing was happening until Lincoln began "stirring up dry bones," wrote an officer on the *Monitor*. "It is extremely fortunate that the President came down when he did—he seems to have infused new life into everything, even the superannuated old fogies [Goldsborough and Wool] began to show some signs of life."[28]

Left behind when the Confederates evacuated Norfolk was the *Virginia*, whose draft was too great to get past shoals in the James River. On May 11 its crew blew her up to prevent capture. With the rebels apparently on the run, Commander John Rodgers of the new ironclad USS *Galena* led four other gunboats, including the *Monitor*, up the James River hoping to force the surrender of Richmond with their guns trained on its streets as Farragut had done at New Orleans three weeks earlier. Eight miles below the city, however, they encountered Fort Darling atop 200-foot-high Drewry's Bluff on May 15. The ships could not run past the fort because the Confederates had driven pilings and sunk several cribs and hulks filled with stones at a narrow point in the river near the fort. The sailors would have to silence the fort's guns before they could remove the obstructions. The *Galena* stopped 600 yards from the fort and opened fire. The *Monitor* came closer but discovered that it could not elevate its guns enough at that distance and had to fall back several hundred yards to where its smoothbore Dahlgrens were less effective. The Confederates concentrated the plunging fire of their seven guns on the *Galena*, hitting her forty-three times and perforating her three-and-a-half-inch armor both above and below the waterline. After five hours of fighting with seventeen killed and seven wounded on the *Galena* (some by sharpshooters concealed along the banks) and his ship holed like Swiss cheese, Rodgers gave up and dropped downriver with his flotilla. The Confederates in the fort suffered only seven killed and eight wounded. Paymaster William Keeler of the *Monitor* (which was hit only three times and had no casualties) went aboard the *Galena* and was appalled by the carnage. "Here was a body with the head, one arm & part of the breast torn off by a bursting shell," he wrote to his wife, "another with the top of his head taken off the brains still steaming on the deck, partly across him lay one with both legs taken off at the hips & at a little distance another completely disemboweled."[29]

Southerners were elated by their victory. Secretary of the Navy Mallory boasted two weeks later that the defenses at Drewry's Bluff and at Chaffins' Bluff across the river were now so strong "that I am afraid the enemy will not make a second attempt to pass them. I want him to try once more." By July, Mallory could declare: "I have got the river so strongly protected now that I earnestly desire the whole Yankee fleet to attempt its passage."[30]

They never did. According to Fox, President Lincoln "was very disappointed at the gunboats not being in Richmond." From Goldsborough came a rejoinder that "without the Army the Navy can make no real headway towards Richmond. This is as clear as the sun at noonday to my mind."[31] But McClellan claimed that he could not spare the troops for a joint operation against Drewry's Bluff. (A month later, Halleck told Farragut the same thing with respect to combined operations against Vicksburg.) Much of the Northern press, which had earlier praised the navy for its successes, now became critical of its failures. Sighing with exasperation, Gideon Welles lamented the public's unrealistic expectations. "They tell us the Navy took New Orleans, why can it not take Richmond?" he wrote. "It overcame obstructions on the Mississippi, why can it not overcome them on the James River? Having done more than was expected, it is now expected we will do impossibilities."[32]

Goldsborough was a prime target of criticism, much of it coming from within the navy itself. "The prevailing opinion among the ships on the [James] river," wrote an officer on the *Monitor*, "is, that the old Commodore has a large fleet of vessels on his hands which . . . he don't know what to do with." Goldsborough "is not the man for the position he occupies. . . . He is coarse, rough, vulgar & profane in his speech, fawning and obsequious to his superiors, supercilious, tyrannical, & brutal to his inferiors." Weighing 300 pounds, he was "a huge mass of inert matter & known throughout the whole fleet" as "Old Guts."[33]

Welles shared many of these sentiments. On July 6 he created the James River Flotilla and gave command of it to Charles Wilkes (of *Trent* affair notoriety), who was instructed to report directly to the Navy Department instead of to Goldsborough. By this move, Welles divested Goldsborough of one-third of the ships in his North Atlantic Squadron. Complaining bitterly that this order "places me in a most humiliating attitude before the public and Navy," Goldsborough asked to be relieved and transferred to an administrative position in Washington. Welles readily complied but tempered the implied rebuke by having Lincoln promote Goldsborough to rear admiral as he was put on the shelf for the rest of the war.[34]

Welles had no illusions about Wilkes, whom he privately described as "ambitious and self-willed . . . unpopular in the Navy . . . interposes his own authority to interrupt the execution of the orders of the Department." But in the light of lingering public acclaim for Wilkes's seizure of Mason and Slidell, Welles found it "almost a necessity that something should be done for Wilkes." The James River Flotilla was the solution, which had the added benefit of easing out Goldsborough.[35]

To replace Goldsborough, Welles appointed Samuel Phillips Lee as the new commander of the North Atlantic Squadron with the rank of acting rear admiral. A native Virginian and a cousin of Robert E. Lee, he had never wavered in his loyalty to the United States. He had proved himself one of Farragut's best fighting captains in the campaigns against New Orleans and Vicksburg. Lee was also well connected in Washington, where his wife, Elizabeth Blair Lee, was the daughter of the prominent politico Francis P. Blair and sister of Lincoln's postmaster general, Montgomery Blair. During the next two years, Lee would earn more prize money from the capture of blockade-runners than any other squadron commander but also more criticism for the large number of runners into and out of Wilmington that his squadron did *not* catch.

One thing Lee did not have to worry about was Wilkes. By the time Lee took up his new command on September 2, Wilkes was gone and the separate James River Flotilla existed no more. After General Robert E. Lee's Army of Northern Virginia drove the Army of the Potomac away from Richmond in the Seven Days Battles, Lincoln and his new general in chief, Henry W. Halleck, decided to withdraw the army from the peninsula. Both McClellan and Wilkes protested this decision, but by mid-August it was a fait accompli. The James River Flotilla performed its last duty in convoying the transports that evacuated the army and returned it to northern Virginia, where part of it fought at Second Bull Run. For the time being, the Confederates owned the James River again as they also owned the Mississippi from Helena down to Port Hudson.[36]

WELLES STILL HAD THE PROBLEM of what to do with Wilkes. At Lincoln's and Secretary of State Seward's behest, on September 8 Welles appointed the headstrong officer to command a "flying squadron" of seven warships to patrol the West Indies in search of Confederate commerce raiders and blockade-runners.[37] American diplomats in Britain and its colonies had gathered intelligence about the "Oreto" and "No. 290," ships that had been built in Liverpool as commerce raiders intended to destroy American merchant ships and whalers. Both vessels had evaded the British neutrality laws and gone to sea as the CSS *Florida* and CSS *Alabama*. Wilkes showed more zeal for trying to capture blockade-runners—which would earn him prize money—than for finding and fighting the *Alabama*, which began her depredations in September 1862. "It is desirable to break up the illicit traffic," Welles told Wilkes, "but the first great and imperative duty of your command is the capture and destruction of the *Alabama* . . . and similar cruisers of a semi-piratical nature."[38]

The launching of the *Florida* and *Alabama* in the summer of 1862 was another element in Confederate efforts to blunt and even reverse the momentum of Union naval success. The origins of this endeavor went back more than a year. At the same time that Naval Secretary Mallory sent James North to Europe to buy or build ironclads for the Confederacy, he also dispatched James D. Bulloch to England to buy or build ships suitable for destroying merchantmen.[39] Bulloch was the right man for the job. A native of Georgia who was a veteran of fourteen years in the U.S. Navy and eight years in commercial shipping, he had the maritime knowledge, business contacts, and financial acumen to acquire suitable vessels and to navigate his way through the obstacles of doing so in a foreign nation that did not recognize the Confederacy. Although Bulloch wanted to command one of these ships himself, Mallory found him so valuable as a procuring agent that he kept him in Europe for the entire war.[40]

In the summer of 1861, Bulloch contracted with shipbuilding firms in Liverpool for the construction of two vessels that became the *Florida* and *Alabama*. Each was rigged as a sailing ship with a steam-driven propeller for added speed and maneuverability when chasing a prize. While cruising under sail alone, the propeller could be lifted into a well under the stern to reduce drag. Each ship carried eight guns to enable it to fight Union warships if necessary. As the vessels neared completion in the spring of 1862, their warlike purpose was an open secret in Liverpool, which was a center of pro-Confederate sentiment. The city had been "made by the slave trade," observed an American diplomat tartly, "and the sons of those who acquired fortunes in the traffic, now instinctively side with the rebelling slave-drivers."[41] The construction of these ships was an obvious violation of British neutrality. The Foreign Enlistment Act prohibited the construction and arming of warships in Britain for a belligerent power. But Bulloch was a master of misdirection. The Confederate government itself was not a party to the contracts he had negotiated. The *Oreto* (*Florida*) was supposedly being built for a merchant of Palermo. The American consul in Liverpool, Thomas H. Dudley, amassed a great deal of evidence that the *Oreto* was intended for the Confederacy. Minister Charles Francis Adams presented this evidence to the Foreign Office.[42] But the *Oreto* was allowed to go to sea in March 1862 as an ostensible merchant ship with a British crew and without any guns or other warlike equipment. In August she took on her armament, ammunition, and supplies that had been separately shipped to an uninhabited cay in the Bahamas.

Confederate navy Lieutenant John N. Maffitt christened the *Oreto* as the CSS *Florida* and took her to Havana to complete fitting out and fill up his crew. But several crewmen were sick with yellow fever, and others succumbed in Cuba. Maffitt decided to make a run for Mobile with a skeleton crew of eighteen men, some of whom, including Maffitt himself, were infected with the deadly fever. As the *Florida* approached the blockade fleet off Mobile in broad daylight, the executive officer wanted to wait until night to slip into the bay. No, said the feverish Maffitt. "We will hoist the English colors as a *'ruse de guerre,'* and boldly stand for the commanding officer's ship; the remembrance of the delicate *Trent* affair may perhaps cause some deliberation and care before the batteries are let loose on us; four minutes of hesitation on their part may save us."[43]

The senior officer on the blockade was Commander George H. Preble, grandson of the famous Captain Edward Preble, who had won renown in wars against the Barbary states. From his flagship USS *Oneida*, Preble hailed the supposed British ship. When he got no response, he fired a shot across her bow. The *Florida* paid no attention. Mindful of orders not to alienate the British by firing on their ships, Preble sent two more shots across the bow to stop the silent vessel, which only sped up. Preble then ordered the *Oneida* to fire in earnest, scoring several hits and wounding half the crew. "The loud explosions, roar of shot and shell, crashing of spars and rigging," wrote Maffitt, "mingled with the moans of our sick and wounded, instead of intimidating, only increased our determination to enter the destined harbor." With her superior speed, the *Florida* finally made it to the protection of Fort Morgan and into Mobile Bay.[44]

Farragut was "very much pained" by this incident, and he reprimanded Preble for a serious error of judgment in not firing directly into the *Florida* after she failed to heed the first warning shot. In his defense, Preble cited the general orders not to antagonize Britain and noted that all of his officers assumed that the ship was British. The Navy Department knew that the *Florida* (which they still called *Oreto*) was in the Caribbean but had not gotten word to Preble. "Had I been officially or unofficially, in any way, informed that a [Confederate] man-of-war steamer was expected or on the ocean," he wrote, "I would have known her true character and could have run her down."[45]

Preble's defense did him no good with Welles, who took the report to Lincoln with a recommendation that Preble should be cashiered. Welles had endured a torrent of criticism for deficiencies in the blockade and for the navy's supposed failure to protect merchant ships from privateers and cruisers. He needed a scapegoat—or as he put it, an example to encourage greater vigilance—and Preble was it. "If that is your opinion," Lincoln told Welles, "it is mine. I will do it."[46]

Preble was a popular officer in the navy and carried a proud name. Pressure built almost immediately for his restoration to rank. Farragut was upset that his reprimand of Preble "should have drawn upon him such summary and severe punishment." After reviewing all the evidence in the case, Lincoln decided—against Welles's advice—to restore Preble to the navy at his rank of commander, but he spent the rest of the war relegated to marginal commands.[47]

The *Florida* would remain bottled up at Mobile for more than four months. Meanwhile, the *Alabama* began her career as the most notable—or notorious—commerce raider. James Bulloch had to perform even greater legal legerdemain to get her out of England than in the case of the *Oreto*. Consul Thomas Dudley matched Bulloch in a contest of spies, double agents, and lawyers to pile up evidence of *No. 290*'s warlike purpose and Confederate ownership. "The United States authorities in this country have used every possible means of inducing the British authorities to seize, or at least to forbid the sailing of, the *Alabama*," wrote Bulloch from Liverpool.[48] But his talents for obfuscation and Foreign Secretary Lord John Russell's initial skepticism about the largely hearsay nature of the evidence of Confederate ownership that Dudley presented caused delays in British investigation of *No. 290*'s real purpose. By the time Russell became convinced that the case required a closer look, it was too late. Receiving word from a double agent that the British government was about to seize the ship, Bulloch took her out on July 29 for a "trial run" from which she never returned. Aware that the USS *Tuscarora* was lying in wait, *No. 290* headed north around the tip of Ireland to avoid her, then south to the Azores for rendezvous with a British merchant ship carrying

"No. 290" in British waters near Liverpool before she took on her guns and became the CSS *Alabama*. (From *Frank Leslie's Illustrated History of the Civil War*)

ordnance and supplies. On August 24, *No. 290* was commissioned as the CSS *Alabama* with the redoubtable Raphael Semmes as captain and a mostly British crew.[49]

During the next three weeks, the *Alabama* captured and burned ten American ships, eight of them whalers. Whale oil made a spectacular bonfire, wrote a midshipman from Georgia, "filling the wide Ocean with smoke and standing as still to her fate as though she were calling down curses on the head of Abe Lincoln and his Cabinet."[50] Gideon Welles did most of the cursing of "the connivance of British authorities" in allowing these "British wolves" to escape and prey on American commerce.[51] An international tribunal eventually agreed with Welles and ruled that the British government must compensate American shipowners for the losses caused by the Crown's negligence in failing to enforce its own neutrality laws.

But that happened ten years later. In 1862 Welles could only gnash his teeth about the *Alabama*'s continued destruction of merchant ships as Semmes moved away from the Azores into the North Atlantic. By November 30 the *Alabama* had burned twenty-one merchant ships or whalers, all of them sailing vessels that could not escape when the *Alabama* put on steam. Semmes used the same tactics he had perfected with the *Sumter*. He would fly the American flag or sometimes British or French colors as he approached a ship, then run up the Confederate flag after she hove to under the *Alabama*'s guns.

Orders went out from Washington to a dozen navy ships to drop everything else and go after the raider. Rumors and reports placed the *Alabama* here, there, and almost everywhere from Cape Verde to Nova Scotia to Bermuda to the Windward Islands to the coast of Brazil. The clamor against the navy for its failure to catch the raider caused even Sophie Du Pont, wife of Rear Admiral Samuel F. Du Pont, to join the chorus of criticism. The admiral tried to explain. "What vexes me," he wrote, "is that so few people know or understand what a needle in a haystack business it is to chase a single ship on the wide ocean."[52]

On one occasion, the USS *San Jacinto* spotted the *Alabama* in the harbor of Fort Royal at Martinique. Under international maritime law, belligerent warships must not fire on each other within three miles of a neutral shore. While the *San Jacinto* waited outside that limit, the Georgia midshipman on the *Alabama* described how the French officials "showed us every kindness imaginable, giving us charts of the harbor and inviting us up to their club rooms."[53] That night the slippery Semmes bribed a double agent to send up rockets in one direction to alert the *San Jacinto* while he escaped from the harbor on the opposite course.[54]

American shipowners and merchants began transferring registry of their vessels to neutral nations, principally Britain, or ownership of the cargoes to citizens of those nations. Since the *Alabama* could not take its prizes into port to determine ownership, Captain Semmes constituted himself the judge of a Confederate admiralty court on board ship. If a captain or supercargo could prove non-U.S. ownership of the cargo on an American ship, Semmes would bond the ship (require the captain to sign a bond for the estimated value to be paid to the Confederate government after the war) and let it go. Semmes followed this procedure with five of the twenty-six American ships he captured by the end of 1862. He required some of these ransomed vessels to take the prisoners that the *Alabama* had captured on ships she burned. In several other cases, however, he judged the papers showing foreign ownership of cargo or vessel to be fraudulent on technical grounds (such as not having a consul's stamp). He then burned them without further ado, in some cases creating great resentment by neutrals that actually did own part of the cargo. Of course,

Semmes had to let many of the ships he stopped go free because both vessel and cargo had legitimate papers showing neutral ownership. As time went on, more and more American ships legally transferred to foreign registry, beginning the "flight from the flag" that crippled the American merchant marine.[55]

The exploits of the *Alabama*, coupled with other Confederate initiatives on land and water from the summer of 1862 through the spring of 1863, ushered in a period of defeat and discouragement for the Union navy as well as for the Union cause in general. The ways in which the navy coped with these unfamiliar experiences would go far to shape the course of the war.

chapter six

Nothing but Disaster

"This whole blockade is and has been unsatisfactory from the beginning," wrote Gideon Welles in July 1862.[1] He was referring specifically to leaks in the blockade of Wilmington, North Carolina. But the same expression of dissatisfaction could have applied to Charleston, Mobile, and other ports. The navy's capture of Hatteras Inlet, Port Royal, Fernandina, New Orleans, and other smaller ports had shut them down. And the occupation of many estuaries and bays along the south Atlantic and Gulf coasts had denied easy access to the shallow-draft schooners and other craft that had run in and out during the war's early months. But some still tried it in 1862, and they constituted the majority of the 390 blockade-runners captured or destroyed in 1862—including four schooners caught along the Gulf coast by the ninety-day gunboat USS *Kanawha* on the single day of April 10, 1862, earning a nice sum of prize money for the crew and their commander, Lieutenant John C. Febiger.[2]

By then, however, the nature of blockade-running had begun to change. Shortages of every sort of war matériel and consumer goods in the Confederacy caused prices to commence their dizzying inflationary rise. Blockade-running became an extremely lucrative enterprise. It attracted investors from the Confederacy and abroad, mainly Britain. Even a few Northern merchants whose eye for the dollar eclipsed their patriotism got into the game. Investors or Confederate agents would buy arms, ammunition, gunpowder, shoes, coffee, salt, wine, silk, hoop skirts, and other goods in Europe and ship them in ordinary merchant vessels to Nassau, Havana, Bermuda, or Halifax, where the cargoes would be transferred to fast steamers to make a run for Charleston, Mobile, Wilmington, or perhaps another port like Galveston, where they would try to slip past the blockaders on a dark, foggy, or stormy night guided by coded signals from shore. There they would load up with cotton or perhaps another Southern product like resin or turpentine and watch for their chance to dash out on the return run.

Merchant ship captains—mostly British—and retired Royal Navy officers were often the commanders and sometimes part owners of these runners. Southern pilots who knew the coast and channels of their home region were paid handsomely for their services. The profit motive was the main attraction for officers and crews of the runners, but the excitement of adventure also played a part. "Nothing I have ever experienced can compare with it," wrote a British officer on a runner. "Hunting, pig-sticking, steeplechasing, big-game hunting, polo—I have done a little of each—all have their thrilling moments, but none can approach running a blockade."[3]

The risk of being shot at, driven ashore, or captured was real, but if they were foreigners (as most were), they would eventually be released—many to return to blockade-running—despite Welles's wish to see them incarcerated. If caught, the ship and its cargo would be seized and evidence of its attempt to violate the blockade taken before a prize court. These courts normally ruled in favor of the U.S. government unless they found that the ship's papers (usually falsified) showing that its cargo was consigned to a neutral port were genuine. If condemned, the ship and its cargo would be sold and the proceeds divided between the navy's pension fund and the crew or crews of the blockade ships that had captured her. The amount of prize money to each member of the crew was prorated by rank, with the squadron commander also getting a cut for each capture. The navy bought many of the captured runners and converted them to blockade ships because they had greater speed than most naval vessels. Despite the risk of capture, there was no shortage of investors because owners could make back their investment in one or two round trips and clear pure profit with every subsequent successful voyage—and in 1862 at least three-quarters of them were successful.

Investors in blockade-running began buying the newest and fastest steamers they could find, paying premium prices. A Scottish newspaper complained in November 1862 that "there will soon be scarcely a swift steamer left on the Clyde."[4] British shipyards began building or converting vessels intended especially for the purpose: sleek in design, fast and shallow drafted, painted lead gray for low visibility, burning smokeless anthracite, and featuring a low freeboard, telescoping smokestacks, and underwater steam-escape valves so that the boat moved almost silently through the water. "The class of vessels now violating the blockade is far different from those attempting it a year ago," wrote a Union ship captain in March 1863. "They are very low, entirely free from top hamper, and almost invisible from the color of their paint." Although his officers and crew "all keep a sharp lookout," it was impossible on dark nights to see a runner until it was almost on top of the blockading ship and going so fast that "vigilance alone without speed is insufficient" to catch it.[5]

An officer on a blockade ship off Cape Fear, North Carolina, unburdened his frustrations in a letter to his wife. "Let no one condemn the occasional running in or out of a vessel till they have experienced some of the difficulties of preventing it," he wrote in April 1863. Because of the length of coast to be guarded, blockade ships sometimes were a mile or more apart from each other. "What is there to prevent a vessel from running between them in the darkness when it is impossible to see more than three or four hundred feet from the ship. They make but little noise as they approach, & that little is difficult to distinguish from the beating of surf on the beach—they come upon us and flit by like a phantom."[6]

The wife of the Confederate agent in Bermuda who organized the cargoes for blockade-runners sailed on one of them from Wilmington with their three children to join him in Bermuda. "I did not altogether relish these 'deeds of darkness,'" she wrote in a journal entry describing the trip. "There is a little feeling of wounded pride, that we must seek the protection of the night, & slip by our foes as noiselessly as we can. . . . The port holes were all closed, & blankets hung over them, the sky light covered, the lights all extinguished." Thus darkened, they passed through the blockade fleet ship by ship over a period of two hours and escaped undetected.[7]

In 1862 most of the criticism of the navy in Northern newspapers and gloating by the Southern press over the porousness of the blockade focused on the South Atlantic coast, especially Charleston. Rumors, exaggeration, and outright fabrication magnified the numbers of ships that were reported to have evaded the blockade. A letter from Nassau published in the *New York Times* of May 3, 1862, listed several vessels running the blockade into or out of Fernandina and Jacksonville, Florida, during the time that Union forces actually *occupied* those ports. American consuls in European and Caribbean ports sent lists and descriptions of ships reported to be departing for Southern ports, and the State Department passed these on to the navy. At one time in the spring of 1862, Flag Officer Du Pont of the South Atlantic Squadron had a list of 160 such vessels, of which only a few "have ever run the blockade, or even ventured to approach the coast."[8]

The captain's clerk on the USS *Flag* (which was credited with nine

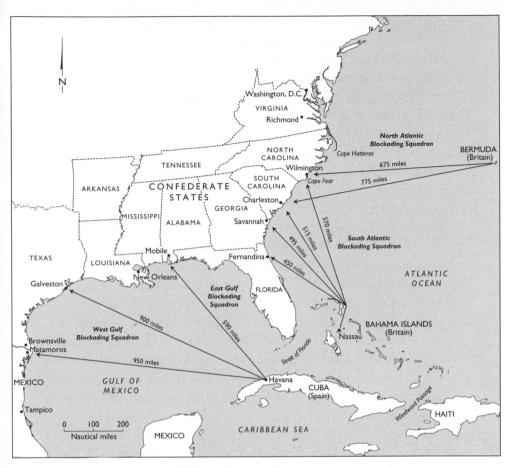

U.S. Navy Blockading Squadrons Showing Distances to the
Ports Favored by Blockade-Runners

prizes during the war) compiled a list of sixty-five vessels reported or rumored to be approaching the South Atlantic coast. Somehow the *Philadelphia Evening Bulletin* managed to publish this list under the headline "Vessels That Have Run the Blockade." In fact, only two of them had done so.[9] The senior officer on the Charleston blockade noted in his journal that "some ten days ago when it was said that 22 schooners had run out, only three started, and two of them grounded in the harbor and put back, and the third was captured by the *Huron*. The greatest number known to go out at one time was six schooners and that [was] about a month ago of which we captured two."[10] A month later, the *New York Times* published a story from a Nassau correspondent that thirteen blockade-runners had recently arrived from Charleston; Du Pont noted that eight of these had actually been captured by Union warships.[11]

Neither Du Pont nor Welles nor any other Union officer, however, denied that a good many runners got through, especially at Charleston, Wilmington, and Mobile. All three of these port cities were difficult to blockade because of multiple navigation channels needing to be blocked. In the case of Charleston, shallow water extended far from the coastline, forcing blockade ships to stand out a substantial distance from the harbor entrance. In 1862 Du Pont could not keep more than a dozen ships guarding a parabolic line about thirteen miles long. At the entrance to Mobile Bay, three Confederate forts kept Union ships at a distance from the navigation channels. Large forts also guarded the two inlets to the Cape Fear River below Wilmington. These two inlets were only a few miles apart as the crow flies but were separated by Smith Island and Frying Pan Shoals extending far into the ocean so that blockade ships guarding each inlet were separated by fifty miles of navigable water. The Confederate commander at Fort Fisher defending New Inlet explained why blockading the Cape Fear River was so difficult, especially in the fall and winter when storms frequently drove ships to shelter: "The prevalence of southeast weather at the main entrance, while it is very dangerous for vessels outside, forces them to the northward of the cape and gives easy access to vessels running the blockade," while "in like manner the northeast gales drive the enemy to shelter to the southward of the cape and clears the New Inlet."[12]

All of the squadron commanders complained constantly to Welles that they did not have enough ships to maintain a tight blockade, that those they did have were too slow, and that their vessels were repeatedly breaking down from the wear and tear of the service. In August 1862 Du Pont acknowledged that at Charleston "the blockade has never been more violated." The main problem, as one of his ship captains put it, was that "with the few vessels we have here I think it almost impossible to keep steamers from running in or out."[13] At the two inlets off the Cape Fear River, wrote officers on those stations, "the force now on either side of the shoal is far too small to make an effective blockade." It was "greatly to our mortification, after all our watchfulness to prevent it, that the enemy succeeded in eluding us. None can be more vigilant than we are—the officer of the watch, with the quartermaster, always on the bridge, lookouts on each bow, gangway, and quarter. . . . I do not see how this can be prevented unless we can string the whole coast with steamers."[14]

The number of ships in each blockade squadron listed on paper bore little relationship to the actual number available on station at any given time. Although by mid-1862 the North Atlantic and West Gulf squadrons had shortened the down time for resupply by establishing additional bases at Beaufort, North Carolina, and Pensacola, Florida (which the Confederates had abandoned), ships were still off their stations periodically to refill their coal bunkers. Du Pont had installed a large repair facility at Port Royal, and minor repairs could be made at Pensacola and Beaufort. But major repairs required ships to make the long trip to one of the Northern navy yards. And such repairs were needed more and more often as hard service took an increasing toll on boilers and machinery—especially of the purchased and converted merchant ships, which had not been built for such service.

No theme comes up more often in the naval records than what Du Pont described succinctly as "lame ducks." "My vessels are coming in all the time broken down, the truth is they have been tried to the utmost," he wrote in July 1862. A month later, one of his ships returned to Port Royal with both machinery and crew worn out. "I think his fires have been out about eleven days in eleven months. You may imagine what [effect] this is on the engineers and firemen." Du Pont's captains lamented that "how we are to keep up the blockade with so many vessels broken down is a problem which my arithmetic cannot solve."[15] From the Gulf, Farragut also reported so many ships "disabled, and requiring so much repairs that I almost despair of getting vessels enough to do efficient service." Assistant Secretary Gustavus Fox told Farragut in September 1862 that "we have our navy yards filled with broken-down vessels, and we know your wants and will exert ourselves to help you, but the more we send the more they seem to come back."[16]

Sailing ships did not have this problem, of course, nor did they need to leave their stations to coal. But by 1862 they were almost useless for blockading large ports like Charleston, because the fast steamers and even schooners that chose their time could nearly always outrun them. Du Pont therefore stationed most of his sailing vessels at what he called his "inside blockade" in the numerous small bays and inlets that pierced the coast from South Carolina to Florida. Flag Officer James L. Lardner of the East Gulf Squadron did the same on Florida's Gulf coast. Because blockade-runners rarely tried to get in or out of these small inlets after 1861, blockade duty there was quite easy but also tedious, as the weeks went by and nothing happened.

The surgeon on the USS *Fernandina*, a bark-rigged vessel converted to a six-gun warship, kept a diary in which he chronicled this kind of duty. The *Fernandina* was shifted from one inlet or bay to another in South Carolina or Georgia every three months or so for a change of scene. Only once in two years did she take a prize—a schooner trying to go out through St. Catherine's Sound with 300 bales of cotton and some turpentine. The rest of the time, the crew had little to do, which gave them leisure for walking on shore, hunting game, buying provisions from contrabands on plantations whose owners had fled to the mainland, catching fish and gathering oysters. Diary entries described the mixed pleasures and tedium of such activities.

December 16, 1862, St. Helena Sound: "The reading of light literature is carried on to a great extent in the service on account of the monotony pervading. No prizes to be seen or captured makes it rather dull work and poor pay. Oh, for a cruise on the briny deep!"

January 23, 1863, St. Simon's Sound: "Taking exercise on shore is a great blessing to us naval officers and a luxury that few on blockade duty enjoy."

April 30, 1863, Doboy Sound, saluting hunters from the ship who killed a young bullock: "We'll eat your healths in some of the juicy beef whenever it is served up. . . . In a month or six weeks we will have watermelons, peaches, oranges, potatoes, etc."

May 6, 1863, still at Doboy Sound: "Between smoking, eating and drinking I managed to kill time and drive dull care away. This blockading is rather a dull affair. We are all anxious to make a journey up North."

May 9, 1863: "We are spoiling for a fight! Our only enemies to contend with at present are mosquitoes, sand flies, and snakes."[17]

Sailors on blockade duty on the "briny deep" also experienced long periods of boredom, especially during daylight hours and moonlit nights when no runners could be expected. These times alternated with the tension and fatigue of dark or stormy nights when every sense had to remain alert. The blockaders at Charleston needed that alertness in the last days of January 1863, when it paid off in one case and the lack of it led to near disaster in another. At 3:15 A.M. on January 29, the large British merchant steamer *Princess Royal* neared the harbor carrying two English-built marine engines for Confederate ironclads, six 70-pound Whitworth rifled cannons and 930 steel-headed shells for penetrating iron armor, 600 barrels of gunpowder, and other military cargo worth altogether nearly half a million American dollars. The shallow-draft spotter ship USS *G. W. Blunt* (a schooner) saw her approaching Rattlesnake Channel and fired a shot, signaling the rest of the squadron. The gunboat USS *Unadilla* drove the *Princess Royal* aground, and the navy was able to secure the prize before the Confederates could salvage or destroy the cargo or ship. It was one of the most valuable prizes captured during the war and did a great deal for the morale of the blockade squadron.[18]

Two nights later, however, the Confederates struck back. Through a thick fog, the two recently completed ironclad rams CSS *Chicora* and CSS *Palmetto State* sortied from Charleston to attack the blockade fleet. The *Palmetto State* rammed the USS *Mercedita* and left her in what appeared to be sinking condition to seek other targets, while the *Chicora* sent several shots through the USS *Keystone State*, killing twenty-five men. This action stirred up a beehive of activity among the Union fleet, as some ships fled to safety and others converged on the Confederate ironclads. They returned to Charleston claiming they had sunk two blockaders and set four others on fire. None of that was true; the two badly damaged ships were towed to Port Royal for repairs, while the rest of the fleet remained at sea and soon resumed their stations. General Pierre G. T. Beauregard asserted that by scattering the fleet, the Confederates had broken the blockade, which under international law could not be reestablished without sixty days' notice. Du Pont rejected Beauregard's claim and continued the blockade as before.[19]

A good many blockade-runners that were headed to or from South Atlantic ports were captured not by the squadrons blockading those ports but by ships 400 miles or more distant in one of the channels through the Bahamian Islands. In the war's first year, Nassau was the principal transshipment port for blockade-runners. It was closer to Confederate ports on the Atlantic than any other neutral port. But all traffic had to funnel through narrow channels in the shallow waters of the Bahamas, where Union blockade ships of the East Gulf Squadron learned to lie in wait. Making their passages in or out of Confederate ports at night, runners often found themselves in the Bahama channels in daylight, where they became prey to blockaders. One of the most successful was USS *Santiago de Cuba*, a big and fast sidewheeler armed with ten guns that captured four runners in seven days in April 1862 and a total of sixteen in the war as a whole—eight of them steamers.

By August 1862 Confederate agents and blockade-running captains were shifting most of their operations to Bermuda, where open, deep water gave them a better chance to evade blockaders despite being 100 to 150 miles farther from Wilmington and Charleston. "The port of Nassau has become so dangerous even as a port of destination for arms in British ships," wrote a Confederate purchasing agent in August 1862, "that I have thought it prudent not to order anything more to that port."[20]

THE PRINCIPAL GULF PORT FOR blockade-runners was Mobile, about 600 miles from Havana. After Farragut's fleet emerged from its frustrating three months in the Mississippi River at the end of July 1862, the new admiral wanted to move against the Alabama port and close it down. With the Confederate abandonment of the old navy yard at Pensacola, Farragut had a new base for coaling and making minor repairs only fifty miles from Mobile Bay. But many of his ships needed major repairs, and his crews were decimated by diseases caught near Vicksburg and by the beginning of the yellow fever season in the Gulf. The Navy Department squelched Farragut's desire to launch a campaign to enter Mobile Bay. "The present condition of your vessels," Welles told him in August, and the absolute necessity to retain enough force at New Orleans to hold it precluded "attempting the concentration of an adequate force at Mobile for the reduction of that place." Instead, Farragut should repair his vessels and concentrate on improving the blockade, especially along the Texas coast, where it had sprung aggravating leaks.[21]

During the fall, Farragut received some new ships and managed to patch up many of his older ones. The government had a new mission for them. In mid-December Major General Nathaniel P. Banks arrived in New Orleans to replace Benjamin Butler as commander of the Department of the Gulf. Banks brought a large number of army reinforcements with him. His orders were to cooperate with the navy in a new campaign to capture Port Hudson and Vicksburg and to occupy key points in Texas. When Farragut learned of these orders, he grumbled to Fox: "Had I my own way, it would be to attack Mobile first & then have the whole available force for the River & Texas."[22] But despite his prominence as America's first admiral, he did not get his own way.

Several of Farragut's gunboats had already seized key points along the Texas coast from the Sabine River on the border with Louisiana south to Corpus Christi. The most important was Galveston, which three Union ships had captured in October 1862. Farragut was well aware that while the navy might be able to take possession of these harbors and inlets, it could not hold them without army troops to fend off land-based Confederate counterattacks. "I have the coast of Texas lined with vessels," Farragut informed Welles in October. "If I had a military force I would go down and take every place from the Mississippi River to the Rio Grande."[23] General Butler, still in command, promised to send troops to hold Galveston, but they did not come. "I fear that I will find difficulties in procuring the few troops we require to hold the place," Farragut told the senior naval commander at Galveston.[24] Farragut's fears were justified; the troops that eventually came were too few and too late.

One of Farragut's biggest headaches in Texas was actually in Mexico: the city of Matamoras (the 1860s spelling), just across the Rio Grande River from Brownsville, Texas. Soon after the war began, a huge increase in trade occurred between Matamoras and other neutral ports, especially Havana. Dozens of ships appeared on the Mexican side of the mouth of the Rio Grande to offload arms and other military supplies and to take on cotton. Union naval officers were certain that the incoming freight was destined for Texas and the cotton came from there. Commander Henry French of the USS *Albatross* boarded several of the ships and found that "their papers are in order, showing that the cotton has been shipped from Matamoras with certificates showing that it is Mexican property." But he was convinced that "every ounce of this cotton comes from Brownsville, and merely goes through the form of transfer to Mexican merchants without a bona fide transfer." French was quite correct. By one estimate, some 320,000 bales of cotton were exported from Matamoras during the war. Even if this estimate was inflated, Matamoras appears to have been the leading port for wartime export of Southern cotton. In September 1862 Commander French asked Farragut what he should do about Matamoros and its cotton trade. "My inclination to lay violent hands on it is very great," French wrote. "I should enjoy real gratification in being able to find authority for seizing all of their 'king cotton.'"[25]

Farragut authorized French to seize these ships and others carrying military contraband into Matamoras but warned him that "you will have to execute that duty with great delicacy toward neutrals, who claim the right to trade with Matamoras, which we do not wish to interfere with when it is legitimately carried on."[26] Farragut's authority came from Welles, who had instructed captains to stop, search, and seize "all vessels . . . without regard to their clearance or destination" carrying contraband of war intended for or exported by the Confederacy even if under a neutral flag. "The abuse of a foreign flag or the destination of a neutral port must not be permitted to shield the conveyance of munitions to the enemy."[27]

Welles here enunciated a corollary to the doctrine of continuous voyage. This doctrine had been established by British blockaders in previous wars to justify seizure of contraband on neutral vessels if there was good reason to believe that it would be shipped onward to an enemy port. Union ships had already exercised that power by capturing some ships traveling from Britain to Bermuda or another neutral port to be transshipped to a blockade-runner. In the case of Matamoras, the contraband was not transshipped by sea to another port but across a river into Texas, so Welles's corollary came to be known as the doctrine of continuous transportation.

The most celebrated case of this doctrine in the Civil War concerned the British merchant steamer *Peterhoff* carrying contraband from England to Matamoras, which was captured in February 1863 in the West Indies a thousand miles from Matamoras by the USS *Vanderbilt* under the command of none other than Charles Wilkes. British merchants protested loudly and the Foreign Office objected mildly. But an American prize court upheld the seizure and the U.S. Supreme Court eventually affirmed it. The British government recorded the precedent and applied it a half century later against goods shipped from neutral America to neutral Holland destined for Germany in World War I.[28]

Matamoras remained a festering problem for the blockade, however. Some prize courts refused to condemn cargoes when their manifests and other papers seemed genuine. Blockade captains found it difficult to stop and search every ship going to or from Matamoras. Some vessels with clearances from U.S. customs agents in New York, New Orleans, or other American ports seemed to have legitimate permission to trade with Mexico, even though Farragut was certain they were trading with the Confederacy through Matamoras. He denounced American merchants "whose thirst for gain far outstrips their patriotism." He vowed that "I shall do all in my power to break up this unrighteous traffic by fraudulent clearances . . . and expose the operations of those ruthless speculators who are dishonoring our cause by taking every possible advantage of 'turning a dollar,' even at the expense of our country's honor."[29] The whole issue was complicated by the existence of a civil war in Mexico, in which the French were intervening with thousands of troops. Some of the shipments of arms to Matamoras were in fact intended for one side or the other in *that* conflict.

Farragut and Welles were convinced that the only way to cut off trade with the Confederacy through Matamoras was to occupy Brownsville and the north bank of the Rio Grande for several miles upriver. Farragut appealed to the Navy Department for shallow-draft gunboats to get over the bar into the Rio Grande, and Welles appealed to the army for troops to occupy Brownsville. Before anything could come of these entreaties, a series of blows struck the Union navy that caused severe setbacks in this theater and elsewhere in the winter of 1862–63.

ON DECEMBER 30, 1862, three companies (260 men) of the 42nd Massachusetts Infantry finally arrived at Galveston to join the five gunboats in possession of that port. The 42nd was perfectly raw, one of the new nine-months militia regiments organized in the fall of 1862. Their presence in Galveston was short-lived. At 5:00 A.M. on New Year's Day, four Confederate steamboats protected by cotton bales and carrying a thousand men launched a surprise attack. Two of the cottonclads rammed the USS *Harriet Lane*, while Texas soldiers scrambled aboard and captured her, killing the captain. A Confederate surgeon who watched this action described how "our boys poured in, and the pride of the Yankee Navy was the prize of our Cow-boys."[30] The USS *Westfield* ran aground, and her commander, William Renshaw, who had led the Union occupation of Galveston three months earlier, ordered her burned to prevent capture. The fire reached the magazine before he could escape, and a dozen sailors plus Renshaw were killed in the explosion. The rest of the Union gunboats fled ignominiously, leaving behind the 260 soldiers and nearly 100 crewmen of the *Harriet Lane* as prisoners of war.[31]

Farragut was appalled by this news and disgusted with the poor showing of his sailors. "The shameful conduct of our forces has been one of the severest blows of the war to the Navy," he admitted to Welles. "The prestige of the gunboats is gone in that quarter until it is again reestablished by some corresponding good conduct on our part." Assistant Secretary Fox echoed Farragut's jeremiad. "The disgraceful affair at Galveston has shaken the public confidence in our prestige," he lamented. "It is too cowardly to place on paper."[32]

Farragut's hope to retrieve the navy's reputation by "good conduct" suffered more setbacks. He sent his second in command, Commodore Henry H. Bell, with the twenty-six-gun USS *Brooklyn* and five gunboats to retake Galveston. "The moral effect must be terrible if we don't take it again," Farragut warned. "May God grant you success for your own sake and the honor of the Navy."[33] Before Bell could make the attempt, however, none other than Raphael Semmes and the CSS *Alabama* appeared on the scene. From reading New York newspapers in one of the merchant ships the *Alabama* captured, Semmes learned of General Banks's expedition to the Gulf. The newspapers speculated that Galveston was Banks's objective, so Semmes decided to head there himself with the audacious purpose of getting among Banks's troop transports and sinking as many as possible.

As it turned out, Banks went to New Orleans. But when Semmes spotted Commodore Bell's warships outside Galveston on January 11, he quickly modified his plan. He would lure one of the Union ships out to check on the *Alabama*, flying the British flag and looking from a distance like a blockade-runner. The ruse worked beautifully. The USS *Hatteras*, a converted sidewheeler ferryboat carrying only five light guns, came out to investigate the strange sail. Turning away as if to escape, the *Alabama* went slowly enough that at dusk the *Hatteras* came up to her and hailed: "What Ship is That?" "Her Majesty's Steamer *Petrel*" came the answer. A boat put off from the *Hatteras* to inspect this suspicious vessel, whereupon the raider ran up Confederate colors and fired a broadside into the *Hatteras*. Stunned and outgunned, the Union ship fought back gamely but was soon full of so many holes that she was sinking. She struck her colors and went to the bottom, while the *Alabama* rescued her surviving crew and made off at top speed before the rest of the Union fleet learned what had happened. The smaller boat's crew got away and reported the sinking. Three days later, Farragut had to begin his report to Welles: "It becomes my painful duty to report still another disaster off Galveston."[34]

This affair delayed Commodore Bell's plan to retake Galveston long enough for the Confederates to emplace a sufficient number of guns there to cause him to abandon the plan. The city remained in Southern possession for the rest of the war. Nor did the sinking of the *Hatteras* drain Farragut's cup of woe. Four days later, the CSS *Florida* escaped from Mobile, where she had been corked up by the blockade for more than four months. The night of January 15–16 was so pitch dark and turbulent that the *Florida* passed within 300 yards of one blockader without being seen. When finally discovered, she was able to outrun her pursuers in a thrilling chase that lasted most of the day on January 16. "Under a heavy press of canvas and steam," wrote the *Florida*'s captain, John N. Maffitt, his ship "made 14½ knots an hour." Within six days, the *Florida* captured three

American merchant vessels whose crews had been unaware of her escape and seized ten more in the next three months.[35]

Five days after the *Florida*'s escape, Farragut's West Gulf Squadron suffered another defeat when two Confederate cottonclad steamers that had worked their way up the inland waterway from Galveston captured the two Union sailing ships holding Sabine Pass on the Louisiana border.[36] "I have nothing but disaster to write to the Secretary of the Navy," sighed Farragut. "Misfortune seldom comes singly," he reflected in a letter to his wife. "This squadron, as Sam Barron used to say, 'is eating its dirt now'— Galveston skedaddled, the Hatteras sunk by the Alabama, and now the Oreto [*Florida*] out on the night of the 16th."[37]

News from other theaters did nothing to ease Northern gloom as 1862 made way for 1863. The previous July, Congress had enacted legislation authorizing the navy to take control of the river gunboats (except Alfred Ellet's ram fleet) from the army. This provision went into effect on October 1, 1862, when Welles upgraded the Western Flotilla to the Mississippi Squadron. He ignored seniority to jump Commander David D. Porter over several captains to take command of the squadron.[38] Welles knew that this appointment would give offense to senior officers, especially since Porter was "impressed with and boastful of his own powers, given to exaggeration in everything related to himself . . . reckless, improvident, and too assuming." But he also "has stirring and positive qualities, is fertile in resources, has great energy," and "is brave and daring like all of his family."[39] Porter did indeed breathe new life into the Mississippi Squadron, which had fallen into lassitude during the final weeks of Charles Davis's command. Porter also cooperated actively with the army in a renewed effort to take Vicksburg.

After Henry W. Halleck went to Washington to become general in chief in July 1862, General Ulysses S. Grant was left in command of Union ground forces in west Tennessee and northern Mississippi. With his principal subordinate, Major General William T. Sherman, Grant planned a two-pronged campaign against Vicksburg. With 40,000 troops, Grant would move overland through northern Mississippi while Sherman would load 30,000 soldiers on transports in Memphis and take them down the Mississippi and up the Yazoo River to operate against Vicksburg from that direction. Porter's gunboats would convoy the transports and lead the way for Sherman's troops to land and carry the bluffs north of Vicksburg.

The squadron's first task was to clear out the hundreds of torpedoes that the rebels were known to have planted in the Yazoo. On December 12, two shallow-draft gunboats functioned as minesweepers moving slowly up the river to cut the wires and fish up the mines or to explode them with rifle fire from the deck. The ironclads *Cairo* and *Pittsburg* protected the minesweepers by shelling Confederate shore batteries and sharpshooters. Growing impatient with what he considered slow progress in this effort, Lieutenant Commander Thomas Selfridge took the *Cairo* forward faster in the main channel. He quickly discovered the wrong way to find torpedoes by running on one or possibly two of them (reports varied), which exploded under his hull and sent the *Cairo* to the bottom in twelve minutes. All of the crew were rescued—as were the guns and iron parts of the *Cairo* a hundred years later, when they were raised and put on exhibit at Vicksburg National Military Park, where they can be seen today.

The sinking of the *Cairo* was the first but far from the last success of Confederate torpedoes. Until December 1862, as Porter reported to Welles, "these torpedoes have proved so harmless . . . that officers have not felt that respect for them to which they are entitled."[40] After the loss of the *Cairo*, they had plenty of respect—perhaps more than necessary, as "torpedo fever" began to eclipse ram fever as a cause of caution among Union officers.

Porter's gunboats plus two of Ellet's rams continued to clear out torpedoes without further sinkings. But the task was complicated by Confederate artillery and rifle fire from the bluffs and banks. "We have had lively times up the Yazoo," Porter wrote to a friend. "We waded through sixteen miles of torpedoes to get at the forts (seven in number); but when we got thus far the fire on the boats from the riflemen in pits dug along the river" killed several men, including Lieutenant William Gwin, one of Porter's best young officers. "The forts are powerful works, out of the reach of ships, and on high hills, plunging their shot through the upper deck, and the river is so narrow that only one could engage them until the torpedoes could all be removed."[41]

The gunboats finally cleared the way for Sherman to land his troops on December 26. Unknown to Porter and Sherman, however, Grant was not coming according to plan. A Confederate cavalry raid had destroyed his supply base at Holly Springs, Mississippi, forcing him to turn back. Another raid farther north by Nathan Bedford Forrest's cavalry had torn down telegraph wires and prevented Grant from informing Sherman of this reverse. Sherman attacked Chickasaw Bluffs on December 29 and suffered a bloody repulse. The second Vicksburg Campaign came to an even more ignominious end than the first one in July 1862, although this time the Mississippi Squadron under Porter had done all that was asked of it.

The navy suffered one of its saddest losses of the war on the last day of 1862. The cause was the ancient foe of mariners—the weather—rather than a human enemy. The story began with a proposal for a combined attack on Wilmington to shut down what was becoming the chief blockade-running port of the Confederacy. "Though the popular clamor centers upon Charleston," Fox wrote to Acting Rear Admiral Samuel Phillips Lee on December 15, "I consider Wilmington a more important point."[42]

Since assuming command of the North Atlantic Squadron in September, Lee had been taking soundings on the bars at the old and new inlets to the Cape Fear River and scouting obstructions near Fort Caswell to determine which of his vessels might be able to get into the river. He also worked on plans for cooperation with army troops commanded by Major General John G. Foster at New Bern. The soldiers would attack (or carry out a diversion against) Wilmington from the north while his gunboats steamed up the river from the south.

Fox promised Lee the *Monitor* and the first of the new and slightly larger monitors, the USS *Passaic*, for this campaign. But it turned out that their draft was too great to get over the bars. Meanwhile, Foster ran into strong Confederate resistance inland from New Bern, making his cooperation impossible. And the "clamor for Charleston" also seemed to override Fox's priority for Wilmington. Nevertheless, when the *Monitor* left Hampton Roads under tow by the powerful sidewheeler USS *Rhode Island* on December 29, their intent was to join Lee's squadron for an attack on Fort Caswell and then to go on to Charleston, where Admiral Du Pont was requesting all the ironclads he could get for an effort to capture that arch symbol of rebellion.[43]

The *Monitor* and the *Rhode Island* had smooth sailing at first, but as they approached that notorious graveyard of ships off Cape Hatteras on December 30, a gale brewed up that grew stronger as the early darkness came on. "I have been through a night of horrors that would have appalled the stoutest heart," wrote the *Monitor*'s paymaster. "The heavy seas rolled over our bow dashing against the pilot house &, surging aft, would strike the solid turret with a force to make it tremble." The bow "would rise on a huge billow & before she could sink into the intervening hollow, the succeeding wave would strike under her heavy armour with a report like thunder & a violence that threatened to tear [her] apart." So much water flooded the engine room that the pumps could not keep up and eventually stopped altogether when the rising water doused the fires.

The *Monitor* signaled the *Rhode Island* that she was sinking. Courageous sailors from the *Rhode Island* manned rescue boats. "Words cannot depict the agony of those moments as our little company gathered on top of the turret . . . with a mass of sinking iron beneath them," peering into the darkness for the boats from the *Rhode Island*. "Seconds lengthened into hours & minutes into years. Finally the boats arrived," while "mountains of water were rushing along our decks and foaming along our sides" and the boats "were pitching & tossing about on them and crashing against our sides."

Somehow, most of the men and officers managed to board the boats, including a fireman who had stayed in the engine room operating the last pump, as he later described it, "until the water was up to my knees and the Cylinders to the Pumping Engines were under Water and stoped [*sic*]." He went topside and was swept off the deck but grabbed a line and was hauled aboard a boat. He survived with forty-six other crewmen while the famous ironclad slipped below the waves at 1:00 A.M. on December 31. Sixteen men went down with her. "The Monitor is no more," wrote her paymaster to his wife after his rescue. "What the fire of the enemy failed to do, the elements have accomplished."[44]

Thus ended the year 1862, which had begun so promisingly for the Union navy. In some respects, things in the new year would get worse before they got better. The "clamor for Charleston" pushed the navy into a major effort to capture the city—but it turned out to be its most disheartening failure of the war.

{ *chapter seven* }

A Most Signal Defeat

T he capture of Charleston had been the ultimate goal of Flag Officer Samuel Francis Du Pont's attack on Port Royal in November 1861. One of Du Pont's principal subordinates, the South Carolina native Percival Drayton, believed that if the raw army troops who accompanied the Port Royal expedition "had been much more than a mob, we could have had either Charleston or Savannah" after the navy captured the forts, "for such a panic as seems to have existed through the low country can scarcely be imagined."[1]

Whether Drayton was correct is debatable. But even if the window of opportunity for easy capture of Charleston was open immediately after the Battle of Port Royal, it soon closed. Even in 1861, Charleston was one of the most strongly defended places in the Confederacy. Scores of heavy guns bristled in nearly a dozen batteries and forts (including Fort Sumter) bracketing the navigation channels for more than four miles from the ocean to the city. A maze of islands, marshes, creeks, and small rivers provided many defensive positions against a land attack. In the end, Charleston proved to be the Confederacy's hardest nut to crack; it never did succumb to naval attacks or combined operations from the coast.

It was not for lack of trying, however. And Northern campaigns against the Cradle of the Confederacy were aided (as elsewhere in the war) by the thousands of contrabands who escaped from slavery to Union ships and gunboats. Modern historical scholarship has shown how the Union army became a powerful force in the liberation of slaves, and how the 180,000 black Union soldiers (most of them liberated slaves) in turn helped the Union army win the war. Less well known is the role of the navy in freeing slaves and the vital contribution of black sailors to the navy's campaigns. In 1861–62 the navy penetrated earlier and more deeply than the army into tidewater regions of the South Atlantic coast and into the valleys of the lower Mississippi River and its tributaries, where much of the enslaved population lived. Du Pont's capture of Port Royal and the adjacent sea islands freed nearly 10,000 slaves in one fell swoop when their masters fled to the mainland and the slaves stayed behind to become free people.

This process of liberation had begun in May 1861, when three slaves escaped by boat from Norfolk across Hampton Roads to General Benjamin Butler's lines at Fort Monroe. Butler ingeniously labeled them contraband of war and refused to return them to their owners. Hundreds more began arriving at army camps in Virginia and hailing Union gunboats on the lower Potomac River and Chesapeake Bay. Volume 4 of the *Official Reports of the Union and Confederate Navies* is full of references to slaves who had paddled their skiffs out to gunboats of the Union's Potomac Flotilla in the summer of 1861 and were taken aboard in groups of three, nine, thirteen, and so on. Officers deluged Secretary of the Navy Gideon Welles with questions about what to do with these people. Welles quietly responded to a pair of such inquiries in July with instructions to allow them to "remain on board and employ them as usefully as possible."[2]

Two months later, Welles announced an official policy: "The Department finds it necessary to adopt a regulation with respect to the large and increasing number of persons of color, commonly known as contrabands, now subsisted at the navy yards and on board ships of war." They could not be returned to slavery nor could they be subsisted indefinitely by the government. "You are therefore authorized, when their services can be made useful, to enlist them for the naval service, under the same forms and regulations as apply to other enlistments." In April 1862 Welles strengthened the word "authorized" to "required." The large number of contrabands "flocking to the protection of the United States flag" along the Mississippi River, he told Flag Officer Charles H. Davis, "afford an opportunity to provide in every department of the ship, especially for boats' crews, acclimated labor. The flag officials are required to obtain the services of these persons for the country by enlisting them freely in the Navy."[3]

The navy was a year ahead of the army in recruiting contrabands. In contrast with the antebellum Regular Army, the navy had always enrolled some African American sailors, paving the way for their proportionally greater role in the Civil War navy. For the war as a whole, the Union navy enlisted twice the percentage of its personnel (about 17 percent) from this manpower pool than did the Union army. When David D. Porter took command of the Mississippi Squadron, he began actively recruiting blacks as coal heavers, firemen, and even gun crews. Porter was pleased with his black sailors. "They do first rate, and are far better behaved than their masters," he declared. "What injustice to these poor people, to say they are fit only for slaves. They are better than the white people here, who I look upon as brutes."[4] A lieutenant commander under Farragut discovered that "the able-bodied negro makes a good artillery man" on shipboard. "In the working of the great guns, for coolness, quickness in handling the rammers, powder, shot, and shell, I found that they were exceedingly apt, and fond of it."[5]

These officers had certainly not been abolitionists before the war. They belonged to one of the most conservative, even aristocratic professions in the antebellum era. If there was an aristocracy in America, Samuel Francis Du Pont, grandson of a French royalist who had been forced to emigrate during the French Revolution, was a member of it. Although not a slaveholder himself, Du Pont had been a defender of slavery. But as with many others, his observations and experiences during the war converted him to abolition. "I have never been an abolitionist," Du Pont explained, "on the contrary most of my life a sturdy conservative on the vexed question." He "defended it all over the world, argued for it as patriarchal in its tendencies," he admitted in 1861. "Oh my! What a delusion. . . . The degradation, overwork, and ill treatment of the slaves in the cotton states is greater than I deemed possible, while the capacity of the Negro for improvement is higher than I believed."[6] Not one officer in his squadron had voted for Lincoln in 1860, Du Pont noted in April 1862, but now "there is not a proslavery man among them."[7] The same probably could not be said of any comparable group of Union army officers at that stage of the war.

Du Pont was especially impressed by the courage of contrabands who risked their lives to escape. "No danger deters them," he wrote, "and they encounter shooting [by rebels] with perfect composure."[8] Some of Du Pont's most valuable sources of intelligence were these escaping contrabands. On the night of April 27–28, 1862, fifteen slaves appropriated the barge of Confederate General Roswell Ripley and rowed it out to the Union blockade fleet. They had belonged to the Quartermaster's Department in Charleston, and according to Du Pont, they provided him with important information on "the various defenses, forts, entrenchments, bridges, etc." in the region. They also reported that three blockade-runners laden with cotton were set to run out, and six runners were expected in from Nassau. This intelligence, noted the senior officer on the Charleston blockade, "caused me to alter the positions of the blockading vessels" for better advantage.[9] Several of these fifteen contrabands were skilled watermen who became valuable to the Union fleet in that capacity.

So did Robert Smalls, who performed one of the most famous escape exploits of the war. Smalls was a twenty-three-year-old slave, married with three children, who knew all the waters around Charleston. He was pilot on the *Planter*, a two-gun sidewheel steamer used as a dispatch boat and transport to carry men and guns to the various forts around the harbor. On the night of May 12–13, the *Planter* was tied up to a wharf ready to transport four big guns to a fort the next day. When the white officers went ashore to their homes, Smalls smuggled his and his brother's family aboard, along with several other slaves (sixteen in all). As dawn approached, they eased away and steamed down the harbor, dipping their colors and sounding the usual signal as they carefully passed Fort Sumter. When out of range, Smalls raised a white flag and crowded on speed toward the blockade fleet. As they approached the USS *Onward*, Smalls stepped on deck, saluted the astonished watch officer, and shouted "Good morning, sir! I've brought you some of the old United States guns, sir!" Smalls subsequently told another officer that "it was the cruel treatment his wife received" as a slave that caused him to make the attempt to escape. "They all express their firm determination not to be taken alive after leaving the wharf, and if fired into to sink rather than stop the vessel well knowing what their fate would be if taken."[10]

Congress granted the usual shares of prize money to Smalls and his crew, and the *Planter* became a useful vessel in Union operations along the South Atlantic coast. Even more valuable was the intelligence Smalls provided. "His information is thorough and complete as to the whole defenses of Charleston," wrote Du Pont. Along with other escaped slaves, Smalls was hired as a pilot for Du Pont's squadron. The admiral praised their services. They "have shown the utmost nautical skill in piloting the gunboats and this *under fire* too—generally smiling and showing their white teeth when a shell exploded over their heads, while many [white pilots] brought up to the business didn't show their white teeth."[11]

Among the most important information supplied by Smalls was that the Confederates had abandoned their fort at the mouth of the Stono River, a navigable stream south of Charleston that served as a sort of back door to the city via artificial cuts to the Ashley River. Du Pont promptly sent gunboats into the Stono to support possible army operations against Charleston itself. James Island and neighboring John Island south of the

Stono contained many cotton plantations and a large slave population. When the gunboats appeared in the Stono River on May 21, panicked planters sought to remove their slaves to the mainland. Commander John Marchand of the USS *James Adger* described the ensuing scene: "About 4 o'clock in the afternoon we heard the most terrific screams ashore, the lookouts at the masthead having previously reported a stampede of slaves on the cotton and corn fields to the south of the river. A company of cavalry was then seen to emerge from the pines . . . charging at full speed among the flying slaves . . . [firing] their pistols on all sides amongst the Negroes. . . . [S]o I directed the gunboats to open fire on the mounted men and a half dozen shells . . . [sent them] scampering in every direction." The gunboats took on seventy-one of the black fugitives; within three days, several hundred more came in. Ships carried them to Port Royal, where they joined thousands of other freedpeople liberated by Du Pont's fleet since November.[12]

Navy gunboats silenced several Confederate batteries and supported the landing of 9,000 Union soldiers on James Island. The Union department commander was Major General David Hunter, who left James Island on June 11 to join his wife, who had just arrived at Hilton Head Island. In Hunter's absence, Brigadier General Hiram Benham ordered an attack on June 16 by 6,000 men against strong Confederate defenses near the village of Secessionville. They were repulsed, and Benham was relieved for disobeying orders.

Two weeks later, Hunter ordered a withdrawal from James Island. Naval officers were shocked and disgusted by this "sudden withdrawing without any earthly reason."[13] The gunboats still controlled the Stono River, and with their support the army could reorganize for a systematic campaign to gain the whole island and take Confederate defenses on the south shore of the harbor from the rear. "This disastrous order" of Hunter's "has ruined us all," wrote Lieutenant Commander John P. Bankhead of the USS *Pembina*. "We will never again have so good an opportunity or position to advance upon Charleston." Another naval officer declared that "from the first day of his arrival" General Hunter "has committed nothing but blunders." Bankhead thought the army should "relieve the old gentleman at Hilton Head [Hunter was sixty] who sits all day in his short sleeves and enjoys himself in the bosom of his family." Du Pont agreed. "Oh those Soldiers," he wrote to Gustavus Fox. "I put them nearly on top of the house in Charleston, but I did not push them into the window, and they came back."[14]

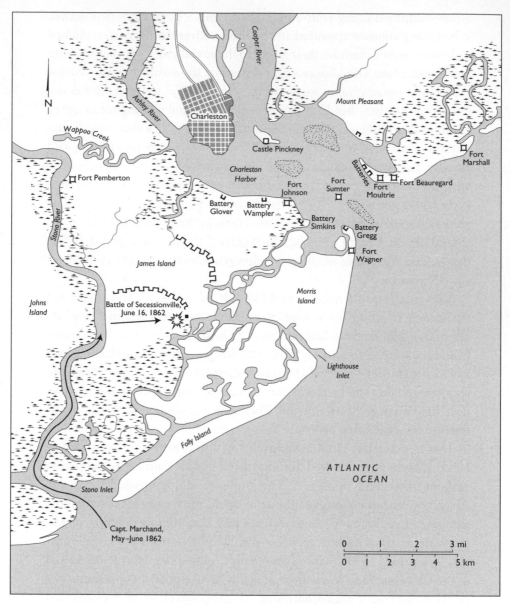

Charleston's Defenses in 1862

In Washington, however, Fox did not seem distressed by the army's withdrawal—quite the contrary. Through the spring and summer of 1862, he carried on a correspondence with Du Pont about the best way to capture Charleston, in which the two men seemed to be talking past each other. Fox wanted it to be entirely a navy operation, as Farragut's capture of New Orleans had been. "Our summer's work must be Charleston by the navy," he told Du Pont. "If we give you the *Galena* and *Monitor*, don't you think we can . . . make it *purely navy*? Any other plan we shall play second [fiddle]" to the army, which "never do[es] us justice, even when we win it" as at New Orleans. "The *Monitor* can go all over [Charleston] harbor and return with impunity. . . . I feel that my duties are twofold; first, to beat our southern friends, second, to beat the Army."[15]

"Do not go it half cocked about Charleston," Du Pont cautioned Fox. "Think coolly and dispassionately on the *main object*," which was to take Charleston, not to glorify the navy. "There is no running the gantlet" at Charleston as there was at the forts below New Orleans. "The whole harbor is ringed with batteries; it is like a 'cul de sac' or bag." In a striking simile that he would repeat frequently, Du Pont described the Charleston defenses as "like a porcupine's hide and quills turned outside in and sewed up at one end." Perhaps the *Monitor* could steam around the harbor with impunity, as Fox maintained, but as her failure and the *Galena*'s misfortunes in the attack on Drewry's Bluff demonstrated, the *Monitor*'s "power of offense is not much." Du Pont told his wife that the Navy Department had been "very quiet since the iron boats could do nothing in the James River at Drewry's Bluff. . . . Charleston should be taken by a large army, squeezed at the same time by a fleet."[16]

In October Du Pont went north for a visit home and for consultations in Washington, where he and Fox discussed their differences face to face. "The number of forts and guns" in the Charleston defenses was "simply fabulous," Du Pont told Fox, to say nothing of obstructions strung across the channel between Forts Sumter and Moultrie consisting of piles, logs strung together with ropes and chains, and torpedoes. But he could not get through to Fox, Du Pont complained. His "Navy feelings are so strong and his prejudices or dislike of Army selfishness so great . . . that he listened unwillingly to combined movements."[17] Du Pont was nettled by Fox's frequent references to New Orleans: if Farragut could do it with wooden ships, why can't you do it with ironclads? "The power of aggression and even endurance of the ironclads are as much overrated by Mr. Fox and others," Du Pont asserted, as "the extent and nature of the defenses of Charleston are underrated . . . in comparison with which those of New Orleans were very slight."[18]

Du Pont returned to Port Royal without settling the question of precisely how the attack on Charleston would be carried out. General Hunter was still commander of the army in the district. The navy had little confidence in him and neither, apparently, did the president. To Lincoln, the talk of combined operations and a slow approach by the army moving on Charleston island by island sounded like McClellan at Yorktown. "*The idea of a siege meets with such disfavor that the President wished me to go down and see you,*" Fox informed Du Pont in February 1863.[19]

Fox did not go; instead, the Navy Department sent monitors of the new *Passaic* class one after another as fast as they were commissioned—seven of them by March 1863, as well as the twenty-gun armored frigate *New Ironsides*. Each of the *Passaic*-class vessels carried one 11-inch and one of the new 15-inch Dahlgren guns in its turret, the latter capable of firing a solid shot weighing 441 pounds or a 350-pound shell. Fox told Du Pont that the other squadron commanders were protesting the dispatch of almost every ironclad to him. But "Farragut and Bailey are and must be, unheeded, to enable that every iron clad possible shall be with you, to insure success."[20]

Welles and Fox made it clear that they expected Du Pont to use all this hardware and firepower to run *past* Forts Sumter and Moultrie to the inner harbor of Charleston "and demand the surrender of all its defenses or suffer the consequences." Fox waxed poetic in his vision of Du Pont "carrying in your flag supreme and superb, defiant and disdainful, silent amid the 200 guns, until you arrive at the center of this wicked rebellion" to "demand the surrender of the forts, or swift destruction. The President and Mr. Welles are very much struck with this programme," while General Halleck "declare[s] that all their defenses must be evacuated if you pass the forts. The sublimity of such a silent attack is beyond words to describe, and I beg of you not to let the Army spoil it."[21]

When Du Pont read these words, he wondered what Fox was smoking when he wrote them.[22] Nevertheless, he replied to Fox that "we'll do it if it can be done—I would like to make you happy." But running silently past the forts was a nonstarter: "I think we shall have to pound and pound beyond any precedent in history." And in a letter to his close friend and confidant, Congressman Henry Winter Davis of Maryland, Du Pont outlined a tactical plan far different from Fox's and Welles's—not to mention Lincoln's—expectations. "They seem to have an idea the ironclads

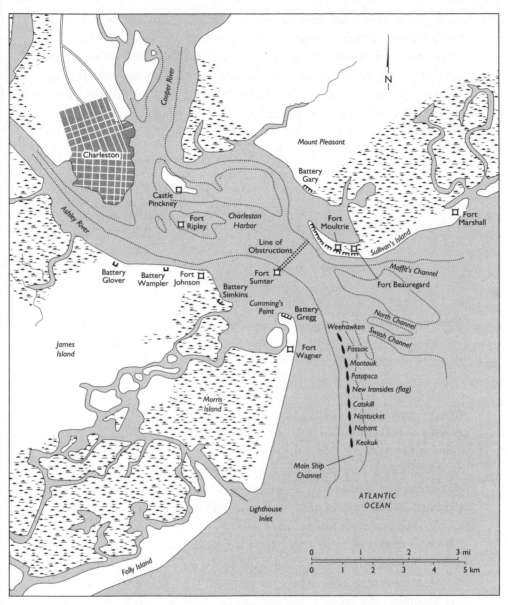

Charleston Harbor and Du Pont's Attack on the Forts, April 7, 1863

can go pirouetting around the harbor and that the forts can be 'run'—a la Mississippi—and that we can get to Charleston," he wrote. But Du Pont intended to "run the Morris Island batteries" a mile or more outside the nexus of Sumter and Moultrie and the obstructions—which Fox had ignored—and then "take the bull (Sumter) by the horns. If we reduce him, which I believe we can, then we can take Morris Island in reverse, and if we can silence them we shall win a base and can get the troops ashore on the Island"—but still five miles from Charleston.[23]

AS THE *PASSAIC*-CLASS monitors began to arrive in January 1863, Du Pont decided to test them in attacks on Fort McAllister, a large earthwork mounting eight guns on the Ogeechee River south of Savannah. On January 27 he sent the USS *Montauk* under Captain John Worden (who had recovered from his wound as captain of the original *Monitor* in its fight with the *Virginia*) accompanied by three gunboats into the Ogeechee. While the wooden vessels stayed back at long range, the *Montauk* went up to the obstructions 1,600 yards from the fort and began a four-hour firefight in which neither ship nor fort did significant damage to the other. The *Montauk* was hit thirteen times without severe injury, which confirmed the ironclads' "impenetrability," Du Pont reported to Welles, but "there was no corresponding quality of aggression or destructiveness as against forts, the slowness of fire [seven or eight minutes between shots] giving full time for the gunners in the fort to take shelter in the bombproofs." To a friend, Du Pont wrote: "I asked myself this morning, while quietly dressing, if an ironclad cannot take eight guns, how are five to take 147 guns in Charleston harbor?" "This experiment," Du Pont informed Welles, only confirmed his conviction that "in all such operations to secure success troops are necessary."[24]

Worden returned to the Ogeechee a month later after learning that the CSS *Nashville*, a former commerce raider and blockade-runner that had been bottled up in the river for eight months, had come down near Fort McAllister preparing to run out but had gone aground. Approaching within 1,200 yards and ignoring the shots rained on the *Montauk* from the fort, Worden shelled the *Nashville*, set her on fire, and blew her up when the fire reached the magazine.[25]

Elated by this demonstration of a single ironclad's power against an enemy vessel if not against forts, Du Pont sent three other monitors (*Passaic*, *Patapsco*, and *Nahant*) to attack Fort McAllister again on March 3.

This time, the ironclads plus their wooden consorts fought the fort for eight hours. They made the sand and turf fly and endured many hits in return, but they knocked out only one of McAllister's guns. "It is wonderful the endurance of these vessels," Du Pont conceded to Welles, but the damage they inflicted on the fort could be repaired in one night.[26] A Confederate artillery officer confirmed this observation. "It would appear that the ironclads are not such formidable monsters after all, particularly against sand batteries," he reported. "The result of this engagement ought to make us feel quite comfortable."[27]

The experiment made Du Pont feel quite *un*comfortable. Even though he received a ninth ironclad—the USS *Keokuk*, smaller with a shallower draft than the monitors and armed with two 11-inch Dahlgrens in stationary turrets—Du Pont's pessimism about an attack grew almost into a self-fulfilling prophecy. "The probabilities are all against us," he told a friend. "Thirty-two guns to overcome or silence two or three hundred, which, however, would not after all disturb me much if it were not for the idea of obstructions. To remove these under fire is simply absurd."[28] Du Pont's gloominess infected some of his monitor captains, who also began to write home that "*we are not very sanguine* of the attack being successful" against enemy defenses "in every conceivable shape, such as torpedoes, obstructions of piles, and innumerable ropes in the channel to foul the propellers of the ironclads." Percival Drayton, commander of the *Passaic*, did not expect the ironclads "to do much damage against my native city."[29]

John Ericsson had designed a raft with explosives to be fitted on the bow of a monitor and pushed ahead of it to detonate torpedoes. But three of these clumsy contrivances had broken loose when being towed to Charleston. Du Pont and his captains had no faith in the remaining raft but attached it to the USS *Weehawken* to give it a try. Two days before the scheduled beginning of his attack, Du Pont forlornly referred to "these operations [for] the capture of Charleston, or what is more probable the *failure* of its capture."[30]

In Washington, Welles and Lincoln were increasingly disturbed by the defeatist tone of Du Pont's dispatches. They reminded Lincoln unpleasantly of McClellan. Welles was also a shrewd if sometimes harsh judge of character. "I deplore the signs of misgiving and doubt that have recently come over" Du Pont, Welles wrote in his diary. "Will and determination are necessary to success," but instead of emulating "the firm and impetuous Farragut," Du Pont "is getting as prudent as McClellan—is very careful—all dash, energy and force are softened under great responsibility. He has a reputation to preserve instead of one to make."[31]

The attack finally came on April 7. Its outcome confirmed Du Pont's pessimism and confounded Washington's hopes. From the start of the ironclads' single-file approach toward Forts Moultrie and Sumter, almost everything went wrong. First in line was the *Weehawken* with the raft to explode torpedoes. But she fouled the grapnels attaching the raft and delayed the whole line for an hour or more while the crew freed them. The raft then caused the *Weehawken* to steer so badly that it was finally cut loose. The ship approached the obstructions anyway, when an explosion that the crew thought was a torpedo but was probably a shell rocked the *Weehawken*. She turned away from the obstructions to engage the two forts, and the other monitors and the *Keokuk* followed suit. All of the ironclads had trouble steering in the strong currents. The flagship USS *New Ironsides* became unmanageable and had to anchor to avoid going aground. Unknown to her crew, she anchored right over a 2,000-pound torpedo, which the Confederates on shore repeatedly tried to explode, without success. (They later discovered that a wagon had run over the wires on Morris Island and cut them.)

This failure was the only thing that went right for Du Pont that day. The *Ironsides* was too far from the forts for its shots to have any effect. It fired only one broadside at Fort Moultrie and none at Fort Sumter for fear of hitting the monitors. The *Keokuk* and monitors crept within a thousand yards or less of Sumter and Moultrie and took enormous punishment without doing much damage to the forts in return. Because of their slow rate of fire, they got off only 151 shots while the forts fired 2,209 shots from 76 guns, of which a remarkable 520 shots struck the ironclads, partly disabling several and holing the *Keokuk* so badly that she sank the next morning. This accuracy was possible because of prepositioned range markers.

Although casualties on the ships were few, Du Pont signaled them to break off the action after two hours and pull back out of range. He intended to renew the attack the next day, but at a conference that evening, the ship captains told him that their vessels were in no condition to do so. "I determined [therefore] not to renew the attack," Du Pont reported to Welles, "for, in my judgment, it would have converted a failure into a disaster."[32]

A Charleston civilian who witnessed the fight seemed to confirm Du

The attack on the Charleston forts by Du Pont's ironclads, April 7, 1863.
The nearer ship on the left is the USS *New Ironsides*; the one in the middle distance
is the USS *Keokuk*. The middle fort is Sumter and the one on the right is Moultrie.
(From *Frank Leslie's Illustrated History of the Civil War*)

Pont's judgment. "It was a most signal defeat for them," he wrote. "We did
not use one half of our guns and had no recourse to rams, torpedoes, etc."
His "only regret is that the fleet did not make more of a fight so as to be
more badly damaged."[33]

In response to criticism that the attack failed because his heart was
not in it, Du Pont wrote to a member of the Senate Naval Affairs Committee that "no officer living could have gone into the experiment with
more earnest zeal than I did."[34] This was disingenuous, to say the least.
Soon after the battle, Du Pont wrote to his wife: "We have failed, as I felt
sure we would. . . . To me . . . there was no disappointment, for I expected
nothing."[35]

A few days after the battle, an article harshly critical of Du Pont appeared in the *Baltimore American*, organ of the powerful Blair family. It
was written by the editor of the paper, Charles C. Fulton, who had gotten
special permission from Gustavus Fox—Montgomery Blair's brother-in-
law—to cover the attack on Charleston. Headlined "A Disgraceful Result,"

the article claimed that the monitors were not badly damaged and that three more hours of fighting would have forced the surrender of Fort Sumter. "Oh, that we had a Farragut here to take command at once, and do what has been so weakly attempted by Admiral Du Pont."[36]

Du Pont was understandably furious. He blamed Chief Engineer Alban C. Stimers for inspiring the article and Fox for allowing it to be published. Both were partisans of Ericsson and his monitors; Du Pont believed that they wanted to blame him rather than the ironclads' deficiencies for the failure. That was partly true, but it was equally true that Du Pont tried to deflect all blame to the monitors, which "are miserable failures where forts are concerned," he insisted.[37]

Six captains of the monitors echoed Du Pont's words in an official report to Welles, including the claim that they were severely damaged by the enemy's fire. Some of them made the same points in private letters. "Four or five of our small number of vessels were also more or less disabled," wrote Percival Drayton. "An hour more would pretty much have finished the fleet, and would have turned into the great disaster of the war what was merely a repulse." Captain John Rodgers of the *Weehawken* told Welles privately that "the vessels were fast getting *hors du combat*," and some might have been captured by the enemy if Du Pont had not withdrawn them when he did. "The Admiral did not choose to risk the chances of a *combat a l'outrance* which, if it went against us, would entail such momentous consequences."[38]

Welles took these reports seriously, but he also recognized that these officers were part of what he later termed a Du Pont clique. The secretary refused to make the reports public because if the monitors did have serious defects, "there was no necessity for us to proclaim that weakness to our enemies. . . . Du Pont is morbidly sensitive, and to vindicate himself wants to publish every defect and weakness of the ironclads and to disparage them, regardless of its effect in inspiring the Rebels to resist them, and impairing the confidence of our own men."[39]

Du Pont wanted to try Alban Stimers by court-martial for furnishing information that Fulton used to defame him. Welles quashed that proceeding and established instead a court of inquiry, which found no grounds for a court-martial. The navy secretary grew increasingly irritated with Du Pont for spending so much time and energy trying to justify himself instead of planning a new campaign against the enemy. In his obsession with the supposed insult to his honor and self-esteem, wrote Welles, "he is evidently thinking much more of Du Pont than of the service or the country." By May 23, almost seven weeks after the battle, the secretary had concluded that Du Pont "is against doing anything [and] is demoralizing others. . . . If anything is to be done, we must have a new commander."[40]

If Du Pont had to go, who would replace him? One eager candidate was Rear Admiral John A. Dahlgren, chief of the Bureau of Ordnance. After the usual cruises as a young midshipman, Dahlgren had spent most of his antebellum career as an ordnance expert in the Washington Navy Yard, where he developed the famous Dahlgren "soda-bottle guns"—so called because their fat breech (to withstand the powder explosion when fired) tapering down to a thinner muzzle reminded observers of a soda bottle. Dahlgren himself was over six feet tall, slender in body and face with a wispy mustache and sideburns. An ambitious officer, he was the victim of the navy's version of Catch-22: promotion came most readily from achievements in service at sea; Dahlgren repeatedly applied for such service after the war began but was denied the chance because Welles considered him too valuable where he was. In the fall of 1862, Dahlgren pressed Welles for assignment to command the forthcoming attack on Charleston. When that was refused, he expressed a willingness to accept command of one of the new *Passaic*-class ironclads to get the sea service on his record. But after endorsing this idea, Welles changed his mind and said that Dahlgren could not be spared from the Bureau of Ordnance.[41]

Remaining in Washington while fellow officers were distinguishing themselves in command of ships and squadrons did give Dahlgren one advantage. He became a good friend of Lincoln, who frequently visited the navy yard to watch ordnance tests. The president asked Welles to promote Dahlgren to rear admiral; Welles resisted, telling Lincoln that such a promotion over the heads of several captains with good combat records would create resentment and discord. On February 17, 1863, Lincoln in effect ordered Welles to promote Dahlgren, and it was done.[42] Welles's apprehensions of resentment were justified. Speaking for some of his friends, Farragut privately commented: "How must some of those poor fellows feel who have had Dahlgren put over their heads, with none of [their] qualities as a naval officer to recommend him . . . over the heads of men who have been fighting for their country ever since the commencement of the war."[43]

Although he was now an admiral, Dahlgren still had no sea duty. He fervently wanted the job as Du Pont's successor, and the president favored him. But Welles instead named his old friend Andrew H. Foote, who had eventually recovered from his Fort Donelson wound and was tired of shore duty as chief of the Bureau of Equipment and Recruiting. Dahlgren finally got his chance, however, when Foote agreed that he could command the ironclad fleet at Charleston while Foote would be the overall squadron commander. As the two men were preparing to depart for Port Royal, Foote fell ill with Bright's disease (nephritis) and died on June 26. Welles had no choice but to give Dahlgren the position as squadron commander—with the condition that as soon as he captured Charleston, he would return to the Ordnance Bureau.[44]

Implicitly recognizing the validity of Du Pont's claim that the navy alone could not take Charleston, Welles instructed Dahlgren to cooperate with the new army commander who had replaced Hunter, Brigadier General Quincy A. Gillmore. The army's leading artillery expert who had commanded the guns that breached Fort Pulaski and forced its surrender more than a year earlier, Gillmore looked forward to working with the navy's foremost ordnance expert. Charleston's defenses were in for a pounding by the army's big Parrott rifles and the Navy's 11-inch and 15-inch smoothbore Dahlgrens.

Du Pont went home a bitter man who could not let go of the controversies that had led to his removal. For the remaining two years of his life, he continued (mostly in private) to defend himself and berate Fox and Welles. Most of these efforts only served to diminish Du Pont's once high reputation. But he did take pride in an important and morale-boosting achievement by ships of his command two and a half weeks before he yielded that command to Dahlgren.

Back in November 1861, the British-built blockade-runner *Fingal*, purchased by James D. Bulloch, had run into Savannah with a valuable cargo of guns, ammunition, gunpowder, and other military supplies. Du Pont had been embarrassed by this breach of the blockade only five days after his victory at Port Royal. The *Fingal* loaded with cotton and resin for a dash out from the Savannah River. But federal seizure of Tybee Island, the capture of Fort Pulaski, and the posting of Union vessels in other outlets had corked up the *Fingal*. The Confederates renamed her the CSS *Atlanta* and rebuilt her as an ironclad ram armed with two 7-inch and two 6.4-inch Brooke rifles, arguably the best naval guns of the war, plus a spar torpedo on the bow.

In June 1863 Union intelligence learned of the *Atlanta*'s intention to sortie from Wassaw Sound south of Savannah. Du Pont sent two monitors, *Weehawken* and *Nahant*, to block the attempt. In a letter to Secretary of

The CSS *Atlanta*, photographed after its capture, with Union sailors on deck.
(Courtesy of the National Archives)

the Navy Mallory, the *Atlanta*'s captain, William A. Webb, boasted that his guns and torpedo would make short work of these vessels. "I assure you the whole abolition fleet has no terrors for me. . . . My plan . . . is to break up and raise the blockade between here and Charleston, and on returning to look into Hilton Head, damaging the enemy there as much as possible, and then to enter the Savannah River, where I can cut off supplies for Fort Pulaski."[45]

It was not to be. Down the Wilmington River into Wassaw Sound came the *Atlanta* at "a fast clip" on the gray morning of June 17, firing its powerful bow gun six times but failing to hit either Union ironclad. The *Weehawken* closed to within 300 yards and hit the *Atlanta* with three of her five shots, including two by the 15-inch gun's 441-pound shot that cracked the *Atlanta*'s armor, knocked out two gun crews, and mortally wounded two pilots. Having run aground, the *Atlanta* struck her colors after less than fifteen minutes.[46] This affair stunned Southerners and elated Northerners starved for good news. It "has created the wildest excitement in the fleet," wrote a Northern reporter, "and has put new life into all hands."[47]

THE CAPTURE OF THE *ATLANTA* gave Welles some relief at a time when he was dealing with two other difficult matters. The first concerned another problematic squadron commander, Acting Rear Admiral Charles Wilkes. When Welles sent him to the Caribbean as commander of a "flying squadron" in September 1862 to search for the *Alabama* and capture any blockade-runners they encountered, he noted prophetically that Wilkes "has given great trouble and annoyance to the Department heretofore and will be likely to give us more trouble."[48] Wilkes soon fulfilled this prediction. As he had done earlier in the capture of the *Trent*, he began twisting the British lion's tail by challenging the port authorities at Bermuda and Nassau over blockade-runners in those harbors. Welles did not mind some tail twisting, but Lincoln and Secretary of State William Seward squelched Wilkes in the interest of keeping the peace with Britain.

Welles was more concerned with Wilkes's failures to hunt down Confederate raiders. When the *Florida* escaped from Mobile in January 1863, two of Farragut's fastest ships chased her to the West Indies. Wilkes arbitrarily incorporated them into his own squadron and dragged his feet when Welles ordered him to return the ships to Farragut. The event that finally brought Wilkes down, however, was his appropriation of the USS *Vanderbilt* for his own flagship. Welles had sent the fast and powerful *Vanderbilt* on a mission to search for the *Alabama* off the coast of Brazil. When she was in the Virgin Islands on her way there, Wilkes pulled rank on her commander and moved into the *Vanderbilt*'s commodious cabin. During the next six weeks, the *Alabama* captured twelve merchant ships off the Brazilian coast while Wilkes was cruising leisurely among the West Indian Islands, spending fifty days at anchor in the months of April and May. Welles was livid. Wilkes was "erratic, impulsive, opinionated. . . . He has accomplished nothing, but has sadly interfered and defeated the plans of the Department" to apprehend the *Alabama*. Despite his lingering popularity with the public, Wilkes had to go. On June 1, 1863, Welles placed him on the retired list (Wilkes was sixty-five) at half pay.[49]

Although Welles worried about the fallout from the simultaneous removal of Du Pont and Wilkes from squadron commands, the rampage of a unique commerce raider along the North Atlantic coasts provoked much greater negative publicity. On May 6 the *Florida* captured her twelfth ship since getting out of Mobile. One of the *Florida*'s officers proposed a bold scheme to Captain John Maffitt. Instead of burning the bark *Clarence*, Lieutenant Charles W. Read wanted to arm her with a 12-pound boat howitzer and take her into Hampton Roads at night to cut out a Union warship. Maffitt approved and gave Read a dozen volunteers for the adventure. A twenty-three-year-old Mississippian, Read had dropped out of the U.S. Naval Academy in 1861 to join the Confederate navy. A classmate at Annapolis described Read as "one of those wiry, energetic fellows who would attempt anything but study."[50] It proved impossible to get into Hampton Roads, so Read started north along the coast and burned three merchantmen. His fourth capture, the bark *Tacony* on June 12, was a faster sailer than the *Clarence*, so he scuttled that ship and continued on with the *Tacony*.

During the next ten days, Read destroyed thirteen more ships and fishing schooners and bonded five—the same days when the Army of Northern Virginia was marching into Pennsylvania. Panicky telegrams poured into the Navy Department appealing for protection against the "pirate." Newspaper editorials berated Welles. Orders went out to navy yards from Philadelphia to Portsmouth, New Hampshire, to "send out anything you have" to "search for this wolf that is prowling so near us." By June 23 some forty warships and quickly chartered steamers were looking for the *Tacony* with its distinctive rig. On that date, Read captured the fishing schooner *Archer* and burned the *Tacony*. Thus disguised, he sailed into the harbor of Portland, Maine, and cut out the U.S. revenue cutter *Caleb Cushing*. But this feat turned out to be Read's last hurrah. Two armed steamers and three tugs crowded with soldiers and militia volunteers caught up with the *Cushing*. Read's crew fired her and took to boats but were captured on June 27.[51]

Despite this denouement, Read's daring raid marked a low point in the war for the Union navy—and the Union cause. The *Alabama* and *Florida* remained at large. Charleston remained untouched and defiant. The Army of Northern Virginia was in Pennsylvania. Vicksburg and Port Hudson still held out. But a change of momentum had already begun on the Mississippi.

chapter eight

Unvexed to the Sea

U nion gunboats nominally controlled the Mississippi River below Port Hudson and above Helena after the withdrawal of Farragut's ships and Charles Davis's Western Flotilla from Vicksburg. But that control remained precarious because of guerrilla attacks on supply steamboats going up and down the river. "The Guerrillas are becoming more alarming every day," wrote one boat captain in July 1862. "They infest the banks of the river throughout its whole length; such is the fear of them that Pilots cannot be engaged at five hundred dollars a month."[1] Usually mounted and sometimes armed with field artillery as well as muskets, these irregular troops carried out hit-and-run attacks on almost everything that floated. Union commanders responded by organizing convoys of supply boats and civilian steamers accompanied by gunboats to shell the banks whenever they encountered guerrillas.

The convoy system worked well enough as a defensive measure most of the time. But when David D. Porter took command of the Mississippi Squadron in October 1862, he initiated a proactive antiguerrilla strategy. Porter immediately obtained authorization to buy a dozen or more light-draft steamboats and arm them with three or four 24-pound and 12-pound howitzers. The engines and boilers were sheathed with a sufficient thickness of boilerplate iron to protect them against light shore-based artillery, and the decks were screened with thinner boilerplate to protect the crew against rifle fire. With a draft of only two to four feet, these "tinclads" could go far up shallow rivers after guerrillas. By the end of the war, some sixty-five tinclads had served on the western rivers.[2]

Porter also used Alfred Ellet's ram fleet as an antiguerrilla force. The Navy Department insisted that the law transferring the river gunboats to the navy included Ellet's fleet. Secretary of War Edwin M. Stanton insisted otherwise. But in November 1862 Stanton lost that battle when Lincoln sided with the navy. Ellet was promoted to brigadier general and his nephew Charles Rivers Ellet became one of the army's youngest colonels. But even though they remained army officers, Lincoln ordered them to "report to [Acting] Rear Admiral Porter for instructions, and act under his direction." Out of this ram fleet grew the Marine Brigade, a flotilla of seven boats carrying soldiers and cavalry horses that could be offloaded on riverbanks to pursue guerrillas into the interior.[3]

Porter took a tough line on guerrillas. Soon after arriving at his new command, he issued a flurry of orders on the subject. Whenever vessels were fired on from shore, the captain should return the fire and then "destroy everything in that neighborhood within reach of his guns," including "houses supposed to be affording shelter to rebels," for this was the only way "to repress the outrageous practice of guerrilla warfare."[4] Gunboat captains were not slow to obey these orders. The executive officer of the timberclad USS *Tyler* reported that when attacked by guerrillas at Ashley's Landing, Arkansas, "we rounded to and shelled the place, and then landed twenty armed men and burned the cotton gin barns and several dwellings owned by men in the rebel army. . . . They will find they are firing into the wrong parties when they open on us, for we shall burn every house within reach."[5]

Porter reported in November 1862 that "Guerrilla warfare has ceased entirely on the banks of the river."[6] This boast was Porter's usual self-serving gasconade, however, for he was soon compelled to issue another order that "persons taken in the act of firing on unarmed vessels from the banks will be treated as highwaymen and assassins. . . . If this savage and barbarous Confederate custom can not be put a stop to, we will try what virtue there is in hanging."[7] When Confederate officials protested this "savage" order, Porter responded that "the hospital vessel of this squadron was attacked in sight of me, and a volley of musketry fired through the windows. . . . A few days since a band of armed desperadoes jumped on the deck of the tug Hercules and killed in cold blood some of the unoffending crew. . . . If General Pemberton is desirous that the war should be conducted on the principle of humanity and civilization, all he has to do is to issue an order to stop guerrilla warfare."[8] But no threats or actions could stop this warfare, which continued as viciously on the rivers as on land in this theater for the rest of the war.

Another task of Porter's squadron and Farragut's gunboats was to prevent Confederate commerce across the Mississippi in either direction. Success in this endeavor was mixed, but the blockade on the Mississippi tightened over time just as the saltwater blockade continued to tighten as the war went on. In October 1862 four gunboats on the lower Mississippi captured an unusual prize. They discovered a herd of 1,500 cattle on the riverbank that had been driven from Texas, intended for Confederate armies in the East. Sailors rounded them up and sent for five transports from New Orleans to come and take them to a suitable pasture near the city. About 200 of the cattle were too unmanageable to get on board, so the captains hired contrabands to drive them down the bank accompanied by a gunboat steaming alongside for protection. Guerrillas ambushed the transports and killed or wounded a few sailors, but the gunboats drove them off. All of the cattle got through, including those that went by land. The senior officer was gleeful about his success as a cattle rustler, "performed at some risk in the midst of a country hostile and alive with guerrillas and armed bands of enemies." He admitted that this feat was "somewhat a novel act of duty for the Navy."[9] One can be certain that these sailors and contrabands ate well for a while.

ONE THIN GLEAM OF CHEER penetrated the gloom of setbacks for the Union navy in the winter of 1862–63. After the repulse of his attack on Chickasaw Bluffs in December, General William T. Sherman proposed a combined operation against Fort Hindman at Arkansas Post forty miles up the Arkansas River. Success there might boost shattered Northern morale, Sherman argued, and prevent enemy use of the river to send supplies and reinforcements to Vicksburg. Porter agreed, and ten gunboats escorting troop transports carrying 30,000 soldiers proceeded up the Arkansas River in the second week of January 1863. The political general John A. McClernand, who outranked Sherman, arrived on the scene and took command of the troops. When Grant in Memphis learned of this expedition, not realizing that it had been his friend Sherman's idea, he complained in a telegram to General Henry W. Halleck that "McClernand has . . . gone on a wild-goose chase to the Post of Arkansas."[10]

If unsuccessful, it might well have gone down as a wild-goose chase. But while the army troops invested the eleven-gun fort, the gunboats, led by three of the Eads city-class ironclads, closed to within 400 yards of the fort and pounded it unmercifully with their big guns. A soldier serving as a volunteer on the USS *Monarch*, one of the Ellet rams, described this bombardment. "Such a terrific scene I have never witnessed," he wrote to his sister. "The fort was riddled and torn to pieces with the shells. The ironclads, which could venture up closer, shot into their portholes and into the mouths of their cannon, bursting their cannon and dismounting them. When most of their batteries were silenced, two of the light draft boats and our boat was ordered to run the blockade to cut off the retreat of the rebels above the F[or]t." Trapped between army troops on three sides and the gunboats in their rear, the Confederate garrison of 5,000 men surrendered on January 11. At the cost of a thousand Union killed and wounded (almost all in the army), this combined operation won a minor but morale-boosting victory that became a springboard for a renewed campaign against Vicksburg.[11]

The ironclads and tinclads suffered relatively little damage because Porter had ordered their pilothouses and casemates greased with tallow and ships' slush, which caused enemy shots that hit at an angle to glance off. It is unclear whether Porter was aware that the Confederates had similarly greased the *Virginia* almost a year earlier. In any event, this practice spread through the Union navy after Porter reported its success at Arkansas Post. The experience could be quite unpleasant for sailors, however, especially in hot weather when the tallow dripped onto the deck, and it was no joy to clean up after action. But it saved lives and reduced damage to ships.[12]

BY 1863 THE CAPTURE OF Vicksburg and Port Hudson had become two of the most important objectives of Union strategy. When General Nathaniel P. Banks departed for his new command at New Orleans in November 1862, General in Chief Halleck instructed him that "the President regards the opening of the Mississippi River as the first and most important of all our military and naval operations." Lincoln believed that "if Vicksburg can be taken and the Mississippi kept open it seems to me [they] will be about the most important fruits of the campaigns yet set in motion."[13]

At the end of January, Grant came down to Milliken's Bend on the Mississippi, about twenty miles upriver from Vicksburg, to make it his headquarters for the campaign against the Confederate bastion. The previous summer, Halleck had told Farragut that he could spare no troops to help the navy take Vicksburg. Now he informed Grant that "the eyes and hopes of the whole country are now directed to your army. . . . The opening of the Mississippi River will be to us of more advantage than the capture of forty Richmonds."[14]

Grant knew that interservice cooperation would be essential in such a campaign. Even though by tradition and law he could not give orders to the navy, nor Porter to the army, the two commanders got on well with each other, just as Grant and Foote had worked well together against Forts Henry and Donelson a year earlier. The task at Vicksburg was complicated by geography and topography. Situated on a 200-foot bluff commanding the lower end of an *S* curve in the river, Vicksburg's defenses made a direct assault from that direction impossible. Extending north from Vicksburg to Memphis, a chain of hills formed an arc of 200 miles and closed in the Delta, low-lying land averaging about fifty miles in width and laced with swamps, rivers, and thick forests. The only dry land suitable for military operations against Vicksburg stretched to the south and east. Grant's problem was to get his army there with enough supplies to sustain a campaign against the land side of the Vicksburg defenses while the navy shelled them from the river and kept open Grant's communications with the North.

The planning for a Vicksburg Campaign in early 1863 included operations against the Confederacy's other major river bastion at Port Hudson, 250 river miles to the south. In the end these actions turned out to be two separate though related campaigns: Grant and Porter against Vicksburg, Banks and Farragut against Port Hudson. But Porter initially conceived of them as a single operation. On February 2 he sent the famous Ellet ram *Queen of the West* past the Vicksburg batteries to roam downriver and capture Confederate supply steamers carrying provisions from the Red River into the Mississippi for the garrison at Port Hudson. The commander of the *Queen* was nineteen-year-old Charles Rivers Ellet, son of the creator of the ram fleet who had been mortally wounded at the moment of triumph in the Battle of Memphis the previous June. "I can not speak too highly of this gallant and daring officer," Porter told Welles. "The only trouble I have is to hold him in and keep him out of danger. He will undertake anything I wish him to without asking questions, and these are the kind of men I like to command."[15]

As the *Queen* ran past Vicksburg, she took several hits from Confederate guns when she diverted to ram the steamer *City of Vicksburg* at the wharf (it later sank). Ellet continued downriver and stopped out of range to repair the damage. During the next three days, the *Queen* captured and destroyed three Confederate steamers carrying $200,000 worth of provisions for Port Hudson. She continued into the Red River and captured another steamboat, *Era No. 5*, on February 14. Seizing the pilot, Ellet forced him to navigate the *Queen* farther up the river, where he ran her into an ambush by a Confederate battery of 32-pounders. Ellet ordered the pilot to back the *Queen* downstream out of range. He backed her instead onto a sandbar that grounded her at point-blank range. The *Queen*'s crew jumped overboard and floated down the river on cotton bales to the *Era No. 5*, leaving the *Queen* to be captured. Because there were wounded aboard, Ellet could not set fire to the *Queen* to prevent her capture.[16]

Meanwhile, the initial reports of Ellet's achievements caused an elated Porter to reinforce success by sending one of his new ironclads, the USS *Indianola*, past the Vicksburg batteries on February 12 to join the *Queen* in playing havoc with enemy shipping. Carrying two 11-inch and two 9-inch guns, the *Indianola* should have been more than a match for anything on the river. As she steamed down from Vicksburg, the *Indianola* met the *Era No. 5* coming up pursued by a fast Confederate gunboat, the *William H. Webb*. Ellet informed the *Indianola*'s captain of the situation and the two boats headed downstream to attack the *Webb*, whose captain turned around and fled when he spotted the formidable ironclad.

Expecting that Porter would send down another gunboat when Ellet told him what had happened, the *Indianola* remained below Vicksburg to blockade the mouth of the Red River. But the Confederates had repaired the captured *Queen of the West*. Along with the *Webb* and two smaller gunboats loaded with infantry for boarding, the *Queen* came down the Red River to attack the *Indianola*, whose captain decided that the odds were too great to fight. He headed back up the Mississippi, chased by the faster Confederate vessels. Waiting until dark on February 24 to minimize the accuracy of the *Indianola*'s guns, they attacked by repeatedly ramming the ironclad, punching holes below the waterline and splintering one of her sidewheels. As the *Indianola* sank in shallow water near the bank, the captain surrendered. Jubilant Confederates prepared to raise and repair her. With the *Webb* and the *Queen*, the *Indianola* would give them a powerful squadron to augment their control of the river between Vicksburg and Port Hudson.[17]

Porter confessed his mortification in a report to Welles. "There is no use to conceal the fact, but this has . . . been the most humiliating affair that has occurred during this rebellion."[18] But Porter had a trick up his sleeve. He directed sailors to build a wooden superstructure on an old coal barge—complete with paddle-wheel boxes, large logs protruding from fake gunports, and two sets of barrels piled on top of each other burning tar to simulate smokestacks—and set the apparition adrift downriver. Coated with tar, this dummy ironclad loomed out of the mist on February 26 looking like a ship of doom to the men in the four Confederate gunboats protecting a working party trying to raise the *Indianola*. The gunboats fled downriver and the working party blew up the *Indianola* to prevent her recapture. "With the exception of the wine and liquor stores of the Indianola, nothing was saved," wrote a Confederate colonel. "The valuable armament, the large supplies of powder, shot, and shell, are all lost."[19]

The next day, several Confederates rowed a skiff out to investigate the false ironclad, which had stuck on a sandbar. On the wheelhouse they found a hand-lettered sign: "Deluded people, cave in." The *Indianola* "would have been a small army to us," lamented the *Vicksburg Whig*. "Who is to blame for this piece of folly?" Nobody came forward to take the blame.[20]

Confederates still controlled that stretch of the Mississippi, however, and supplies for both Vicksburg and Port Hudson still came down the Red River from Texas and Louisiana. Because most of Porter's remaining vessels were cooperating with the army's attempts to get at Vicksburg through Delta waterways to the north, Admiral Farragut decided to move into Confederate territory north of Port Hudson. "Porter has allowed his boats to come down one at a time, and they have been captured," Farragut told his second in command, "which compels me to go up and recapture the whole, or be sunk in the attempt. The whole country will be in arms if we do not do something."[21]

On the night of March 14–15, Farragut, in his beloved flagship, *Hartford*, led seven ships in an attempt to steam past Port Hudson. Behind the *Hartford* came two other steam sloops, the USS *Richmond* and the new USS *Monongahela*. Lashed to the port sides (away from Port Hudson's guns) of each was a smaller river gunboat. These three pairs were followed by the venerable sidewheeler USS *Mississippi*. They were supported by two other gunboats and six mortar schooners that poured shells into enemy batteries in an effort to keep down their fire on Farragut's ships as they struggled upriver against the current.

The night was dark and still, with an atmospheric inversion that prevented the dissipation of smoke from the funnels and guns and made it extremely difficult for the pilots to see where they were going. As they approached the hairpin bend in the river, the *Hartford* and her consort, the USS *Albatross*, ran aground. The *Hartford*'s surgeon, who kept a running account in a small diary strapped to his left wrist, described in spare prose what happened next: "Got off again in ten minutes. Going ahead fast with very heavy firing. The first wounded brought below. Our escape so far has

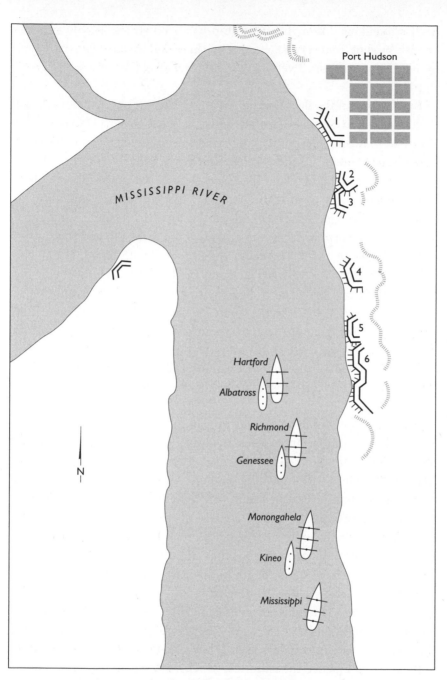

The Attempt to Pass Port Hudson, March 14–15, 1863

been miraculous. Midnight—Our ship has been struck heavily and frequently by shot from very heavy guns on shore and we are delivering quick broadsides at intervals. Twelve-thirty—Passed all of the batteries. Cheered ship!"[22]

But the rest of the fleet had no reason to cheer. Captain James Alden of the *Richmond* described her fate and that of her consort USS *Genessee*: "As we were turning the point almost past the upper batteries we received a shot in our boilers . . . and another shot went through our steam drum. Our steam was all gone," and the *Genessee* was not powerful enough to keep the pair going against the current. "Torpedoes were exploding all around us, throwing water as high as the tops[;] . . . shells were causing great havoc on our decks; the groans of the wounded and the shrieks of the dying were awful. The decks were covered with blood."[23] The two ships finally drifted downriver and out of the fight. Behind them, the *Monongahela* and her consort also went aground, and the crank pin of the *Monongahela's* engine broke when she backed off, so they also drifted downstream. Bringing up the rear, the *Mississippi* then ran aground in the smoky darkness. Port Hudson's guns now could concentrate on her and pounded her relentlessly. The captain ordered the crew to abandon ship before she blew up. Most of them got away, but sixty-four were killed or missing.[24]

When Farragut sat down the next day to write his report to Welles, he began with the words: "It becomes my duty again to report disaster to my fleet."[25] Only later did he learn that except for the *Mississippi,* the other ships had survived with reparable damage. And Welles did not think it a disaster at all, but a valiant action in which the *Hartford* and the *Albatross* had gained a position to contest control of this 250-mile stretch of the river with the Confederates. Assistant Secretary Fox no doubt gladdened Farragut's heart with the assurance that "the President thinks the importance of keeping a force of strength in this part of the river is so great that he fully approves of your proceeding."[26]

At Vicksburg, General Grant sent a loaded coal barge drifting past the batteries at night down to Farragut. Charles Rivers Ellet took two of his rams past Vicksburg two days later. They got started late, so it was daylight when they passed the batteries, which sank the *Lancaster* and damaged Ellet's flagship, *Switzerland*. She was repaired and joined Farragut's two ships at the mouth of the Red River to choke off supplies to Vicksburg and Port Hudson. They soon learned that they would not have to worry about a challenge from the *Queen of the West*. She had gone from the Red

River into the Atchafalaya River, where on April 14 the USS *Calhoun* sank the *Queen* with her first shot from a 30-pound Parrott rifle at a distance of three miles.[27]

When General Banks finally brought Port Hudson under attack and siege in May 1863, a dozen or more of Farragut's warships both below and above helped bombard the Confederate defenses day and night for nearly two months. In looking back on these operations, however, Farragut believed that his most important contribution to the campaign was the initial passage of Port Hudson in March and the subsequent blockade of the Red River. "My last dash past Port Hudson was the best thing I ever did, except taking New Orleans," he wrote to his wife in July. "It assisted materially in the fall of Vicksburg and Port Hudson."[28]

THE FALL OF VICKSBURG did not come easily. While Farragut was performing his heroics downriver, Porter and Grant appeared to be floundering in their efforts to get troops and supplies onto dry land east of Vicksburg. Soldiers and contrabands resumed digging the canal across the De Soto Peninsula formed by the loop in the river to provide a new channel to bypass Vicksburg altogether. If it worked, gunboats and troop transports could get downriver out of range of Confederate batteries and cross troops to the east bank. Porter had little faith in this enterprise because the start of the canal was in the wrong place—where the current formed an eddy rather than scouring into the opening. And the Confederates proved that they could shift guns to command the canal's exit by firing on a dredging machine and forcing it to decamp.

The canal was eventually abandoned. In the meantime, one of Grant's corps tried to carve out a new navigation channel through a maze of bayous, lakes, and tributary rivers in Louisiana that could get boats through to the Red River and then into the Mississippi far south of Vicksburg. This effort also proved fruitless.

More promising was the so-called Yazoo Pass Expedition, in which several of Porter's gunboats, including two river ironclads, played an important part. Army engineers blew up a levee opposite Helena, allowing roiling water from the Mississippi to flood into a series of streams leading to the Tallahatchie River. This river in turn flowed into the Yazoo, theoretically making these waterways navigable to landing places northeast of Vicksburg near the place where Sherman's troops had assaulted the bluffs the previous December.

Porter's initial reports about this expedition were optimistic. But the lieutenant commander in charge of the gunboats was ill when the operation began, and his experiences soon made him sicker. His vessels continually ran aground; overhanging trees damaged their chimneys (smokestacks); enemy axemen chopped down trees to block the channel; and sharp bends in the river required the boats to back and fill. At one bend in the Tallahatchie halfway between Helena and Vicksburg, the Confederates erected a fort of dirt, sandbags, and cotton bales that commanded a straight channel only wide enough for one gunboat to use its bow guns. The surrounding swamplands made an assault by the expedition's 5,000 infantry difficult if not impossible—though Porter thought they should have tried. He blamed the army for the failure of this operation—as was becoming his habit. "If you could only once have to co-operate with the soldiers and see the inefficiency of some of them," he told Fox privately, "you would wonder that we ever did anything together."[29]

Porter changed his tune about the army during another operation commanded personally by himself and his favorite general, William T. Sherman. Labeled the Steele's Bayou Expedition, it involved pushing eleven gunboats (including four of the Eads city-class ironclads) through a series of bayous and rivers that were often not much wider than the boats. Tough willow trees with interlocking branches over the water slowed their progress to about one mile per hour. Confederates again felled trees across streams ahead and behind the gunboats, while possums, raccoons, snakes, and all manner of wildlife dropped from branches onto decks and sailors swept them off with brooms. Confederate sharpshooters along the banks fired at anyone who showed himself on deck.

This nightmare threatened to end badly for Porter. He penned a hasty note to Sherman and gave it to a contraband for delivery to the troop transports several miles to the rear: "Dear Sherman, Hurry up, for Heaven's sake. I never knew how helpless an ironclad could be steaming around through the woods without an army to back her."[30] Sherman disembarked his soldiers to wade through swamps and drive off the Confederates. Recognizing that the expedition had failed, Porter had his sailors unship the rudders, and the gunboats backed slowly downstream the way they had come and returned after "the most severe labor officers and men ever went through," he reported to Welles on March 26. "With the end of this expedition ends all my hopes of getting into Vicksburg in this direction."[31]

Grant was discouraged by these failures. And the country was discouraged with Grant, who came under attack from newspapers and politicians of all persuasions. Lincoln stood by Grant and Porter, but Fox reported confidentially that the president "is rather disgusted with all the flanking expeditions and predicted their failure from the first." On March 29 Lincoln dropped in to John Dahlgren's office at the Washington Navy Yard. "He looks thin and badly," reported Dahlgren, "and is very nervous. Complained of everything. They were doing nothing at Vicksburg or Charleston."[32]

Porter thought Grant should take his army back to Memphis and launch an overland campaign from there against Vicksburg.[33] So did Sherman. But Grant had tried that route without success back in December. Instead, he proposed a different plan that he had been forming in his mind for some time. He would march troops south on the west side of the river, building roads as they went. He asked Porter to run enough gunboats past the Vicksburg batteries to spearhead a crossing of the troops to the east bank and to protect supply vessels that would sustain Grant's operations against Vicksburg from that direction. Porter was reluctant. He told Grant that "when these gunboats once go below we give up all hopes of ever getting them up again." But when Welles learned of Grant's request, he pressed Porter to comply with it. Success in such a movement would be "the severest blow that can be struck upon the enemy," Welles told Porter, and was therefore "worth all the risk." Porter finally gave in, though as he later informed Fox, "I am quite depressed with this adventure, which as you know never met with my approval—still urged by the Army on one side, the President's wishes and the hints of the Secretary [Welles] that it was most necessary, I had to come."[34]

Porter prepared seven river ironclads (including two new ones), a wooden gunboat, and three transports to run the batteries on the moonless night of April 16–17. Loaded coal barges were lashed to their port sides, and they were also protected by heavy logs and bales of wet hay to absorb shells and snuff their fuses. At 11:00 P.M. the squadron drifted silently downriver with paddle wheels barely turning for steerageway. Suddenly, the river was brightly lit with bonfires set by Confederate pickets along the bank who had spotted the boats. They crowded on steam and fired blindly at the Vicksburg bluffs, where the dug-in batteries sent off 525 rounds at the fleet, only sixty-eight of them finding a target because "we ran the Vicksburg shore so close that they overshot us most of the time," according to a master's mate on one of the boats. All of the gunboats and two of the three transports got through with only fourteen wounded. One of the transports went to the bottom (the crew was rescued); another tried to turn back, but Porter had stationed the new ironclad USS *Tus-*

cumbia at the rear to prevent precisely such misbehavior by its civilian crew, and the gunboat herded it onward.

In a private letter to Fox, Porter reported that his fleet had suffered more damage than he had stated in his official report, "as it will not do to let the enemy know how often they hit us, and show how vulnerable we are. Their heavy shot walked right through us, as if we were made of putty." Six nights later, five of seven transports got through with supplies and ammunition; one was sunk and another turned back. They were manned by army volunteers because their regular crews had refused to go.[35]

Grant now had two-thirds of his army below Vicksburg supported by a powerful gunboat fleet. (Sherman's corps had gone up the Yazoo River to make a diversionary feint.) Grant planned to cross his troops to the east bank at Grand Gulf forty miles below Vicksburg, where there were road and rail connections to the interior of Mississippi. The Confederates had fortified Grand Gulf with two heavy batteries, so on April 29 Porter's gunboats pounded these defenses to prepare the way for a landing by troops. They silenced several of the guns but in return took more of a beating than in the run past Vicksburg, with twenty-four killed and fifty-six wounded. "It was the most difficult portion of the river in which to manage an ironclad," Porter reported, "strong currents (running 6 knots) and strong eddies turning them round and round, making them fair targets."[36]

Meanwhile, a contraband had informed Grant of an unguarded crossing another ten miles downriver, with a road leading to Port Gibson and the rear of Grand Gulf. That night, the entire fleet ran past the remaining guns at Grand Gulf, with the gunboats providing covering fire while the supply transports slipped behind them with full steam and the current speeding them through safely.[37] As the vessels began ferrying the troops across the river on April 30, Grant stepped onto Mississippi soil with "a degree of relief scarcely ever equaled since," as he recalled it more than twenty years later. "I was now in the enemy's country, with a vast river and the stronghold of Vicksburg between me and my base of supplies. But I was on dry ground on the same side of the river with the enemy. All of the campaigns, labors, hardships and exposures, from the month of December previous . . . were for the accomplishment of this one object."[38] And it could not have been accomplished without the navy.

During the next three weeks, Grant's army marched 130 miles, won five battles over detachments of the Confederate Army of Mississippi that if united would have been nearly as large as the 44,000 men in Grant's Army of the Tennessee, and penned up the Confederates in the Vicksburg defenses. While Grant was carrying out this whirlwind campaign, Porter took most of his fleet up the Red River as far as Alexandria, destroying the batteries at abandoned Fort De Russy on the way. When part of General Banks's army occupied Alexandria while the rest invested Port Hudson, Porter brought most of his squadron back to Vicksburg to support Grant. He left several gunboats in the Red River to keep up the blockade of that Confederate supply route.

By the end of May 1863, the two separate armies of Grant and Banks had Vicksburg and Port Hudson under siege by land, and the naval squadrons of Porter and Farragut sealed them off by water. The big guns of the warships and mortar boats of both squadrons joined the armies' field artillery to pound the Confederate defenses around the clock.[39] The Vicksburg batteries gave as good as they got during the early days of the siege. Grant asked Porter for fire support during his May 22 assault on Confederate lines. Porter cheerfully complied, and his gunboats absorbed a heavy cannonade in return. "It is useless to try to remember the different times the vessels were hit," wrote a master's mate on Porter's flagship.[40] Five days later, a plunging shot through the deck of the USS *Cincinnati* sank this hard-luck ironclad for the second time (she had been raised after Confederate rams had holed her at Plum Point Bend a year earlier). Like Lazarus, however, the *Cincinnati* was raised from the dead and refitted once more after the fall of Vicksburg. She lived to fight again.[41]

While maintaining the stranglehold on Vicksburg, Porter had enough gunboats to carry out auxiliary operations. Learning that two Confederate brigades were approaching Milliken's Bend and anticipating a diversionary attack on the two uncompleted black regiments posted there, Porter sent the new ironclad USS *Choctaw* and veteran timberclad USS *Lexington* to the bend. On June 7 the Confederates drove outnumbered and untrained black soldiers back over the levee to the river, where the gunboats "opened on the rebels with shell, grape, and canister," Porter reported, "and they fled in wild confusion, not knowing the gunboats were there or expecting such a reception. They retreated rapidly to the woods and soon disappeared. Eighty dead rebels were left on the ground, and our trenches were packed with the dead bodies of the blacks, who stood at their post like men."[42]

At about the same time, Porter sent gunboats up the Yazoo River to capture Confederate transports after the Southerners had evacuated their navy yard and destroyed uncompleted ironclads they had been building there. A month later the Confederates returned, so Porter sent another

David Dixon Porter, photographed after his promotion to rear admiral. (Courtesy of the Library of Congress)

expedition to accompany a division of Union soldiers to capture and destroy the base for good. They succeeded, though two torpedoes exploded under the Eads ironclad USS *Baron de Kalb* and sent her to the bottom. Nevertheless, Porter claimed, "we are somewhat compensated for the loss of the *de Kalb* by the handsome results of the expedition," which included the seizure of 3,000 bales of cotton worth several times the cost of the *de Kalb*. The Confederates also sank or blew up nineteen steamboats to prevent their capture. "There are no more steamers on the Yazoo," Porter informed Welles in August. "The large fleet that sought refuge there, as the safest place in rebeldom, have all been destroyed."[43]

By then, there were no more Confederates except civilians at Vicksburg either. After a siege of forty-seven days, General John C. Pemberton surrendered its 30,000 defenders to Grant on the Fourth of July. Porter totaled up the navy's contribution to this result in the way of firepower:

7,000 mortar shells rained on Vicksburg; 4,500 shot and shells fired by gunboats; another 4,500 rounds fired by naval guns landed on shore and manned by sailors; and 6,000 shot and shells supplied to army guns.[44]

Porter also rushed the first news of Vicksburg's surrender to Washington. He sent a fast gunboat up the river to the nearest available telegraph office, at Cairo, which dispatched the message to Welles on July 7. The secretary went immediately to the White House to give Lincoln the news. Coming just three days after the president had learned of the outcome at Gettysburg—and when he was beginning to fret about General George G. Meade's caution in pursuit of the retreating Confederates—the telegram from Porter produced unalloyed pleasure. Putting his long arm around Welles, Lincoln exclaimed: "What can we do for the Secretary of the Navy for this glorious intelligence? He is always giving us good news. I cannot, in words, tell you my joy over this result. It is great, Mr. Welles, it is great!"[45]

Once Vicksburg fell, the fate of Port Hudson was sealed. Its commander surrendered the post and its 7,000 defenders to General Banks on July 9. The Mississippi now did flow unvexed to the sea—except for Confederate guerrillas, who continued to be very vexatious indeed. Lincoln promoted Porter to rear admiral, and Welles gave him control of the entire Mississippi down to New Orleans. Farragut enthusiastically endorsed this reduction in the scope of his command, delighted to get himself and his ships back to salt water.[46]

After the capture of Vicksburg and Port Hudson, what next for the soldiers and sailors who had accomplished these results? Grant and Banks wanted to mount a campaign against Mobile. Farragut had wished to go after that objective for more than a year. But other priorities eclipsed Mobile for the time being. Another year would pass before Farragut finally got his chance. The great Union victories in July 1863 had swung the momentum over to the North again, but the war was far from over, and the navies of both sides continued to confront each other at home and abroad.

chapter nine

Ironclads, Torpedoes, and Salt, 1863–1864

The nation of Mexico was plagued by its own civil war during the same years as the American conflict. Unlike the United States, however, the Mexican government could not prevent foreign intervention in its troubles. In December 1861 a joint military expedition by France, Britain, and Spain invaded Mexico to force the payment of debts owed to citizens of those countries. The British and Spanish contingents pulled out after negotiating a settlement, but Napoleon III kept French troops there and increased their numbers to 35,000 by 1863. They helped the forces of the church and large landowners overthrow the liberal government of Benito Juárez in June 1863. Napoleon began planning to install the Archduke Ferdinand Maximilian of Austria as emperor of Mexico in an audacious bid to restore the French suzerainty in the New World that his uncle Napoleon Bonaparte had given up when he sold Louisiana to the United States in 1803.

Confederates began fishing in these troubled waters. They made contacts with anti-Juárez chieftains in northern Mexico who profited from the contraband trade across the Rio Grande with the Confederacy. Southern diplomats sought an agreement with France whereby the Confederacy would recognize Napoleon's puppet regime in Mexico in return for French recognition of the Confederacy.

This pact was never consummated, but in the summer of 1863 an alarmed Lincoln administration was afraid it might come to pass. Secretary of State Seward convinced the president that the United States must send a warning message to France by invading Texas. Not only was the French presence in Mexico a violation of the Monroe Doctrine; the possibility of French-Confederate cooperation also represented a clear and present danger to the Union cause. When Generals Grant and Banks, backed by Admiral Farragut, proposed a campaign against Mobile after the fall of Vicksburg, therefore, Lincoln told them that Mobile must wait until they had planted the American flag firmly in Texas. A campaign against Mobile, Lincoln told Grant, "would appear tempting to me also, were it not that in view of recent events in Mexico, I am greatly impressed with the importance of re-establishing the national authority in Western [eastern?] Texas as soon as possible."[1]

The troops for such a campaign would come from Banks's Army of the Gulf and the supporting naval force from Farragut's squadron. Banks decided to invade Texas via Sabine Pass—the outlet of two Texas rivers to the Gulf on the border with Louisiana—and to move inland to cut the railroad between Beaumont and Houston. He selected Major General William B. Franklin to command 5,000 troops for this expedition. This choice did not augur well for success. A McClellan favorite who had botched his mission to rescue the Harpers Ferry garrison in the Antietam campaign and had failed to reinforce success at Fredericksburg, Franklin had been exiled to Louisiana by Lincoln for intriguing to get McClellan restored to command. Farragut's warships were also in poor shape for this campaign. On the eve of departing for the North in the *Hartford* for a much-needed rest for himself and repairs to his flagship, Farragut warned Welles that most of his ships were worn out or damaged and in need of repairs before they could become efficient again.[2]

The acting squadron commander in Farragut's absence was Henry H. Bell, who assigned four small gunboats to support Franklin's troops. These vessels were converted river steamboats, sidewheelers with "decayed frames and weak machinery, constantly out of repair," in the words of General Banks. But they were the only available vessels with a shallow enough draft to get over the bar into the river to attack the six-gun Confederate battery sited to control both channels.[3]

Farragut happened to be visiting Welles at the Navy Department when they learned of the planned attack. The admiral predicted failure. "Army officers have an impression that naval vessels can do anything," he said. They would expect the gunboats to silence the battery so they could walk ashore. Farragut thought Franklin should land his troops out of range of the battery and attack it from the rear while the gunboats shelled it from the water. "But that is not the plan," Farragut lamented. "The soldiers are not to land until the navy has done an impossibility, with such boats," so "you may expect to hear of disaster."[4]

Farragut's gloomy prophecy proved accurate. The gunboats attacked on September 8. Firing with the benefit of preset range markers, the Confederate guns knocked out two of them with shots through one's boiler and the other's steam drum. Another gunboat ran aground, and the fourth turned tail when her captain saw what had happened to the others. Just as Farragut had predicted, Franklin waited for the gunboats to silence the battery instead of cooperating with them. When the gunboats were silenced instead, Franklin's troop transports returned to New Orleans without a single one of his soldiers having set foot on Texas soil. The forty-seven Texas gunners commanded by a Houston saloon keeper named Dick Dowling became Southern folk heroes for having put more than 5,000 Yankees to flight and capturing two steamers.[5]

The ignominy of this defeat was hard to live down. But General Banks and the navy did something to retrieve their reputations by carrying out an operation long urged by the Navy Department: occupying the north bank of the Rio Grande at Brownsville to cut off the contraband trade through Matamoras. In November 1863, 6,000 soldiers, commanded by a general with the imposing name of Napoleon Jackson Tecumseh Dana and escorted by three powerful warships, splashed ashore near Brownsville. The troops moved upriver almost 100 miles to Rio Grande City, driving Confederate defenders before them. Gunboats also pushed up the coast along the inland waterway nearly 300 miles to Port Lavaca.[6]

These successes severely curtailed the contraband trade across the Rio Grande as well as blockade-running into and out of ports in southeast Texas. The Confederates still managed to get some war matériel in and cotton out through Matamoras, but now they had to go far inland to Laredo to do it. Because of the fall of Vicksburg and Port Hudson and the active patrolling of the Mississippi by David Porter's tinclads, almost none of this freight could get across the big river, so the reduced contraband trade was confined to the trans-Mississippi theater. But this incursion into Texas had less impact on the Confederate war effort than the capture of Mobile Bay would have had. And it had no apparent impact at all on the French in Mexico or Napoleon III in Paris.

TEXAS WAS FAR AWAY from the center of gravity in the military campaigns of both sides. For the Union navy and its Confederate adversaries on shore, Charleston remained the main focus of attention in the latter half of 1863. Most of the navy's monitors plus the ironclad frigate *New*

Ironsides remained there, and the harbor defenses commanded by General Pierre G. T. Beauregard featured the largest concentration of fortified heavy artillery in the Confederacy.

When Rear Admiral John A. Dahlgren took command of the South Atlantic Squadron on July 6, he immediately began to plan a joint operation with Major General Quincy Gillmore to assault Confederate defenses on the south end of Morris Island. They intended to land troops there for an advance against Battery Wagner on the north end as the first step in a grinding fort-by-fort advance toward Charleston. Supported by the 11-inch and 15-inch Dahlgren guns in four monitors, with their inventor in his flagship USS *Catskill*, blue-clad soldiers crossed Lighthouse Inlet in barges and launches and splashed ashore on the morning of July 10 to attack Confederate batteries and infantry already crippled or demoralized by the monitors' fire.

During a blistering hot day in which soldiers on shore and sailors in the ironclads suffered more casualties from heatstroke than from enemy fire, Union soldiers moved up the island accompanied by the monitors staying as close to shore as they could and pouring grapeshot into Confederate ranks. As the ships and soldiers approached Battery Wagner, Confederate guns in that large earthwork reinforced with palmetto logs zeroed in on the *Catskill* flying the admiral's flag. The least damaged of the monitors in the April 7 attack on Fort Sumter, the *Catskill* took the most hits on July 10 — sixty in all. "Our attack on Sumter before is nothing to this," wrote the *Catskill*'s executive officer. "Thank God we have all come out safely, except two or three wounded on this vessel & several used up from exertion & the heat." Dahlgren narrowly escaped injury when a bolt in the pilothouse flew past him after a direct hit by an enemy shot.[7]

For the next week, the monitors and the *New Ironsides*, with its 150-pound pivot rifles and 11-inch guns in broadside, pounded Battery Wagner night and day while Gillmore's shore-based artillery seconded their efforts. (The Federals called it Fort Wagner because from their perspective it appeared to be an enclosed work.) General Beauregard tried to get the Confederate naval commander at Charleston, Captain John R. Tucker, to send his two ironclads against the Union fleet. On July 12 Beauregard told Tucker that it had "become an urgent necessity to destroy, if possible, part or all of these [enemy] ironclads" by a night attack. Six days later, he again pleaded with Tucker to do something. "I consider it of the utmost importance to the defenses of the works at the entrance to the harbor that some

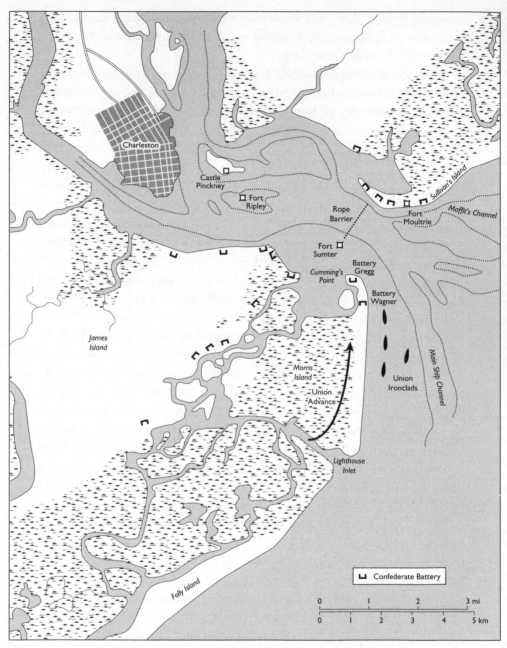

Charleston

Castle
Pinckney

Fort
Ripley

Rope
Barrier

Fort
Moultrie

Sullivan's Island

Maffit's Channel

Fort
Sumter

*Cumming's
Point*

Battery
Gregg

Battery
Wagner

*James
Island*

*Morris
Island*

Union
Ironclads

Main Ship Channel

Union
Advance

*Lighthouse
Inlet*

Folly Island

⊔ Confederate Battery

0   1   2   3 mi

0   1   2   3   4   5 km

The Attack on Morris Island and Battery Wagner

effort should be made to sink either the *Ironsides* or one of the monitors." But Tucker did not want to risk his ships. They remained at anchor near Fort Sumter.[8]

On July 18 the bombardment of Battery Wagner was especially heavy to soften it up for an infantry assault that evening. "Such a crashing of shells and thunder of cannon and flying of sand and earth into the air" he had never seen, wrote Dahlgren in his diary. As the tide rose, he had the monitors move to within 300 yards of shore, while the *New Ironsides*, with its deeper draft, remained farther out and fired over them. "The gunnery was very fine," declared Dahlgren, "the shells of the 'Ironsides' going right over the 'Montauk,' so we had it all our own way." At dusk the Union infantry, led by the celebrated black regiment, the 54th Massachusetts, began their attack, and the Federals no longer had it all their own way. "There could be no more help from us," noted Dahlgren, "for it was dark and we might kill friend as well as foe."[9] Desperate fighting by Confederates in Battery Wagner repulsed the attack by two Union brigades, inflicting a seven-to-one ratio of casualties on the attackers.

Gillmore and Dahlgren were compelled to settle down for a siege that encompassed Battery Gregg at the northern tip of Morris Island and Fort Sumter itself as well as Battery Wagner. Gillmore moved up his 100-pound and 200-pound Parrott rifles close enough to begin reducing Fort Sumter to rubble, while the ironclads and other warships continued to pulverize Batteries Wagner and Gregg. But heat exhaustion, disease, and expiring enlistments began to decimate Union naval crews. Welles promised to send more sailors from the North, but he also ordered Dahlgren "to enlist for service in the squadron as many able-bodied contrabands as you can. . . . There is a great demand at present from all quarters for seamen, and the contraband element must be used where it can with advantage."[10]

Casualties and illness also devastated the Union army in South Carolina. Gillmore pleaded in vain with General in Chief Halleck for reinforcements. Concerned that the campaign might be discontinued if no additional troops were sent, Dahlgren wrote to Welles, who asked Gustavus Fox to see Halleck about the matter. The general in chief insisted that he had no troops to spare from other theaters. Welles went over his head to Lincoln, who ordered Halleck to send 10,000 men from the Army of the Potomac and from North Carolina.[11]

By August Dahlgren also was suffering from the enervating heat and humidity. "My debility increases," he wrote in his diary on August 18, "so

Rear Admiral John A. Dahlgren standing next to one of the guns
named after him. (Courtesy of the Library of Congress)

that to-day it is an exertion to sit in a chair. I feel like lying down. My head
is light. How strange—no pain, but it feels like gliding away to death."[12]

However exhausted Union sailors were, their guns kept pounding
away. From July to September, the *New Ironsides* alone fired 4,439 projectiles against Confederate defenses on Morris Island and Fort Sumter,
and the monitors fired 3,577 more.[13] The commander at Battery Wagner
reported on September 5 that "a repetition of to-day's fire will make the
fort almost a ruin. . . . Is it desirable to sacrifice the garrison?" The next
day, General Beauregard telegraphed Richmond: "Terrible bombardment
of Wagner and Gregg for nearly thirty-six hours . . . nearly all guns disabled . . . Sumter being silenced. Evacuation of Morris Island becomes
indispensable to save garrison; it will be attempted tonight."[14] That night
the Confederates quietly pulled out, and Morris Island became Yankee
territory.

This achievement effectively closed Charleston to blockade-runners by making it possible for Union ships to remain in the channels inside the bar. "The completeness with which four little monitors, supported by an ironclad frigate, have closed this port is well worth noting," Dahlgren boasted to Welles in January 1864. "For several months not a vessel has passed in or out."[15]

But the Confederate flag still flew over Fort Sumter. "Old Sumter has suffered fearfully and is now a wreck, utterly powerless for offensive purposes," acknowledged a Charleston merchant, "but held by its garrison under orders from the General [Beauregard] with a tenacity and gallantry which is wonderful. . . . But even if it should be completely destroyed, the enemy are very far from getting the city. We have remaining an inner line of batteries, and Sullivan's Island, from the Cove to the Moultrie House, is one continuous battery so that you can see their work has hardly commenced."[16]

Dahlgren thought the same. He wanted to remove the obstructions and torpedoes from the vicinity of Fort Sumter so that his ironclads could move closer to attack Fort Johnson and other batteries defending the city. Sumter had been so badly battered that the Confederates had removed most of its big guns, but riflemen and field artillery in the fort could still impede efforts to take up the obstructions. So Dahlgren planned a surprise boat attack on Fort Sumter for the night of September 8–9 by 500 sailors and marines.

By coincidence, General Gillmore was planning a similar attack with two regiments the same night. Until this time, the cordial cooperation between Dahlgren and Gillmore had been a textbook example of combined operations. But on this night, the cooperation began to break down. When each commander learned of the other's intention only hours before the planned attacks, Gillmore proposed that they coordinate their efforts under command of an army officer. Dahlgren replied rather haughtily: "I have assembled 500 men and I can not consent that the commander shall be other than a naval officer." Gillmore replied, just as haughtily, that "why this should be so in assaulting a fortification, I can not see." The two men finally agreed that each group should attack from a different direction under officers of their own service and arranged a password so they would not fire on each other.

In the event, the navy's attack came first, while the army boats were delayed by low tide. The assault was a fiasco. Back in April, the Confederates had picked up the *Keokuk*'s signal book floating into shore after that vessel had sunk. The navy had not changed its code, so the Confederates were able to read the flag communications about the boat attack and were ready for it. When the first boats landed, the marines and sailors were immediately pinned down by rifle fire and hand grenades. Several were killed and wounded, and more than a hundred were captured. In the darkness, the attackers could scarcely see anything, while the defenders, who had been there for months, knew every inch of the ground. "I could see nothing but the utmost confusion," reported a marine lieutenant who escaped. Some navy boats turned back, and when the officers commanding the army boats finally approached and saw what was happening, they called off their own attack.[17]

In the aftermath of this affair, relations between Gillmore and Dahlgren deteriorated. Even though the Confederates still occupied Fort Sumter, the admiral wanted to go ahead and clear an opening through the obstructions for his monitors. He asked Gillmore for army fire against the fort to keep its sharpshooters in their bombproofs. Gillmore did not think his guns could do the job, causing Dahlgren to complain (in his diary) that "having expended my means for sixty days in helping *him* to clear Morris Island, he demurs at the first step in help of me!"[18]

Dahlgren must have reflected ruefully on his eagerness to get this command and wondered if he should have heeded the old adage: "Be careful what you wish for; you might get it." Plagued by continuing friction with the army, criticism from Northern newspapers because he had not yet "taken" Charleston, and sniping from what Welles called the Du Pont clique and other naval officers who still resented his promotion to rear admiral, Dahlgren was depressed by "wearing anxieties, with slander and base abuse . . . miserable lies which corrode the good name of a whole life."[19]

But he had a squadron to command, a blockade to maintain, and a continuing campaign against Charleston to consider, so he could not indulge in self-pity for long. On the night of October 5, the Confederate navy finally answered Beauregard's plea for an attack on one of the Union ironclads—the biggest one, the 3,486-ton *New Ironsides*. A cigar-shaped, semisubmersed vessel only fifty feet in length named *David* slipped almost invisibly through the dark waters, planted a 60-pound canister of powder against the Union Goliath's starboard quarter, and blew a hole in it. Two of the *David*'s crew abandoned ship and were captured, but the other two got her back to Charleston and a heroes' welcome. At first, the damage to the *New Ironsides* did not appear serious, but later inspection showed that it was more severe. She stayed in the squadron and was patched up well enough at Port Royal to remain on station until she returned to the North in June 1864 for extensive repairs.[20] The *David*'s success spawned the construction of several other *David*-class torpedo boats in the South, one of which inflicted minor damage on the USS *Minnesota* at Hampton Roads in April 1864.

After the *David*'s attack on the *New Ironsides*, Dahlgren ordered all his ironclads inside the bar to fit outriggers and netting around each vessel when anchored and to row patrols around them from dark to dawn. But the Confederates were preparing an even more startling surprise for the blockade fleet at Charleston. Dahlgren learned from deserters of a torpedo vessel called the "American Diver," developed in Mobile and shipped by rail to Charleston. It "is nearly submerged and can be entirely so," Dahlgren reported to Welles in January 1864. "It is intended to go under the bottoms of vessels and there operate." Dahlgren's sources were remarkably well-informed, even to the extent of telling him that in trials, this submarine "has drowned three crews, one at Mobile and two here, 17 men in all."[21]

Modern historians are not certain about whether there was a drowning in Mobile. But there were indeed two at Charleston, not involving the *American Diver* but its successor, the *H. L. Hunley*, which was actually the vessel brought to Charleston. One of these accidents took the life of the inventor Horace L. Hunley, after whom the submarine was named. The *Hunley* was a notable combination of the old and new. It was powered by a propeller turned with hand cranks and equipped with diving fins and water tanks for ballast. Like the *David*, it carried a torpedo on a bow spar to be exploded against a ship's hull. On the night of February 17, 1864, a nine-man crew took the *Hunley* outside the bar, where blockade ships had not taken protective precautions, and sank the ten-gun wooden screw sloop USS *Housatonic*. The *Hunley* never returned from this mission, and its crew achieved status as martyr-heroes in the South. With this first combat action by a submarine, the *Hunley* became the most famous warship of the Civil War next to the *Monitor*—in part because, like the *Monitor*, its position was later discovered and much of it has been raised. The *Hunley* can be seen today in Charleston.[22]

After the sinking of the *Housatonic*, Dahlgren ordered ships outside the bar to remain under way at night, or if anchored to put out netting on outriggers and row patrols.[23] The successful attacks on the *New Ironsides* and *Housatonic* raised Confederate morale and dampened Union spirits. They may have contributed to a decision to forgo any more major naval efforts to capture Charleston. On October 18, 1863, Dahlgren had told Fox that "the public demand for instantly proceeding into Charleston is so persistent that I would rather go in at all risks than stand the incessant abuse lavished on me." But four days later, the admiral called a rare council of war with his eight ironclad captains and two staff officers. For six hours, they discussed whether to break the obstructions and fight their way to Charleston once the repairs on the monitors were completed or wait until new ironclads promised for sometime in the winter became available. They voted six to four to wait.[24] Welles told Dahlgren that with the virtual cessation of blockade-running into Charleston, the capture of the city would be merely symbolic and not worth the cost. "While there is an intense feeling pervading the country in regard to the fate of Charleston," Welles acknowledged, "the Department is disinclined to have its only ironclad squadron incur extreme risks when the substantial advantages have already been gained."[25]

Gillmore and many of his troops were transferred to Virginia in the spring of 1864 to become part of the Army of the James to assist the Army of the Potomac in the big push against Richmond. Dahlgren was no doubt relieved to see Gillmore go, but the departure of troops made a combined operation against Charleston that year even less likely. Fox had also become "averse to any attack on Charleston," Dahlgren learned in March. "He suggests letting Farragut have the new monitors for Mobile," which was now a navy priority.[26]

One reason for the Navy Department's reluctance to renew the effort to capture Charleston was the danger from the Confederacy's increasing numbers and effectiveness of torpedoes. Northern naval officers had ambivalent attitudes toward these "infernal machines." In February 1863 Du Pont had denounced Confederate use of them and refused to consider fighting fire with fire—that is, using them himself against the enemy. "Nothing could induce me to allow a single one in the squadron for the destruction of human life," he fumed. "I think that Indian scalping, or any other barbarism, is no worse."[27] The commander of Union ships on the St. Johns River in Florida, where several vessels had been sunk or damaged by mines, warned that he would "deal summarily with anybody caught putting down torpedoes in the river." Dahlgren threatened to hang the two captured crew members of the David after they had torpedoed the New Ironsides "for using an engine of war not recognized by civilized nations."[28]

Needless to say, Dahlgren never did so. By 1864 some Union commanders were using torpedoes themselves, especially in the James River to discourage Confederate ironclads at Richmond from making a sortie against Union transports and gunboats in the river. Dahlgren even advised the Navy Department "to block the Confederates with their own game and let loose on them quantities of torpedoes." He rigged up a torpedo raft loaded with several hundred pounds of gunpowder to float up to Fort Sumter and blow out the outer wall. It did not work.[29] In any case, by 1864 naval mines had become a feared but legitimate weapon of war in the eyes of most Union officers.

THE CLOSURE OF CHARLESTON to blockade-runners forced most of them to use Wilmington, which now became the busiest Confederate port. Acting Rear Admiral Samuel Phillips Lee's North Atlantic Squadron captured or destroyed fifty runners in 1863 and fifty-four in the first nine months of 1864, most of them going to or from Wilmington.[30] But of course a larger number got through. Some of those, however, did not have the full cargo with which they had left port. Many of them had piled their decks as well as holds with as much cargo as the vessel would bear. When spotted and chased, they would jettison the deck cargo (usually cotton bales outbound, lead and munitions inbound) to gain speed in order to get away. Many of these runners were extremely fast, having been built especially for the purpose, and when lightened of part of their load, they could usually outrun a blockader—whose crew could console themselves by picking up the floating bales worth up to $200 each. More than one Northern skipper was accused of breaking off pursuit to pick up bales to win the prize money before another ship could get them.

By the fall of 1863, Phillips Lee finally had enough ships to tighten the Wilmington blockade at both entrances to the Cape Fear River. Experience had refined his tactics. At each inlet, he posed small shallow-draft vessels as close to the bar as possible to detect runners going out. When they did, the picket ship fired a gun and a rocket to alert larger and faster vessels patrolling a couple of miles out and to indicate the direction the runner was heading. Farther out still, sometimes fifty miles or even more toward Bermuda or the Bahamas, was another cordon of blockade ships that intersected the expected routes of outbound runners at a time and place calculated by a complicated formula that combined the times of the beginning of the ebb tide and the rising or setting of the moon (if there was one) with the distance to be traveled and the estimated speed of the runners. For inbound runners, the time of moonrise or -set and of the flood tide could also help blockaders guess when and where runners might appear.

The captain's clerk of the USS *Florida* (not to be confused with the Confederate raider of the same name) described his ship's capture of the valuable blockade-runner *Calypso* carrying armor plates for ironclads when the *Florida* was patrolling the offshore route from Nassau. After an exciting chase of several hours, the *Florida* finally caught the *Calypso*. "Here was our chance at last to show what we are worthy of," he wrote in his diary. "The welcome relief from a monotony of months, that had nearly driven the men crazy, had come at last. There was a chance now to refute the calumnies with which the press, at home, branded the inefficiency of the Wilmington blockade"—and, he might have added, a chance at some welcome prize money.[31]

The captains of blockade-runners were quick learners; they changed direction or speed and began carrying rockets of the same type as the navy, which they fired in the opposite direction they intended to go. In this cat-and-mouse game, the runners continued to have the advantage, especially on dark, foggy, and tempestuous nights, but the blockade did continue to tighten. In the fall of 1863 the British agent for a cotton importer informed London that five out of seven runners carrying cotton from Wilmington had been recently captured. There was no cotton in Bermuda, so "you may not expect to receive over 300 Bales in the next three months" and "the European markets must advance to higher rates than ever yet known."[32] The wife of the Confederate agent in Bermuda was depressed by these captures, which included two of the fastest runners, the *R. E. Lee* and the *Margaret and Jessie*. "We can ill afford to lose any more," she wrote in November 1863. But three weeks later, Union ships captured two more runners. "What a list of trophies for those mercenary hirelings," she mourned.[33] The Union navy added insult to injury by converting the *R. E. Lee* and the *Margaret and Jessie* into blockaders and renaming them the USS *Fort Donelson* and the USS *Gettysburg*.

The Confederate publicist in England, Henry Hotze, inadvertently testified to the effectiveness of the blockade. Editor of the *Index*, a pro-Confederate newspaper in London, Hotze wrote many articles claiming the illegality of the "paper blockade." But in a letter to Confederate Secretary of State Judah Benjamin in January 1864, he complained that "at the present rate of exportation through the blockade . . . it would take 20 years to export the cotton now in the Confederate states."[34]

Nevertheless, with every report of ships getting through the blockade, critics in the North upbraided Welles. The harassed navy secretary in turn reproved his squadron commanders—especially Lee, because Wilmington was his responsibility. "Five steamers containing 6,300 bales of cotton have arrived within one week at Bermuda," he told Lee in July 1864. "It is of great importance that a careful examination of the blockade should be made by yourself, and such arrangements devised as will insure greater vigilance."[35] Lee's blockade fleet had been thinned out during the past two months because so many of his ships were in the James River supporting the army's operations against Richmond and Petersburg.

Next to munitions and shoes, one of the most important products that the Confederacy tried to import through the blockade was salt. This seemingly humble item was necessary for the curing and preservation of meat in that prerefrigeration era and for preserving hides during leather manufacture. Despite ample domestic sources of salt, the South had imported most of what it needed in the antebellum era from the North or abroad. Early in the war, some of the largest potential salt deposits in the Upper South were occupied by Union troops. Many of the blockade-runners captured early in the war, especially sailing ships, were carrying salt.

To compensate for these losses, the Confederacy established salt-making works to boil and evaporate seawater along the coast from North Carolina to Texas, especially on Florida's Gulf coast. These works were usually located a few miles up tidal estuaries or rivers too shallow for Union gunboats to raid. But Northern sailors and marines learned to carry out raids up these rivers in cutters and launches armed with boat howitzers that were useful not only for driving away workers and guards but also for blowing holes in boilers and pans used for evaporating the briny water.

The navy raided hundreds of saltworks. In one ten-day period in December 1863, boats from the bark USS *Restless* destroyed 290 saltworks in St. Andrew's Bay, Florida, including 529 boiling kettles averaging 150 gallons each and 105 boilers of much larger capacity—not to mention 4,000 bushels of salt. Not to be outdone, boats from the steam gunboat USS *Tahoma* went up the St. Marks River in Florida two months later and destroyed 8,000 bushels of salt along with kettles and boilers with the capacity to make 2,500 bushels per day.[36] Such raids helped drive the price of salt in the Confederacy to unimaginable heights and exacerbated the inflation that almost wrecked the Confederate economy. They also broke up the monotony of blockade duty and raised sailors' morale by demonstrating that they could go on the offensive and take the war to the enemy on the beach.[37]

SAMUEL PHILLIPS LEE thought that the large number of gunboats he had to keep in the North Carolina sounds to support the army's occupation of several coastal towns was a wasteful diversion of resources. He may have been right, but Confederate leaders considered these forces a potential threat to the interior of North Carolina and its communications with Virginia. In 1864 they laid plans to use the ironclad they had been building up the Roanoke River to help drive the Federals out of Plymouth as the first step toward regaining the sounds.[38]

The senior Union naval officer at Plymouth, Lieutenant Commander Charles W. Flusser, had good intelligence about Confederate progress in completion of the CSS *Albemarle*. A smaller version of the *Arkansas*, the *Albemarle* was armed with only two guns, but both were 6.4-inch Brooke rifles. In a rare (for the Confederates) combined operation, the *Albemarle* came down the Roanoke on April 19 to cooperate with three brigades of Confederate infantry in an attack on the single brigade of Union soldiers garrisoning Plymouth. With his two sidewheel double-enders (rudders on both ends so the vessels could operate in narrow streams without having to turn around), the USS *Miami* and the USS *Southfield*, Flusser prepared to fight the *Albemarle*. He chained his ships together to try to trap the *Albemarle* between them. But the ironclad rammed the *Southfield* and tore a huge hole in her side. As the *Southfield* was sinking, Flusser on the *Miami* personally fired the bow gun point blank at the *Albemarle*. It was loaded with a shell intended for use against Confederate infantry instead of a solid ball; the shell exploded against the *Albemarle* and shrapnel rebounded straight back and killed Flusser, one of the navy's most promising young officers.[39]

A seventeen-year-old surgeon's steward on the *Miami* described the uneven battle with the *Albemarle*. "We fired about thirty shells at the ram but they had *no* effect on her," while her shots in return caused havoc on the *Miami*. "As fast as the men were wounded, they were passed down to us and we laid them one at a time on the table . . . and extracted the balls and pieces of shell from them. . . . Dr. Mann and I looked like butchers . . . our shirt sleeves rolled up and we covered with blood. . . . The blood was over the soles of my boots. . . . When Captain Flusser fell, the men seemed to lose all heart, and we ran away from the ram into the sound."[40] Deprived of naval support, the Union commander of the Plymouth garrison surrendered his surviving force the next day.

This victory encouraged Confederates to plan a similar combined attack on New Bern.[41] But Phillips Lee organized a task force of Union ships to swarm around the *Albemarle* if she emerged into the sound, fire into her smokestack and gunports, ram her, and do whatever it took to disable her no matter what the cost to the attackers. On May 5 the *Albemarle* ventured into her namesake sound. Six Union gunboats carried out the swarming tactics. They hit the ironclad with at least sixty-four shots, one of which dismounted a gun while others riddled the smokestack so that her fires would scarcely draw, forcing her to limp back to Plymouth.[42]

Her retreat ended the plan for a combined attack on New Bern. The *Albemarle* did not venture into the sound again. But her presence at Plymouth constituted a continuing threat that tied down a number of Union vessels that might otherwise have been on blockade duty. In July 1864 the former commander of the CSS *Florida*, Captain John N. Maffitt, was assigned command of the *Albemarle*. Rumors soon circulated that the intrepid Maffitt intended to take her out and challenge the Union gunboats again. But the army commander of the North Carolina district that included Plymouth was alarmed by this possibility. "There is great danger of her capture if she goes out into the sound," he warned, which "would be irreparable and productive of ruin to the interests of the Government, particularly in this State and district."[43] Maffitt soon took command of a government blockade-runner and the *Albemarle* stayed at Plymouth.

She remained a thorn in Acting Rear Admiral Lee's side, however, and he came up with a plan for "a torpedo attack, either by means of the india-rubber boat . . . or a light-draft, rifle-proof, swift steam barge, fitted with a torpedo."[44] Lee had in mind just the man for this job: twenty-one-year-old Lieutenant William Barker Cushing, who had proved his worth as a sea commando in several daring raids behind Confederate lines in the Cape Fear River. In August 1863 Cushing had led a cutting-out expedition at New Topsail Inlet that captured a schooner and destroyed extensive saltworks. In February 1864 he led a raid by small boats past Fort Caswell to capture a Confederate general. The general had gone up to Wilmington that day, but the Yankees captured the chief engineer of the Confederate garrison and brought him away. Then in June 1864 Cushing took a cutter up the Cape Fear almost to Wilmington itself in a scouting mission that lasted four days and gained valuable information about Confederate defenses. He outwitted several boats sent to capture him and escaped without harm to his party.[45]

Cushing enthusiastically embraced Lee's idea of a torpedo attack on the *Albemarle*. He went to New York to supervise the construction of a special steam launch for the purpose. On the night of October 27, he led fifteen men up the Roanoke River to Plymouth, passing Confederate pickets without detection. They approached the *Albemarle*, which was tied to a wharf and surrounded by a boom of logs. Circling around, they were detected, and Cushing made straight for the *Albemarle* through a hail of bullets, bounced up over the logs, planted his torpedo on the hull, and exploded it at the same instant that one of the *Albemarle*'s guns shot a hole in the launch that sank it. Cushing and his men jumped into the river and swam for it. "The most of our party were captured," he wrote in his official report, "some were drowned, and only one escaped besides myself, and he in another direction. . . . Completely exhausted, I managed to reach the shore. . . . While hiding a few feet from the path, two of the *Albemarle*'s officers passed, and I judged from their conversation that the ship was destroyed."[46]

Cushing made his way back to the fleet, where he was hailed as a hero. He received the Thanks of Congress and was promoted to lieutenant commander. Eight Union gunboats steamed up the Roanoke River and recaptured Plymouth, which remained in Union hands for the rest of the war. Despite the derring-do in North Carolina waters during 1864, however, this theater remained marginal to the crucial course of events elsewhere in that year.

chapter ten

From the Red River to Cherbourg

From the fall of Forts Henry and Donelson in February 1862 to the fall of Vicksburg and Port Hudson in July 1863, the Mississippi River and its tributaries were one of the most active theaters of the war. And this vast region was anything but tranquil and routine thereafter. Rear Admiral David Dixon Porter's Mississippi Squadron remained responsible for suppressing guerrillas, monitoring trade, convoying supplies to General William S. Rosecrans's Army of the Cumberland, carrying out combined operations with General Nathaniel P. Banks's Army of the Gulf on the Red River in the spring of 1864, and a host of other activities necessary to maintain Union control of the Mississippi valley and help repel Confederate counteroffensives.

In the fall of 1863, Porter established several "divisions" of his squadron on the Mississippi River from Cairo to New Orleans. Each division had several gunboats, and each of these vessels was responsible for patrolling a section of the river ten or twelve miles in both directions from its station to suppress guerrillas and prevent the enemy from crossing men and supplies. "The protection of the river since the fall of Vicksburg has been left entirely to the navy," wrote Porter, "the army only occupying a few prominent points on the Mississippi, making no expeditions away from those points."[1]

The guerrillas operated in bands of 20 to 100 men, often with one or two pieces of field artillery. An acting master's mate commanding a tinclad on the lower Mississippi described a typical encounter with a band that possessed artillery near Gaines' Landing, Arkansas. "As soon as I discovered what they were, I ran down to the gun deck to beat to quarters," he recounted. "Imagine the confusion and delay possible, when half of the men and the Drummer boy were out of their hammocks. . . . But with all this confusion, I had the Port battery manned and gave them one broadside before the thieves had given us their second round." A furious duel ensued, and the boat was hit several times, but "we drove them off firing the last shot."[2]

Guerrillas were not the only enemy that gunboat crews had to confront. "You have no conception of what mosquitoes are down here," wrote a sailor on the tinclad USS *Silver Cloud* patrolling between Fort Pillow and Helena. "They are perfect devils. . . . I'm also favored with a large company of cockroaches. . . . They devour all the provisions I buy. They eat my thread, clothes & paper & I think they tried to devour my needles. . . . I have become so used to them that I can go to sleep while they are performing pedestrian tours up my legs and over my body generally."[3]

One problem with using gunboats against guerrillas was the ability of these mounted men to move out of range and reappear along the banks of rivers somewhere else. The Marine Brigade created out of the ram fleet by Alfred Ellet thus became one of the Mississippi Squadron's main antiguerrilla outfits. With seven gunboats carrying several hundred cavalry and infantry, they could land horses and men to chase guerrillas into the interior. But even this technique often failed to catch the swift rebels, who knew every byway in the region. The Marine Brigade therefore decided to carry out proactive patrols. They captured some mules to mount their infantry, and in September 1863 they tried the new tactics of landing cavalry and mule-mounted infantry to sweep through the interior, stopping at plantations suspected of harboring guerrillas. While the main body surrounded one plantation, an advance company moved on to the next, and the group thus leapfrogged across country "so rapidly that we kept ahead of the reports of our presence in that section," explained an officer, "thus securing any persons who were loitering around these plantations waiting to concentrate at some given point on the river to fire upon passing transports." Having secured several prisoners, the brigade returned to their gunboats at a prearranged point.[4]

As time went on, however, discipline in the Marine Brigade became more lax. Operating away from both army and navy control, they sometimes plundered the houses and farms they raided, regardless of whether they found any guerrillas there or not. Horses, men, and the gunboats of the brigade began to break down. The warfare against bands that seemed to disappear from one place and pop up again somewhere else became exhausting. In June 1864 an officer in the brigade described "daily sharp, short skirmishes with the roving bands of guerrillas, varied with the roving bands of those almost intangible enemies, the flies by day and mosquitoes by night," the "malarial water we are compelled to drink, and the excessive hot weather." By August 1864 the Marine Brigade had outlived its usefulness and was disbanded.[5]

The navy learned that the best way to deal with guerrilla attacks on supply transports was a convoy system. A large number of transports would gather at a supply depot such as Cairo, Illinois. Several gunboats would space themselves through the fleet and convoy them to their destination. In the winter and spring of 1862–63, cavalry raids by Generals Nathan Bedford Forrest and Joseph Wheeler cut rail and road routes to Union General William S. Rosecrans's army at Murfreesboro. Rosecrans was dependent on supplies that came up the Cumberland River to Nashville in weekly convoys of thirty or more steamboats guarded by four to six gunboats on each trip. "Our line of convoy up the Cumberland is sometimes 4 or 5 miles in length," wrote the navy officer in charge in February 1863. "All of Rosecrans' supplies are sent up that way." From January to June 1863 the gunboats convoyed four hundred transports and 150 barges to Rosecrans "without loss of a single steamer or barge." These convoys enabled the general to build up the huge depot of supplies that supported his Tullahoma and Chattanooga Campaigns.[6]

Forrest's and Wheeler's cavalry made a major effort to stop this supply pipeline by attacking the Union garrison at Fort Donelson on February 3, 1863. The Confederates outnumbered the 800 Union defenders five to one. The Northern soldiers held out all day until they were almost out of ammunition. A convoy was approaching Fort Donelson with six gunboats, which raced upriver when they received news of the attack. Arriving at about 8:00 P.M., they found the Confederates deploying dismounted for a final attack in bright moonlight. The Confederate left wing was positioned in a ravine leading to the river. "This position gave us a chance to rake nearly the entire length of his line," wrote the senior officer of the gunboat flotilla. "Simultaneously the gunboats opened fire up this ravine, into the graveyard, and into the valley beyond, where the enemy had his horses hitched. . . . The rebels were so much taken by surprise that they did not even fire a gun, but immediately commenced retreating."[7]

Convoys also supplied General Ambrose E. Burnside's operations in East Tennessee during the fall of 1863, when the Cumberland River rose enough to get them to the junction of the Cumberland and the Big South Fork River above Nashville. When Grant took control of Union forces besieged in Chattanooga after the battle of Chickamauga, he ordered Sherman to bring four divisions from Vicksburg to Chattanooga. Porter mobilized a flotilla of gunboats to convoy the troops and transports as far as Eastport, Mississippi, from which Sherman had to depend on rail communications the rest of the way. "We are much obliged to the Tennessee, which has favored us most opportunely," wrote Sherman to Porter as he prepared to move overland after debarking at Eastport. "I am never easy with a railroad which takes a whole army to guard, each foot of rail being essential to the whole; whereas they can't stop the Tennessee, and each boat can make its own game."[8] Four gunboats convoying transports up the White River to De Vall's Bluff in Arkansas also supported the campaign of Major General Frederick Steele that captured Little Rock in September 1863.[9]

One of the more spectacular feats of the Mississippi Squadron was performed by six tinclads of the Ohio River Division during General John Hunt Morgan's raid north of that river in July 1863. After Morgan's 2,000 cavalry crossed into Indiana, Lieutenant Commander Le Roy Fitch concentrated his gunboats and moved upriver parallel to the raiders, "keeping boats both ahead and in his rear, guarding all accessible fords." As pursuing Union cavalry closed in at Buffington Island, Morgan tried to cross there but the tinclads "shelled most of them back, killing and drowning a good many." Most of the raiders were captured there; Morgan and 350 men kept on and were eventually run down and captured near Salineville, Ohio. One of the army officers in charge of the pursuit declared that the "activity and energy with which the squadron was used to prevent the enemy recrossing the Ohio, and to assist in his capture, was worthy of the highest praise."[10]

In the spring of 1864, General Nathan Bedford Forrest led a raid into West Tennessee and Kentucky. In Paducah, Kentucky, at the junction of the Tennessee and Ohio Rivers, his 2,700 men attacked 800 Union defenders, driving them back into Fort Anderson. Two tinclads swept the streets of the town, firing 700 rounds that finally drove Forrest's raiders away. "We kept putting the shell and grape into them from all the guns we could get to bear," wrote a gunner on the USS *Peosta*. "Their riflemen and some of the people of the town got into the buildings down by the river and pelted us with musket balls but we soon gave them enough of that for we directed our whole fire on them at short range with shell grape and canister and soon fetched the bricks around their eyes. . . . They would have had the fort and the city if it had not been for us, for they were out of ammunition in the fort."[11]

Almost three weeks later, however, the sole gunboat on the scene when Forrest attacked Fort Pillow on the Mississippi, the USS *New Era*, could do little to help the defenders. The *New Era* drove off the attackers on the south side of the fort, but dense timber protected them on the north side. When the Confederates carried the fort, murdering many of the black soldiers and white Tennessee Unionists after they surrendered, the captors turned the fort's artillery on the lightly armored tinclad and drove it out of range.[12]

In addition to countering guerrillas and raiders and convoying supply transports, one of the most important tasks of the Mississippi Squadron was regulating Northern trade with occupied territory. Porter conceived of this duty as analogous to the blockade against trade in contraband goods, imposed on the rivers instead of on the high seas. But to foster the reopening of commerce in occupied Southern territory, the Treasury Department issued trade licenses to Northern merchants to purchase cotton from and sell goods to Southerners who took an oath of allegiance to the United States. Much trade in contraband goods under fraudulent licenses went on from such cities as Memphis and Helena, however, and these items found their way into Confederate possession. "I have reason to know that the Board of Trade in Memphis has granted licenses to carry contraband goods into rebel places," wrote Porter on one occasion. "I have directed the officers under my command not to recognize any permits from any board of trade. . . . I claim to have jurisdiction on the water, and I intend that all rebel depots shall be hermetically sealed."[13]

Such actions brought Porter into conflict with the Treasury Department, and he was forced to recognize legitimate trade permits. Yet there were many gray areas where the navy continued to seize shipments that officers suspected were intended for the enemy and confiscated cotton that was traded for such goods. "Can we not stop this cotton mania?" Porter asked Grant in February 1863. "I have given all the naval vessels in the river strict orders to permit no trade in rebel territory, but to seize all rebel cotton for the Government."[14]

Just as blockade ships on blue water captured runners carrying cotton, Porter's squadron therefore laid hold of cotton shipments on the rivers and even sent men ashore to take cotton from plantations and transport it north as prizes. The district court at Springfield, Illinois, however, ruled that most of this cotton was owned by individuals who claimed to be Unionists and who had Treasury Department permits to ship it. Porter asserted in 1864 that of the 8,000 bales his squadron had seized, the court recognized only 1,000 as prizes. "The trickery and corruption practiced is beyond conception," Porter fumed. "The claims put in by the Treasury Department are preposterous. . . . The court at Springfield is admitting claimants to plead when cotton is actually marked C.S.A."[15]

Porter's motives were not entirely patriotic. If ruled a prize, half of the proceeds from sale of the cotton would have gone to the naval pension fund and 45 percent to the members of the crew that had seized it, with 5 percent going to Porter himself as squadron commander. That percentage of the proceeds from 7,000 bales would have been a tidy sum. And there is evidence that some of the cotton seized from plantations was indiscriminately stamped "C.S.A." by its captors. That was particularly true of cotton sent north from the Red River Campaign in the spring of 1864, which turned out to be a fiasco for the Union army and nearly a calamity for Porter's squadron.

SEVERAL POLITICAL AND STRATEGIC purposes impelled the invasion of northern Louisiana via the Red River by General Banks's Army of the Gulf and Porter's Mississippi Squadron. Banks was overseeing the creation of a Unionist government in the state under Lincoln's 10 percent Reconstruction plan; to gain control of more of Louisiana would give that process greater legitimacy. The continuing concern about French actions in Mexico caused the Lincoln administration to recommend a greater military presence in Texas, which could be achieved by continuing the movement up the Red River into that state. General Grant wanted Banks's army to capture Mobile instead, as he had been advising since the previous summer. If it were purely a matter of military strategy, General Halleck informed Grant, a thrust against Mobile would make more sense. But as "a matter of political or State policy, connected with our foreign relations," the president still considered it important to "occupy and hold at least a portion of Texas" in addition to Brownsville.[16] Admiral Porter and General Sherman were concerned about the reported construction of Confederate ironclads and other gunboats at Shreveport that might threaten Union control of the Mississippi where the Red River entered the big river. Taking advantage of the spring rise in the Red to go above the rapids at Alexandria, they proposed to "clear out Red River as high as Shreveport by April." To do the job thoroughly, Porter intended "to take along every ironclad vessel in the fleet."[17] And then there was all that cotton reported to be waiting along the banks of the Red River to feed the New England mills and enrich the sailors and soldiers who seized it as a prize.

Porter did indeed take almost every ironclad in his squadron into the Red River in March 1864—thirteen of them, plus another thirteen tinclads and various tugs, tenders, dispatch boats, and supply vessels. This muscle-bound fleet was far larger than needed for the purpose, especially given the difficult navigation on the upper stretches of the river and the lesser spring rise than usual. Why Porter brought so many vessels is not clear, but it may have had something to do with the large amount of cotton they gathered—some 3,000 bales.

The campaign started well. The gunboats and a division of soldiers drove the Confederates out of Fort De Russy thirty miles up the river on March 14. "The surrender of the forts at Point De Russy is of much more importance than I at first supposed," Porter reported to Welles. "The rebels had depended on that point to stop any advance of the army or navy into this part of rebeldom."[18]

That was about the last good news from the expedition, however. While the gunboats worked their way upriver to within thirty miles of Shreveport, the army moved inland and ran into the Confederates under Major General Richard Taylor at Mansfield on April 8. Taylor defeated Banks and drove the Federals back to Pleasant Hill, where another battle took place on April 9. This one was a tactical Union victory, but Banks decided to give up the campaign anyway and retreat to Alexandria.

When word of this retreat reached Porter, he too decided to return downriver, especially since the water level was dropping rapidly and threatening to strand several of his vessels. "The army has been shamefully beaten by the rebels," Porter informed his friend General Sherman. "I was averse to coming up with the fleet [this was untrue], but General Banks considered it necessary . . . and now I can't get back again, the water has fallen so much. . . . I can not express to you my entire disappointment with this department."[19]

The gunboats continually went aground and were pulled off on the way down. Confederate artillery and cavalry began appearing on the riverbank and shelling the fleet. At Blair's Landing, a full-scale battle took place between 2,000 troops and three gunboats—two of them aground. In the turreted ironclad USS *Osage*, Lieutenant Commander Thomas O. Selfridge made the first known use of a periscope to aim his 11-inch guns. One of his

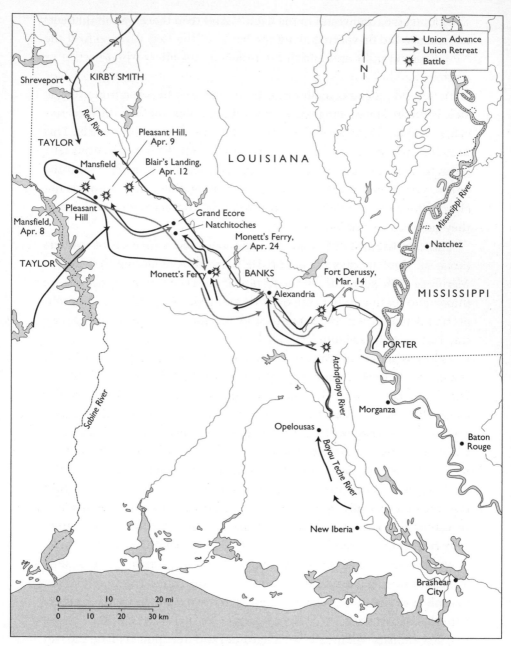

The Red River Campaign, March–May 1864

shots killed the commander of the Confederate troops, which caused them to break off and disappear inland.[20]

On April 15 the largest of Porter's ironclads, the USS *Eastport*, struck a torpedo, and her captain ran her aground to be repaired. They finally got her afloat, but she grounded eight more times on the way down to Alexandria, where she went aground again at the rapids—for the last time. It proved impossible to get her off, so on April 26 her captain lit a match to a fuse leading to 3,000 pounds of gunpowder and blew her up. During the attempt to get her off, Confederates had attacked her consorts and two pump boats, putting both out of action and sending a shot through the boiler of one that scalded to death a hundred contrabands on board who were being carried to freedom.

A substantial part of Porter's fleet was stranded at the rapids above Alexandria when the river dropped too low for them to get through. Porter was profoundly depressed by the career-ending prospect of having to blow them up to prevent capture. "It can not be possible that the country would be willing to have eight ironclads, three or four other gunboats, and many transports sacrificed without an effort to save them. It would be the worst thing to happen in this war."[21]

One of Porter's officers suggested the possibility of building a coffer dam at the falls to raise the water enough to float the vessels through the chute. But it was an army officer, Lieutenant Colonel Joseph Bailey of Wisconsin, who organized the actual construction of the dam. An engineer with experience in building dams to float logs downstream in Wisconsin, he put several thousand soldiers to work on the project at the lower falls. Two barges anchored to extend the dam to midstream broke loose, but four of the gunboats got through while the water was still high. Porter described the scene as the first of them, the timberclad USS *Lexington*, entered the chute. She "steered directly for the opening in the dam," he wrote, "through which the water was rushing so furiously that it seemed as if nothing but destruction awaited her. Thousands of beating hearts looked on anxious for the result; the silence was so great as the Lexington approached the dam that a pin might almost be heard to fall." She entered the chute "with a full head of steam on, pitched down the roaring torrent, made two or three spasmodic rolls, hung for a moment on the rocks below, was then swept into deep water by the current and rounded to, safely, into the bank. Thirty thousand voices rose in one deafening roar."

Three more gunboats got over before the water level dropped. Undaunted, Bailey and the soldiers built two new wing dams at the upper

One of Porter's gunboats going through the chute created by
Colonel Joseph Bailey's dam at Alexandria, Louisiana.
(From *Frank Leslie's Illustrated History of the Civil War*)

falls, and on May 11 and 12 the rest of the squadron made it through the
rapids. "Words are inadequate to express the admiration I feel" for Bailey,
remarked Porter with great relief. "This is without doubt the best engi-
neering feat ever performed."[22] Bailey earned the Thanks of Congress and
eventual promotion to brigadier general.

While these adventures were taking place, two tinclads escorting two
troop transports downriver ran into a Confederate ambush several miles
above Fort De Russy. Both transports were sunk and, after a firefight of
several hours, the same fate befell the tinclads. Most of the soldiers on the
transports escaped and were picked up by a third tinclad, the USS *Forest
Rose*, after it too ran the gauntlet of Confederate field guns and riflemen.
"A shell from the enemy's gun struck us in the port side amidships and just
under the waterline," reported the executive officer of the *Forest Rose*. "I
ran down and had just reached the port gun, aft the boilers, when another
shell struck us on the casemate just over the gun and burst, driving a hole
through the casemate and sending splinters in every direction." The *Forest Rose* stayed afloat but broke off the fight and continued down with 300
soldiers and sailors who had escaped from the other vessels.[23]

Both the Union army and navy finally got out of the Red River without
further serious mishap. The campaign reflected no credit on either. As
Sherman put it after reading the reports from Porter, who blamed Banks
for mismanaging everything, it was "one damn blunder from beginning
to end."[24] Banks lost his field command of the Army of the Gulf, though

he retained theater command. Porter's mistakes were less egregious, and the near miracle of saving his fleet at Alexandria imparted a positive glow. Porter kept his command and even went on to greater things in the war's final months, but the Red River Campaign left something of a stain on his reputation.

THE JAMES RIVER also became an active theater of operations again in 1864. After the withdrawal of the Army of the Potomac from the Virginia peninsula in August 1862, the James was a relatively quiet sector as the main action moved to northern Virginia and Maryland. For a time in the spring of 1863, however, actions along the Nansemond River, which flowed into the James from the south about fifteen miles west of Norfolk, had seemed to portend major fighting in this theater. Reports that Union troops planned an advance on Petersburg from their base at Suffolk on the Nansemond alarmed General Robert E. Lee. He sent General James Longstreet with two divisions to the south side of the James to counter this anticipated thrust.

When no movement by Union forces materialized, Longstreet converted his operations into a foraging expedition to obtain provisions for the Army of Northern Virginia from this region as yet lightly touched by the war. With 20,000 men, Longstreet also contemplated an attack on Suffolk. Detecting Confederate movements to the Nansemond, Federal commanders feared an effort to recapture Norfolk itself. "If Suffolk falls," Acting Rear Admiral Samuel Phillips Lee warned Welles on April 14, "Norfolk follows."[25]

To help the army defend Suffolk, Phillips Lee sent a half dozen shallow-draft gunboats—converted ferryboats and tugs—into the narrow, crooked river. These fragile craft became the Union's first line of defense, doing more fighting and suffering more damage in artillery duels with Longstreet's guns than did the Union soldiers. In one brilliant operation led by navy Lieutenant Roswell H. Lamson on April 19, a gunboat landed troops plus boat howitzers manned by sailors and captured five field guns and 130 prisoners. The loss of this battery was "a serious disaster," Longstreet reported. "The enemy succeeded in making a complete surprise."[26] Two weeks later, after the battle of Chancellorsville, his divisions were recalled to the Army of Northern Virginia on the Rappahannock. The James River lapsed into quiescence again.[27]

But with the opening of Grant's Overland Campaign in May 1864, the James became a key focal point of Union operations. For political reasons,

President Lincoln had felt it necessary to give General Benjamin Butler another command after his removal from New Orleans. In November 1863 Butler became head of the Department of Virginia and North Carolina, the army counterpart of the North Atlantic Blockading Squadron. Butler formed the Army of the James in April 1864. Grant gave him the assignment of moving up that river against Richmond, while the Army of the Potomac began its campaign against General Robert E. Lee across the Rapidan River. Phillips Lee's gunboats on the James would have a crucial role in this effort.

On May 5, 1864, Butler's 30,000-strong army boarded transports and steamed up the James River to a landing at City Point nine miles from Petersburg. Convoyed by five ironclads and seventeen other gunboats, several of which dragged for torpedoes, the meticulously planned movement went off without a hitch. The next day, however, a 2,000-pound torpedo blew the USS *Commodore Jones* into splinters with the loss of forty men killed. And on the following day, the USS *Shawsheen*, dragging for torpedoes near Chaffin's Bluff far up the river, was disabled by a shot through her boiler and captured along with most of her crew.[28]

Confederates had planted hundreds of torpedoes in the river and had prepared torpedo boats to attack Lee's ships. Lee decided to create what amounted to a minesweeping fleet of three gunboats, which he named the "Torpedo and Picket Division." He put Lieutenant Lamson in charge of this division. Lamson had been assigned to command of the USS *Gettysburg*, a captured blockade-runner converted into the fastest blockading ship in the squadron. Lee asked Lamson to give up this plum assignment, at least temporarily, to take up minesweeping duty.[29]

Lamson threw himself into this dangerous task and in his first day fished up and disarmed ten torpedoes, one of them containing almost a ton of gunpowder.[30] Within three weeks his minesweeping fleet had expanded to eight gunboats, ten armed launches, and 400 men. Lamson explained how he turned the Confederates' weapons against them. "I have had some of the large torpedoes we seized on our way up refitted and put down in the channel above the fleet" as protection from Confederate ironclads at Richmond if they came down. "I have [also] made some torpedoes out of the best materials at hand here, and have each one of my vessels armed with one containing 120 pounds of powder. . . . The Admiral expressed himself very much pleased with them and is having some made for the other vessels."[31]

Butler had advanced up the James as far as Drewry's Bluff only eight

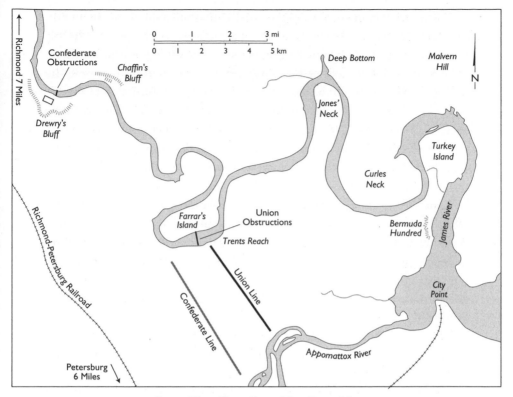

James River Operations, May–June 1864

miles from Richmond. But the Confederates under General Beauregard attacked and drove him back to the neck of land between the James and Appomattox Rivers. Meanwhile, Grant had been fighting and flanking Robert E. Lee's army down to Cold Harbor east of Richmond. Rumors and reports abounded that the Confederate James River Fleet of three *Virginia*-class ironclads and seven gunboats would sortie down the river to attack the Union fleet. Phillips Lee reported "reliable" intelligence that the "enemy meditate an immediate attack upon this fleet with fire rafts, torpedo vessels, gunboats, and ironclads, all of which carry torpedoes, and that they are confident of being able to destroy the vessels here."[32] The Confederates did indeed "meditate" such an attack, but they were delayed by difficulties in getting the ironclads through their own obstructions at Drewry's Bluff. They found the Union fleet on alert and called off the sortie, instead exchanging long-range fire with Union ironclads across a narrow neck where the James made a large loop creating a peninsula known as Farrar's Island.[33]

The possibility of such a sortie caused Union officials to consider sinking hulks at Trent's Reach to create obstructions to prevent it. Phillips Lee was opposed; he wanted to fight enemy ironclads, not block them. "The Navy is not accustomed to putting down obstructions before it," he declared. "The act might be construed as implying an admission of superiority of resources on the part of the enemy"—in other words, Lee might be accused of cowardice. Instead, he and his officers "desire the opportunity of encountering the enemy, and feel reluctant to discourage his approach." Lee also hoped that a successful fight with enemy ironclads would get him promoted to rear admiral.

General Butler urged the sinking of obstructions; Phillips Lee told him bluntly that if they were to be placed, "it must be your operation, not mine." Butler responded that he was "aware of the delicacy naval gentlemen feel in depending on anything but their own ships in a contest with the enemy," but "in a contest against such unchristian modes of warfare as fire rafts and torpedo boats I think all questions of delicacy should be waived." Exasperated, Lee countered that he would only sink the hulks "if a controlling military authority [that is, Grant] requires that it be done."[34]

Grant did so order it when he decided to cross the army over the James and attack Petersburg. Phillips Lee reluctantly ordered Lieutenant Lamson to do it, which he did on June 15. And sure enough, the Northern press accused Lee of being afraid to fight the rebels. Lee was especially outraged by an article in the *New York Herald*, his chief tormentor, which declared that the placing of obstructions "has called an honorable blush to the cheek of every officer in his fleet. . . . [Lee] has ironclad vessels enough to blow every ram in the Confederacy to atoms; but he is afraid of the trial." The *Herald* subsequently backed down and admitted that Grant had ordered the obstructions, but in a parting shot the newspaper stated that he did so because "he has no confidence" in Lee.[35]

By late June 1864, Grant had troops in place in front of both Petersburg and Richmond and settled in for a partial siege. Affairs on the James River also settled into a stalemate in which the two fleets remained behind their respective obstructions. The Union warships continued to convoy the steady stream of supply steamers up the river to Grant's base at City Point. Welles ordered Lee to turn over the James River Fleet to Captain Melancton Smith and to move his own headquarters to Beaufort, North Carolina, where he could give more attention to the blockade.

With the concentration of so many vessels on the James River in May and June, the blockade off North Carolina had suffered some relapse.

More and more runners were getting through. One of the most egregious violations of the blockade was accomplished by the CSS *Tallahassee*. Built in England as a fast cross-channel steamer named *Atalanta*, it became a blockade-runner in 1864 and made several successful runs to and from Wilmington. Because of its speed and strong construction, the Confederate navy purchased it in July 1864 and converted it into a commerce raider armed with rifled guns. Renamed the *Tallahassee*, she slipped out of New Inlet on the night of August 6, avoided two blockaders that fired on her in the dark, and cruised north along the Atlantic coast on the most destructive single raid by any Confederate ship. In the next nineteen days, she captured thirty-three fishing boats and merchant ships, burning twenty-six, bonding five, and releasing two. Naval ships hunted her from New York to Halifax and back to the Cape Fear River, which she reentered August 25 just ahead of pursuing blockaders.[36]

The *Tallahassee*'s exploits intensified Northern criticism of Phillips Lee and the Navy Department. Lee issued a flurry of new orders to tighten the cordon of ships off the two inlets of the Cape Fear River.[37] By September these measures were paying off. Major General William H. C. Whiting, Confederate commander of the District of North Carolina and Southern Virginia, lamented "the loss of seven of the very finest and fastest of the trading fleet" in September. "The difficulty of running the blockade has been lately very great. The receipt of our supplies is very precarious." One reason for the navy's success in catching these runners was that the *Tallahassee* had taken all the anthracite coal available in Wilmington for her cruise. Left with only bituminous coal, the runners spewed clouds of black smoke that revealed them to the blockade fleet.[38]

DESPITE ITS SHORTCOMINGS, the blockade was clearly hurting the Confederate war effort by 1863–64. In Britain and France, however, Commander James D. Bulloch was trying his best to do something about that by contracting for ironclad cruisers to break the blockade and for more commerce raiders to prey on American merchant ships at sea.

Once Bulloch had provided for construction of the raiders that became the *Florida* and the *Alabama*, he turned his attention to the project of getting ironclad rams built in Britain. In July 1862 he signed a contract (ostensibly as a private citizen, not a Confederate agent) with the same Laird firm that had built the *Alabama* for construction of two formidable ironclads. They were to displace 1,800 tons, carry six 9-inch guns in three turrets, and be fitted with a seven-foot iron spike on the prow for ramming enemy ships below the waterline. The number of turrets was subsequently reduced to two, with pivot guns added fore and aft. These two ships—one scheduled for completion in March 1863 and the other two months later—would have been capable of wreaking havoc on the Union blockade. Although the presence of turrets made the warlike purpose of these "Laird rams" hard to disguise, Bulloch hoped to evade the British Foreign Enlistment Act by not having the ships armed and equipped in Britain—the same subterfuge that had allowed the *Florida* and the *Alabama* to escape.[39]

Meanwhile, in November 1862 Matthew Fontaine Maury had arrived in Britain to join the already crowded field of Confederate agents looking to buy or build ships for the navy. A famed hydrographer who had charted the ocean currents and had also developed torpedoes for the Confederacy, Maury managed to purchase a steamer named the *Japan* suitable to take on guns and become a commerce raider. In March 1863 she was ready to sail from the obscure port of White Haven. Maury sent coded messages to various Confederate and British officers to rendezvous there. The British Foreign Office decided to stop the *Japan,* but the telegram to White Haven sat in an outbox in London on March 31 until the port's telegraph office had closed for the day. After midnight the *Japan* sailed, took on guns and ammunition off Ushant, and went to sea as the CSS *Georgia.* During the next six months, the *Georgia* destroyed nine prizes before limping into Cherbourg in broken-down condition, never to sail again as a raider.[40]

The embarrassment caused by the *Georgia*'s escape made the Foreign Office determined to prevent any more such occurrences. And in March 1863 the House of Commons had undertaken an investigation of the earlier cases of the *Florida* and the *Alabama.* Its report condemned the government for laxness in enforcement of British neutrality. At the same time, the American consul in Liverpool, Thomas H. Dudley, and Minister Charles Francis Adams flooded the Foreign Office with evidence of the Laird rams' Confederate provenance. They also pressed Foreign Secretary Lord Russell to seize the *Alexandra,* a small steamer just completed in Liverpool as another commerce raider.

In April the government did seize the *Alexandra.* The Court of Exchequer ruled the seizure illegal on the grounds that there was no proof of Confederate ownership or of the arming or fitting out of the vessel in England. That was technically true—it had been built for Fraser, Trenholm, and Company, a British firm that just happened to be the Confederacy's financial agent in London. The government appealed the Exchequer's decision and continued to detain the *Alexandra*. The officer slated to command that ship pronounced its Confederate epitaph. "It is clear that the English Government never intends to permit anything in the way of a man-of-war to leave its shores," he wrote. "I know Mr. Adams is accurately informed of the whereabouts and employment of every one of us, and that the Yankee spies are aided by the English Government detectives.... With the other vessels the same plan will be instituted as with the *A[lexandra]*. They will be exchequered, and thus put into a court where the Government has superior opportunities of instituting delays."[41]

Recognizing the impossibility of getting the two Laird rams out of England under these changed circumstances, Bulloch arranged for the dummy purchase of them by Bravay & Company of Paris acting as agents for "his Serene Highness the Pasha of Egypt." This subterfuge fooled no one. Thomas Dudley continued to amass evidence of their Confederate ownership, while Adams bombarded the Foreign Office with veiled threats of war if the rams were allowed to escape. On September 6, 1863, the British government detained the ships and subsequently bought them for the Royal Navy.[42]

In Glasgow, James North had signed a contract with the Thomson Works to build a 3,000-ton ironclad frigate for the Confederacy. Delays and cost overruns plagued the project. By the time the ship neared completion in late 1863, Bulloch acknowledged that "the chances of getting her out are absolutely nil." North finally arranged for the sale of the ship to Denmark for more than the Confederacy had paid for it.[43]

Bulloch shifted his efforts to the apparently more friendly environs of France. Napoleon III and the French Foreign Ministry seemed willing to look the other way from Confederate intrigues to secure warships. Using funds and credit from the bond issue floated for the Confederates in Europe by the banking firm of Emile Erlanger, Bulloch contracted with French shipbuilders for construction of four "corvettes" as commerce raiders and two ironclad rams in 1863. In June 1864, however, Bulloch was forced to report the "most remarkable and astounding circumstance that has yet occurred in reference to our operations in Europe." Napoleon had changed his mind and ordered the corvettes seized and sold to "bona fide" purchasers—that is, those not fronting for the Confederacy.[44]

Napoleon had evidently concluded that his delicate relations with the United States concerning French intervention in Mexico should not be complicated by allowing French-built warships to fall into Confederate hands. One of the two ironclads was sold to Sweden, which in turn sold it to Denmark, which was then at war with Prussia. Bulloch tried to arrange the sale of the second one also to Sweden to be then resold to the Confederacy. The U.S. legation in Paris discovered evidence of this fictitious sale and presented it to the French Foreign Ministry, which quashed the effort. The Confederate envoy in Paris, John Slidell, informed Secretary of State Judah Benjamin that "no further attempts to fit out ships of war in Europe should be made at present. . . . This is a most lame and impotent conclusion to all our efforts to create a Navy."[45]

These disappointments caused Bulloch "greater pain and regret than I ever considered it possible to feel."[46] But he did not give up completely. In both France and England, he purchased and contracted for the construction of a dozen or more fast steamers as blockade-runners for the Confederate Navy Department, using money from the forced sales of the Laird rams and James North's ironclad frigate.[47]

In the midst of all this activity came startling news from Cherbourg. On June 11, 1864, the CSS *Alabama* put in at this port for much-needed repairs. The USS *Kearsarge* arrived three days later to blockade the rebel raider. The *Alabama*'s captain, Raphael Semmes, decided to challenge the *Kearsarge*, which was commanded by Captain John A. Winslow, a shipmate of Semmes during the Mexican War. Semmes informed Flag Officer Samuel Barron, chief Confederate naval officer in Europe, that "I shall go out to engage her as soon as I can make the necessary preparations. . . . The combat will no doubt be contested and obstinate, but the two ships are so equally matched that I do not feel at liberty to decline it."[48]

The *Alabama*'s armament consisted of six 32-pounders, a 68-pound smoothbore, and a 7-inch (110-pounder) British-made Blakely rifle. The *Kearsarge* was armed with four 32-pounders, two 11-inch Dahlgrens, and a 30-pounder rifle. She also had chain cables strung over vital parts of her hull to protect the engines and boilers. The *Alabama* steamed out of Cherbourg on the morning of June 19 as thousands gathered to watch the duel. The two ships met six or seven miles outside the harbor. They steamed in circles while pounding each other with starboard broadsides and their pivot guns. The *Alabama* fired faster but wilder, logging 370 shots to the *Kearsarge*'s more disciplined and accurate 173. One of the *Alabama*'s 110-pound rifle shells smashed into the *Kearsarge*'s sternpost—a potentially fatal shot, but it failed to explode.

Indeed, many of the *Alabama*'s shells did not explode because the powder was old and defective. The *Kearsarge*'s more accurate fire began to tell. After sixty-five minutes, the *Alabama*, in a sinking condition, struck her

The duel between the USS *Kearsarge* (in the foreground) and the CSS *Alabama*,
June 19, 1864. (Courtesy of the Library of Congress)

colors and sent a gig to the *Kearsarge* to ask for help to rescue her men
from the water. Winslow sent his two undamaged boats and also signaled
the *Deerhound*, an English yacht that had been watching the action, to
come to their aid as well. The *Deerhound* picked up Semmes and most
of his officers along with two dozen sailors, a total of forty-one men, and
sailed for England, while an outraged Winslow, whose boats were res-
cuing other survivors, watched helplessly. "The Deerhound ran off with
prisoners which I could not believe any cur dog could have been guilty of
under the circumstances, since I did not open upon him," wrote Winslow
in disgust.[49] The *Kearsarge* rescued seventy-seven of the *Alabama*'s crew,
including twenty-one wounded; twenty-six were killed or drowned. On
the *Kearsarge* only three were wounded, of whom one died.[50] When the
news arrived across the Atlantic, it produced elation in the North and
mourning in the South for the loss of the famous raider, which had burned
fifty-five merchant ships, ransomed nine, and sunk the USS *Hatteras*.

The *Florida* was still in action, but not for much longer. She captured
and burned her last prize off the coast of Brazil on September 26, 1864,
then put into the port of Bahia on October 4. The next day, Commander
Napoleon Collins steered his USS *Wachusett* into the harbor. He had been
on the lookout for the *Florida*; now that he had found her, he did not

intend to let her go. Maintaining that the *Florida* had violated Brazil's neutrality by bringing three prizes into one of its ports the previous year, Collins considered her fair game. At 3:00 A.M. on October 7, while the *Florida*'s captain and several officers were ashore, the *Wachusett* got up steam and rammed the raider on the starboard quarter. Failing to sink her, the *Wachusett* took her in tow and steamed out of the harbor.

Brazilian guns fired on the *Wachusett* but failed to hit her, and Collins got away with his prize. He brought it back to Hampton Roads to a big welcome but also an international outcry about violation of Brazilian sovereignty. Brazil demanded the return of the *Florida* and an apology. She got the latter, but the *Florida* sank at Hampton Roads after an "accidental" collision with an army boat. Collins was tried by court-martial and dismissed from the navy in April 1865, but sixteen months later, Welles restored him to command, and he later retired as rear admiral.[51]

While the Union navy basked in the glow of success in the sinking of the *Alabama*, it suffered embarrassment over the fiasco of the *Casco* class of shallow-draft monitors. These twenty single-turret, two-gun ironclads were initially designed by John Ericsson to have a six-foot draft, but they were repeatedly altered by Chief Engineer Alban Stimers and by Fox, so that when the first one, the USS *Chimo*, was launched in May 1864, it seemed to have been designed by a committee—each member of which knew nothing of what the others were doing. Without turret and stores, the *Chimo* floated with only three inches of freeboard; if fully loaded and equipped, it would have sunk. The builders made modifications and finally launched another ship of this class, the USS *Tunxis*, which almost foundered in September 1864 before it could get back to the dock. Only eight of the class were completed by the time the war ended, and none of them ever went into action.[52]

The failure of these vessels contrasted sharply with the success of the turreted river monitors in the Mississippi valley designed by James B. Eads, which did good service, especially in the Battle of Mobile Bay in August 1864. With that victory and with the capture of Fort Fisher and Wilmington six months later, the Union navy made two of its most significant contributions to ultimate victory in the war.

chapter eleven

Damn the Torpedoes

ver since the spring of 1862, several high-ranking Union officers—Farragut, Grant, and Banks—had been proposing attacks on Mobile. But other priorities always took precedence: control of the Mississippi; the attack on Charleston, which tied up most of the ironclads; Banks's expeditions to Texas in the fall of 1863; and the Red River Campaign in the spring of 1864. In February 1864 Farragut champed at the bit once again. He wrote to his son, a cadet at West Point, that "if I had the permission I can tell you it would not be long before I would raise a row with the Rebels in Mobile."[1] With the abandonment of the Red River Campaign in May 1864 and the removal of Banks from field command, the stage was finally set for a combined operation against Mobile Bay with Farragut's fleet and soldiers from the Army of the Gulf, now commanded by Major General Edward Canby.

The Confedcrate defenses of Mobile Bay had been much improved by then. The South's only admiral, Franklin Buchanan, had taken command at Mobile in September 1862 and had built a naval squadron around the ironclad CSS *Tennessee* and two other uncompleted ironclads. Afflicted by shortages of everything from armor plate to experienced crew, Buchanan nevertheless put up a bold front that convinced Farragut in May 1864 that the Confederate fleet might come out and attack his blockaders. Buchanan did think of doing so, but he never managed to come out. Farragut was disappointed. "I . . . wish from the bottom of my heart that Buck would come out and try his hand upon us," Farragut wrote in June. "We are ready to-day to try anything that comes along, be it wood or iron. . . . Anything is preferable to lying on our oars." In July Farragut's squadron finally got ironclads of its own: the double-turreted river monitors USS *Chickasaw* and USS *Winnebago* arrived off Mobile Bay. Soon to follow were the sea-

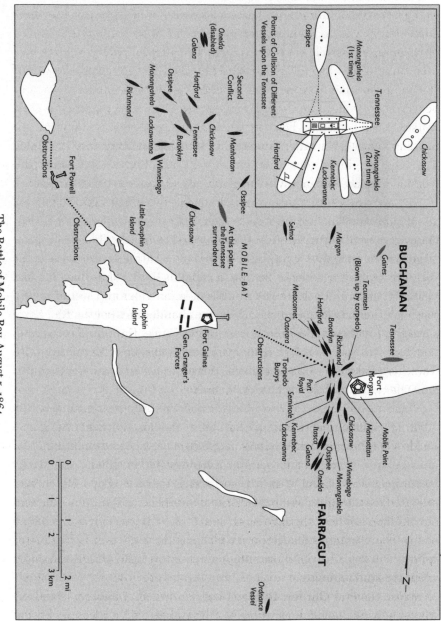

The Battle of Mobile Bay, August 5, 1864

going monitors USS *Manhattan* and USS *Tecumseh*, each carrying two 15-inch Dahlgrens in its turret.[2]

The *Manhattan* and the *Tecumseh* were the newest monitors, but they were just as uncomfortable as their predecessors. A lieutenant in the *Manhattan* on its way to Mobile complained in his diary on July 1: "The day has been so excessively hot that I am almost melted. . . . Everything is dirty, everything smells bad, everybody is demoralized. . . . A man who would stay in an ironclad from choice is a candidate for the insane asylum, and he who stays from compulsion is an object of pity." The next day was even worse. "I can't imagine how the firemen and coalheavers stand it," the lieutenant wrote. "The thermometer in the fireroom stands at 135° to 138°. The Chief Engineer goes in there semi-occasionally to superintend the work and comes out again wringing wet, [cursing] all the ironclad fleet."[3]

By the end of July, Farragut had his fleet assembled and his plan of attack laid out. The four ironclads would lead the way on the right flank closest to Fort Morgan, the main Confederate defensive work at the mouth of the bay with eighty-six guns. The fourteen wooden ships would go in on their left, lashed together in seven pairs with the larger ships to starboard to absorb the fire from Fort Morgan. The Confederates had laid some 189 torpedoes across the channel, leaving an opening of perhaps 200 yards closest to Fort Morgan for blockade-runners. It was through this opening that Farragut planned to take his ships. After running this gauntlet, he would engage the *Tennessee* and the three Confederate gunboats in the bay. The eighteen Union ships would outgun the four Confederate vessels 147 to 22.

The paymaster's clerk on the USS *Galena* described the preparation of his ship for the anticipated battle. The *Galena* had been rebuilt from the unsuccessful ironclad of 1862 into a three-masted wooden screw sloop. Its equipage was typical of the wooden vessels at Mobile Bay. "We are well prepared for the fight," wrote the clerk. "The topmasts & yards are all sent down, chain Cable on the side, sand bags all around the boilers, cable over engine room hatch, sails & Hammocks around the wheel to protect it, splinter netting all around the ships sides, all the railing & stanchions of whatever kind removed."[4]

Major General Gordon Granger had landed on Dauphin Island on August 3 with 1,500 troops to invest Fort Gaines, three miles across the entrance from Fort Morgan, while five gunboats attacked Fort Powell at Grant's Pass, a shallow channel another five miles to the northwest. On the morning of August 5, the main fleet weighed anchor and proceeded

the principal entrance to the bay. A southwest breeze blew the
toward Fort Morgan, which opened on the ships as they came
ange. The leading monitor, *Tecumseh*, struck a torpedo and went
...n in less than a minute, taking ninety men with her. The USS *Brooklyn* and her consort, the USS *Octorara*, hesitated at the line of torpedoes,
and the whole parade of ships came to a halt under the punishing guns of
Fort Morgan.

Next in line was Farragut's flagship, the USS *Hartford*. He ordered the
Hartford and her consort, the USS *Metacomet*, to pass the *Brooklyn*, and in
that moment a legend was born. "Damn the torpedoes! Full speed ahead!"
Farragut supposedly shouted. A marine on the *Hartford* standing near
Farragut later said that he had not heard any such cry.[5] Whether Farragut
said these words or not, he certainly did order the *Hartford* to go ahead.
Percival Drayton, the captain commanding the flagship, described these
events. When the *Tecumseh* went down, "our line was getting crowded
and very soon we should all have been huddled together, a splendid mark
for the enemy's guns," Drayton wrote. "The Admiral immediately gave the
word to go ahead with the Hartford and pass the Brooklyn. We sheered
to port, passing the Brooklyn on our starboard side. . . . We passed directly over the line of torpedoes planted by the enemy, and we could hear
the snapping of the submerged devilish contrivances as our hull drove
through the water—but it was neck or nothing, and that risk must be
taken. All the other vessels followed in our wake and providentially all
escaped."[6] The rapid and shifting currents in the channel off Fort Morgan
had evidently broken loose some of the torpedoes and caused others to
leak, dampening the powder.

As the *Hartford* forged ahead dueling with the guns of Fort Morgan,
Farragut climbed the rigging for a better view above the smoke and was
lashed to the shrouds by the boatswain. A rifleman on the *Tennessee* fired
several shots at him. If the shooter had managed to hit him, Farragut
would have been a martyred hero like Horatio Nelson at Trafalgar instead
of merely the hero of Mobile Bay.[7] Once past Fort Morgan and into the
bay, the *Hartford* and the *Brooklyn* engaged the *Tennessee*, which tried
to ram them in turn but was too slow. The *Hartford* cut loose its consort,
the *Metacomet*, which went after the Confederate gunboat *Selma* and captured her. One of the other Southern gunboats was sunk by gunfire from
several Union ships, and the third fled thirty miles up the bay to Mobile.

The *Tennessee* retreated temporarily under the protection of Fort Morgan, while the Union ships rendezvoused out of range to decide what to do

The capture of the CSS *Tennessee* by the Union fleet in Mobile Bay, August 5, 1864. The ship about to ram the Confederate ironclad is the USS *Hartford*, with Rear Admiral Farragut's pennant flying on the foremast. The double-turreted river monitors USS *Winnebago* (on left) and USS *Chickasaw*, plus the single-turreted USS *Manhattan*, combine with two other sloops of war to surround the crippled *Tennessee*. (From *Harper's Pictorial History of the Civil War*)

next. Suddenly the *Tennessee* came at them, alone, in a do-or-die mission to take on the whole fleet. Several of Farragut's ships rammed the *Tennessee* without much effect, while the monitor *Chickasaw* hung on her stern and peppered her with 11-inch bolts while the monitor *Manhattan* fired her 15-inch guns at point-blank range. With the *Tennessee*'s smokestack riddled, her steering chains cut, and Admiral Buchanan badly wounded (he would recover), the Confederate ironclad finally struck her colors.[8]

During the action, a twenty-year-old ensign in charge of a section of guns on the USS *Monongahela* described an adrenalin-fueled high as his ship rammed the *Tennessee* twice and poured broadsides into her. "I felt such pride and such a-good-all-over feeling that I wonder I did not go up in smoke," he wrote to his father two days later. "During the battle, the wildest enthusiasm prevailed. . . . I'll go through a dozen battles to feel that way again."[9]

Taking stock of the casualties after the fighting was over, however, sobered men quickly. The lieutenant from the *Manhattan* who boarded the *Tennessee* to take possession of her colors wrote that "her decks looked like a butcher shop. One man had been struck by the fragments of one of our 15-inch shot, and was cut into pieces so small that the largest would not have weighed 2 lbs."[10] The *Hartford* was the hardest hit of the Union ships (except the *Tecumseh*), with twenty-five killed and twenty-eight wounded. A marine-corps private on the *Hartford* reported that "our ship presented a fearful sight after the action. A shell burst in the steerage tearing everything to pieces. A great many shots came in on the berth deck. . . . Our cockpit looked more like a slaughter house than anything else. At night twenty-one dead bodies were sewed up in hammocks . . . and taken away for burial."[11]

In addition to the ninety men drowned in the *Tecumseh*, the Union fleet altogether suffered fifty-two killed and 170 wounded. Confederate casualties were only twelve killed and twenty wounded—plus 243 captured. By the standards of land battles in the Civil War, this was a small butcher's bill for such an important victory, which sealed off Mobile from blockade-runners.

But the victory was not complete until the Confederate forts surrendered. The *Chickasaw* poured a heavy fire into Fort Powell on the afternoon of August 5, and the Confederates evacuated it that night. The next day, the monitors pounded Fort Gaines while 3,000 Union troops moved against its land face. On August 8 it also surrendered. Fort Morgan proved a tougher prospect. For two weeks, Union warships—now including the repaired *Tennessee*—fired tons of metal into the fort while General Granger's troops moved inexorably forward and added army artillery to the mix. On August 23 Fort Morgan finally surrendered.

Ironically, this was the same day that President Lincoln penned his "blind memorandum" (so called because he asked his cabinet members to endorse it sight unseen) stating that because of Northern war weariness and the lack of important victories in 1864, he was likely to be defeated for reelection. News of the capture of all the forts at Mobile Bay reached the North a few days later. A neighbor of the Farraguts at Hastings-on-the-Hudson in New York wrote to the admiral that this news was "doing a great deal more than perhaps you dream of, in giving heart to the people here, and raising their confidence. Your victory has come at a most opportune moment, and will be attended by consequences of the most lasting and vital kind to the republic."[12] General Sherman's capture of Atlanta on September 2 further electrified the North. In combination with other Union successes during the fall of 1864, Mobile Bay and Atlanta helped assure Lincoln's reelection after all.

With complete control of Mobile Bay, Farragut advised against efforts to capture the city itself. "I consider an army of twenty or thirty thousand men necessary to take the city of Mobile and almost as many to hold it," Farragut told Welles. Even if captured, "I can not believe that Mobile will be anything but a constant trouble and source of anxiety to us."[13] For the time being, Farragut's advice prevailed. General Canby provided a small force to garrison the forts, and several gunboats maintained a presence in the bay. The following spring, a combined operation did capture Mobile—after the navy lost seven vessels to torpedoes there, including two monitors. The city of Mobile surrendered on April 12, 1865—three days after Appomattox.

FOLLOWING THE SUCCESS at Mobile Bay, Welles had a new mission for Farragut. After much backing and filling, both the army and the navy were finally in accord about a major effort to capture Fort Fisher and close down the port of Wilmington. Since the winter of 1862–63, Acting Rear Admiral Samuel Phillips Lee had come up with several proposals for a combined operation against Fort Caswell, Fort Fisher, or both. But General Halleck could never spare the troops for such a campaign, and Charleston continued to have priority for the ironclads and troops that were available. By September 1864, however, Grant seemed ready to provide enough troops to cooperate with the navy for an attack on Fort Fisher. Lee expected to command the naval part of this effort, but Welles thought he was not the man for the job. Lee "is true and loyal, careful, and circumspect almost to a fault," wrote Welles in his diary, "but while fearless he has not dash and impetuous daring."[14] Farragut had those qualities in abundance, so Welles selected him to take Lee's place as commander of the North Atlantic Squadron. Lee would switch with Farragut and take over the Gulf Squadron.

Welles's letter to Farragut, however, crossed with one from Farragut to him in which the officer stated that constant service in the Gulf and on the Mississippi had broken down his health, and he requested a respite. Welles granted the request and turned instead to David D. Porter to command the Fort Fisher attack. "It will cut Lee to the quick," Welles acknowledged, "but again personal considerations must yield to the public necessities." Welles ordered Porter east to take over the North Atlantic

Squadron and sent Lee west to replace Porter as head of the Mississippi Squadron.[15]

Porter took command with the energy and determination Welles expected of him. He assembled a large fleet for the attack. The army still dragged its feet, reluctant to take troops from the siege of Petersburg and Richmond. Grant finally detached 6,500 troops from the Army of the James and put twenty-nine-year-old Major General Godfrey Weitzel in command of them. The navy would land them north of the L-shaped Fort Fisher to attack its land face while the fleet bombarded the huge earthen fortification from the sea. Weitzel's superior, Benjamin Butler, decided to accompany the expedition and, in effect, to supersede Weitzel.

The controversial Butler also came up with a scheme to fill an old ship with gunpowder, take it as close to the sea face of Fort Fisher as possible, and explode it. He had read of the accidental explosion of two powder barges at the British port of Erith, which had leveled nearby buildings. If the explosion of a ship could do the same to Fort Fisher, it might dismount many guns and stun the garrison. Butler presented his idea to the Navy Department. Porter and Fox were enthusiastic. They consulted several engineers and weapons experts, some of whom expressed skepticism. But in a memorandum dated November 23, 1864, Porter summarized the majority consensus: "The explosion would injure the earthworks to a very great extent, render the guns unserviceable for a time, and probably affect the garrison to such a degree as to deprive them of the power to resist the passage of naval vessels by the forts and the carrying of these works by immediate assault."[16]

Porter supervised the loading of the USS *Louisiana* with more than 200 tons of powder and ordered Commander Alexander Rhind to take her as close to Fort Fisher at night as he could get, anchor her, and set the timers that were designed to explode the powder when the escape ship got far enough away. "Great risks have to be run, and there are chances that you may lose your life in this adventure," Porter told Rhind, "but the risk is worth the running, when the importance of the object is to be considered and the fame to be gained by this novel undertaking. . . . I expect more good to our cause from a success in this instance than from an advance of all the armies in the field."[17]

After delays because of bad weather, the *Louisiana* finally went in on the night of December 23–24. Rhind reported that he anchored her within 300 yards of the fort (it was actually 600 yards), set the timers, lit backup slow fuses in case the timers did not work, and departed on the escape ship USS *Wilderness*. As thousands of eyes in the fleet several miles away watched anxiously, the moment of 1:18 A.M. for the timed explosion went by, then more minutes until at 1:46 A.M. on December 24, an explosion lit the sky—actually four explosions, for the timers did not work and the various powder compartments exploded separately, with the first explosion probably blowing some of the unexploded powder overboard. The force of the blast was thus much diminished, and the current had also dragged the insecurely anchored ship farther from the fort. As a consequence, the explosion did almost no damage. Butler took some ridicule for this fizzle— but it was not a fair test of the scheme.[18]

This failure left it up to the naval bombardment to soften Fort Fisher for an assault by Butler's troops. Porter's fleet steamed into position by noon on December 24, with each of the thirty-seven ships (including five ironclads) assigned a particular area of the fort as a target. Nineteen smaller gunboats were held in reserve. For five hours, the fleet poured 10,000 rounds of shot and shell into the fort, setting barracks on fire, knocking out a few guns, and causing other damage. But many of the shells buried themselves in the sand and sod before exploding, doing little harm. The fort fired back sparingly, for Colonel William Lamb, its commander, knew that he had only 3,000 rounds for his forty-four guns and needed to save some for the infantry assault.

Butler's troops arrived that evening, the general furious with Porter for attacking before they got there. The two men had maintained ill will toward each other since feuding during the New Orleans campaign back in 1862. On Christmas morning, Porter renewed the bombardment, pouring another 10,000 rounds into the fort, while part of the fleet covered the landing of troops a few miles to the north. An advance unit reconnoitered the land face of the fort. Weitzel concluded that the defenses were too strong and insufficiently damaged by the shelling for an attack to succeed. Butler decided to call it off and reembark his troops.

Porter was furious. After only an hour and a half of firing on the first day, he had reported that the batteries in the fort "are nearly demolished. . . . We have set them on fire, blown some of them up, and all that is wanted now is the troops to land and go into them." After Butler withdrew, Porter could scarcely find words to denounce the army for "not attempting to take possession of the forts, which were so blown up, burst up, and torn up that the people inside had no intention of fighting any more. . . . It could have been taken on Christmas with 500 men, without losing a soldier. . . . I feel ashamed that men calling themselves soldiers should have left this

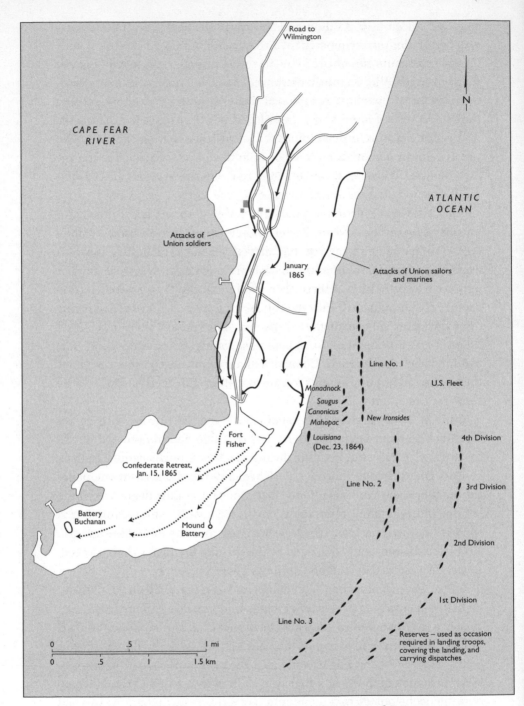

Road to
Wilmington

CAPE FEAR
RIVER

ATLANTIC
OCEAN

N

Attacks of
Union soldiers

January
1865

Attacks of Union sailors
and marines

Line No. 1

U.S. Fleet

Monadnock
Saugus
Canonicus
Mahopac

New Ironsides

Louisiana
(Dec. 23, 1864)

4th Division

Fort
Fisher

Confederate Retreat,
Jan. 15, 1865

Line No. 2

3rd Division

Battery
Buchanan

Mound
Battery

2nd Division

1st Division

Line No. 3

Reserves – used as occasion
required in landing troops,
covering the landing, and
carrying dispatches

0   .5   1 mi
0   .5   1   1.5 km

U.S. Naval Bombardment of Fort Fisher, December 1864 and January 1865 place so ingloriously; it was, however, nothing more than I expected when General Butler mixed himself up in this expedition."[19]

Porter's claims of damage to the fort were greatly exaggerated. Colonel Lamb reported that on the first day, the fleet's fire "tore up large quantities of the earthworks, splintered some of the revetments, but did not injure a single bombproof or endanger any magazine." On the second day, "a few more quarters were burned, more of the earthworks were displaced, but none seriously damaged, and [only] five guns were disabled by the enemy." The Cape Fear district commander, Major General William H. C. Whiting, noted that the naval fire was concentrated mainly on the sea face of the fort, leaving the land face and its nineteen guns relatively intact. Because of the smoke and dust, Union gunners used the fort's flag as an aiming point. Noticing this, Lamb had moved the flag back toward the Cape Fear River, causing many of the shots to fly harmlessly over the fort.[20]

Whatever the truth of these contrasting reports, Porter's claims resonated with Grant, who had been looking for an excuse to get rid of Butler. He told Porter to keep his fleet ready and he would send the troops back under a new commander. At Grant's behest, Lincoln relieved Butler, and Grant named Brigadier General Alfred Terry to command a beefed-up contingent of 8,000 troops for a renewed attack on Fort Fisher.

Porter and Terry hit it off, and the second attack was much better planned than the first. In an implicit admission that the shelling on December 24–25 did not inflict as much damage as he had reported, Porter issued special orders to his gunners to fire at the fort's gun emplacements, not the flagstaff.[21] On January 13 the fifty-nine vessels of the fleet opened a deadly barrage. The *New Ironsides* and four monitors moved to within a thousand yards and systematically knocked out all but one of the heavy guns on the land face, breached the stockade in many places, and plowed up the land mines and their wires in front of the stockade.

For two days, this shelling continued. On the evening of January 14, Porter and Terry planned for a coordinated assault at 3:00 P.M. the next day. Two thousand sailors and marines would land on the beach and attack the bastion at the corner of the land and sea face while 4,000 soldiers would charge the other end of the land face. A week earlier, Porter had written to Fox: "I don't believe in any body but my own good officers and men. I can do anything with them, and you need not be surprised to hear that the web-footers have gone into the forts. I will try it anyhow, and show the soldiers how to do it." He armed 1,600 sailors with cutlasses and

Part of the land face of Fort Fisher after the Union naval bombardment
and army assault on January 15, 1865. Note the dismounted gun next to
one of the traverses and the stockade splintered by Union shells.
(Courtesy of the Library of Congress)

revolvers and ordered them to "board the fort in a seaman-like way," while
the 400 marines "will form in the rear and cover the sailors."[22]

On January 15 the sailors and marines landed on the beach and rushed
the parapet. They were a few minutes ahead of the soldiers, so the fort's
defenders crowded the bastion and decimated the sailors with heavy fire.
Porter blamed the marines for the failure of this attack: "The marines
could have cleared the parapets by keeping up a steady fire, but they failed
to do so" and then broke and ran.[23]

But if the sailors did not succeed in their effort to "board the fort," their
attack diverted the defenders so that when the soldiers attacked the northwest corner, they got into the fort with minimal opposition. They then
fought their way from traverse to traverse against increasingly furious
opposition. In a striking example of coordination in that pre-radio age,

the warships (especially the *New Ironsides*) brought down fire on each of thirteen traverses just ahead of the Union troops as they cleared one after another. Fighting in the front lines with their men, Colonel Lamb and General Whiting were wounded (the latter mortally). Desperate resistance continued after dark, but the Union forces finally prevailed. At the cost of about a thousand casualties, they captured more than 2,000 Confederates and all of the fort's guns and equipment.[24]

It was the crowning achievement of combined operations in the war. Naval ships entered the Cape Fear River through New Inlet to shell Fort Caswell from the rear. The Confederates evacuated that fort and blew it up. Three blockade-runners, unaware that the river was in Union hands, were decoyed in by Lieutenant Commander William B. Cushing's operation of the range lights. "We are having a jolly time with the blockade runners, which come into our trap," Porter told Fox. "We almost kill ourselves laughing at their discomfiture, when they find they have set out their champagne to no purpose, and they say it is 'a damned Yankee trick.' . . . This is the greatest lark I ever was on."[25]

The capture of Fort Fisher closed the last blockade-running port except faraway Galveston. (A few runners had been getting into Charleston in recent months by using Maffitt's Channel close to Sullivan's Island. The last one got in just before the evacuation of Charleston on the night of February 17–18, 1865.) Confederate Vice President Alexander Stephens considered the loss of Fort Fisher "one of the greatest disasters which has befallen our Cause from the beginning of the war."[26] The advance up the river by Porter's gunboats and army troops to capture Wilmington on February 22 was something of an anticlimax. The same was true of the occupation of Charleston when the Confederates evacuated it on February 18 after Sherman's army cut the city's communications with the interior on their march through South Carolina. Clearly, the end of the Confederacy was in sight. But action continued on several fronts during the winter and spring of 1864–65.

While part of the James River Fleet was absent on the Fort Fisher campaign, Confederate Secretary of the Navy Stephen Mallory ordered Flag Officer John K. Mitchell, commander of the South's own James River Fleet, to attack Grant's supply base at City Point. Heavy rains in the James River's watershed raised the river level enough that Confederate ironclads had a chance to get over the Union obstructions at Trent's Reach twenty river miles above City Point. "I regard an attack upon the enemy . . . at City Point to cut off Grant's supplies, as a movement of the first importance,"

Mallory told Mitchell. "You have an opportunity . . . rarely presented to a naval officer and one which may lead to the most glorious results to your country."[27]

With three ironclads carrying four guns each—the *Virginia II*, the *Fredericksburg*, and the *Richmond*—and eight smaller consorts, including two torpedo boats, Mitchell came down on the night of January 23–24. The Union fleet of ten gunboats, including the double-turreted monitor USS *Onondaga* with its two 15-inch Dahlgrens and two 150-pound rifles, dropped several miles downriver to a spot where they had maneuvering room against the enemy—or so their commander, Captain William A. Parker, later explained. But to General Grant, it looked like a panicked retreat. Grant himself untypically pushed the panic button. He fired off telegrams to Welles and ordered naval vessels back up to the obstructions on his own authority, complaining that "Captain Parker . . . seems helpless." Two of the three Confederate ironclads ran aground at the obstructions; army artillery blasted them and the *Fredericksburg*, which had gotten through but was forced to return; the *Onondaga* came back upriver and added its big guns to the heavy fire that sank two Confederate gunboats and compelled the rest to retreat.[28]

In the end, this affair seemed like much ado about very little. But it resulted in the replacement of both fleet commanders. Lieutenant Commander Homer C. Black replaced Parker despite the latter's pleas for a second chance. He was later tried by court-martial and found guilty of "keeping out of danger to which he should have exposed himself." But the court recommended clemency in view of his thirty-three years of honorable service, "believing that he acted in this case from an error of judgment." Welles accepted the clemency recommendation, but Parker's career was essentially over.[29] On the Confederate side, Mallory replaced Mitchell with Raphael Semmes, recently promoted to admiral and without a command.[30] Semmes's principal accomplishment as chief of the James River Squadron was to order its ships blown up when the Confederates evacuated Richmond on the night of April 2–3, 1865.

SAMUEL PHILLIPS LEE was indeed "cut to the quick" by Welles's decision to replace him as commander of the North Atlantic Squadron just before the Fort Fisher campaign. But Lee went to work as head of the Mississippi Squadron with an earnest will. He was greeted soon after his arrival by a minor disaster at Johnsonville on the Tennessee River about thirty miles south of Fort Henry. Union forces in Tennessee had established a large supply depot at Johnsonville on the east bank connected by rail with Nashville. Many of the supplies for Sherman's army in Georgia came up the Tennessee River by convoy and were shipped by rail from Johnsonville to Nashville and then south to Sherman. On November 4, 1864, 3,500 Confederate cavalry under Nathan Bedford Forrest appeared on the west bank and opened fire on the eleven transports and eighteen barges unloading at Johnsonville under the protection of three tinclads. The latter exchanged fire with Forrest's guns for a half hour but could not maneuver in the narrow river full of sandbars and shoals. The crews set fire to the gunboats and other vessels, while Forrest's guns shifted their fire to the unloaded supplies and warehouses, destroying them as well. Forrest subsequently crossed the river and joined General John Bell Hood's army in its invasion of Tennessee.[31]

The autumnal rise in the Cumberland River made it navigable to Nashville in November 1864, so the Mississippi Squadron shifted its supply convoys to that river to support Major General George H. Thomas's confrontation with Hood. Phillips Lee sent two tinclads and the ironclads *Neosha* and *Carondelet* to Nashville, where they prevented Hood's left wing from crossing the Cumberland above the city and bolstered Thomas's crushing attack that routed Hood's army on December 15 and 16. As he pursued the retreating Confederates, Thomas asked Lee to send gunboats up the Tennessee River as far as they could go to find and destroy boats and pontoon bridges that the Confederates could use to cross the river. Hood was forced to cross above Muscle Shoals at a point the gunboats could not reach, but the navy's active patrolling of 175 miles of the river below Muscle Shoals cut off the retreat of hundreds of stragglers, contributing to the demoralization and disintegration of the Confederacy's second-largest army.[32]

Hood's invasion and retreat were the last gasp of Confederate forces in the West. After the fall of Richmond and the flight of the Confederate government, Secretary Welles sent an alert to naval forces to be on the lookout for Jefferson Davis and his cabinet, reported to be on their way to Texas to continue the war. Lee mobilized his entire squadron for intensive patrols of the Mississippi and its tributaries, hoping to catch the biggest prize of all.[33] But it was not to be; Davis got no farther than Irwinville, Georgia, where Union cavalry captured him on May 10, 1865.

NEWS OF THE END OF THE WAR traveled slowly across the oceans, where two Confederate warships were still in action, or hoping to be. Despite repeated failures to get ships out of Britain and France in 1863–64, James D. Bulloch kept trying. Secretary of the Navy Mallory wanted him to buy a fast ship to prey on the American whaling fleet. "The success of this measure would be such an effective blow upon a vital interest as would be felt throughout New England," wrote Mallory in late 1864. "I regard a vigorous attack upon this interest as one of the heaviest blows we can strike the enemy"—surely an example of wishful thinking.[34]

In September 1864 Bulloch managed to buy in England a large vessel involved in the Bombay trade, the *Sea King*. He took elaborate precautions to disguise Confederate ownership and sent her to Madeira with an English crew to meet the Confederate commander, James I. Waddell. Taking on her armament and supplies there and changing her name to CSS *Shenandoah*, she steamed southward around the Cape of Good Hope, into the Indian Ocean, and finally to the whaling grounds in the Bering Sea in June 1865. Unaware that the war had ended, the *Shenandoah* captured and destroyed thirty-two whaling ships (having burned six merchant vessels earlier) before finally learning in August 1865 from a British ship that the war was indeed over. Waddell sailed his ship all the way back to Liverpool and turned it over to the British government after circumnavigating the globe.[35]

Even more futile in forwarding the Confederate cause was the saga of the CSS *Stonewall*. This ship was none other than one of the ironclad rams Bulloch had originally contracted for in France that was sold to Denmark. Its delivery was delayed until the Danish war with Prussia over Schleswig-Holstein had ended, when Denmark sold it back to the French builder. Using a go-between and complicated codes to keep the process secret, Bulloch acquired the ship for the Confederacy in December 1864.

Flag Officer Samuel Barron had big ambitions for this vessel, signified by naming it the *Stonewall*. It was armed with a 300-pound rifle, two 70-pound rifles, and a lethal ram at the bow. Its first task would be to break the blockade of Wilmington, then to capture the California gold steamers between Aspinwall and New York, and finally "a dash at the New England ports and commerce might be made very destructive. . . . A few days cruising on the banks may inflict severe injury on the fisheries of the United States."[36]

The *Stonewall* headed for the South Atlantic coast in March 1865 but got only as far as the port of Ferrol in northwest Spain, where it put in because of bad weather and needed repairs. The USS *Niagara*, a large steam frigate armed with thirty-two heavy guns, arrived at Ferrol to maintain a watch on the *Stonewall* and was soon joined by the ten-gun USS *Sacra-*

mento. On March 24 Confederate Captain Thomas J. Page took the *Stonewall* to sea expecting to fight the two Union warships. Living down to his name, Captain Thomas T. Craven of the *Niagara* watched the *Stonewall* go without firing a shot. "The odds in her favor were too great," Craven explained to Welles, "to admit of the slightest hope of being able to inflict upon her even the most trifling injury, whereas, if we had gone out, the *Niagara* would undoubtedly have been easily and promptly destroyed. So thoroughly a one-sided combat I did not consider myself called to engage in."[37]

Captain Page could scarcely believe he had gotten away without a fight. "This will doubtless seem as inexplicable to you as it is to myself," he wrote to Bulloch. "To suppose that these two heavily armed men-of-war were afraid of the *Stonewall* is to me incredible."[38] Welles found it incredible, too, and when the *Niagara* returned to the United States, he ordered a court-martial trial of Craven, which convicted him and sentenced him to suspension for two years with leave pay. Welles was furious at this light sentence and set aside the verdict because he did not want it on record. Craven was subsequently promoted to rear admiral and retired in 1870.[39]

Meanwhile, the *Stonewall* made it to Havana, where Captain Page learned that the war was over. He sold the *Stonewall* to Spain, which in turn sold her to the United States. Thus ended the story of Confederate commerce raiders, except for the *Shenandoah*, which was still destroying whalers 5,000 miles from the now-defunct Confederacy.

Conclusion

The total military expenditures of the U.S. government in the Civil War were $6.8 billion. Of this amount, the navy cost $587 million—one-twelfth of the total.[1] By any measure of cost-effectiveness, the nation got more than its money's worth for this one-twelfth. In the war as a whole, some 671 warships of all types carrying 4,610 guns fought in the Union navy. All but 112 of these were steamers, and 71 of them were ironclads. The Navy Department purchased 418 ships during the war and contracted for the construction of 208 more. This buildup of what was by 1865 the world's largest navy was an extraordinary achievement, for which Gideon Welles deserves much of the credit. An excellent administrator who put in long hours at his desk, Welles endured recriminations by merchants whose ships and cargoes fell victims to the *Alabama* or other raiders and indictments by the press for the escape of runners through the blockade. Welles eschewed public responses to these accusations, confining his comments to his diary and retaining the full confidence of President Lincoln.[2]

In the asymmetrical war on the waters, the Confederacy could not come close to challenging Union domination. Yet Stephen Mallory and his associates built a technologically advanced naval force almost from scratch that built or bought some 121 warships carrying about 400 guns, including twenty ironclads, eight torpedo boats, and two submarines.[3] In conjunction with the Confederate Submarine Battery Service, the navy scattered thousands of "torpedoes" in waters frequented by enemy vessels. If the destruction or capture of 252 merchant ships and whalers by eleven Confederate commerce raiders and several privateers did not significantly hinder the Union war effort, it did weaken the blockade by diverting its ships into fruitless hunts for the raiders and cripple the merchant marine by causing 700 vessels to seek foreign registry.

Yet these achievements paled in comparison with the Union navy's contribution to Northern military operations. The navy won some of the most strategically important victories by itself (Hatteras Inlet, Port Royal, Fort Henry, New Orleans, Memphis) or as an essential partner in combined operations with the army (Fort Donelson, New Bern, Island No. 10, Vicksburg, Port Hudson, Mobile Bay, Fort Fisher).

Even the much-maligned blockade was a crucial factor in the war's outcome. It is true that five out of six blockade-runners got through—some 8,000 successful trips compared with about 1,500 runners captured or destroyed. Most of the successful runners, however, were intracoastal vessels early in the war from one Confederate port to another. The ratio for steamers bringing in goods from abroad or shipping cotton out was lower: of some 1,300 attempts, about 1,000 got through.[4] During the war, the Confederacy managed to export between half a million and a million bales of cotton through the blockade. At least 400,000 rifles were carried in by blockade-runners, 3 million pounds of lead, more than 2 million pounds of saltpeter (the main component of gunpowder), a million pairs of shoes, and thousands of tons of other supplies, consumer goods, and so on. Blockade-running was the "lifeline of the Confederacy," as the title of a book on the subject puts it.

Yet without a blockade, the Confederacy might well have prevailed. The most important statistic is not how many blockade-runners got through, but how many ships and how much cargo would have come in and gone out of Confederate ports if there had been no blockade. Twenty thousand vessels entered and cleared Southern ports in the four antebellum years, most of them with greater cargo capacity than the 8,000 successful runners of the war years. The half a million to a million bales of cotton exported from 1862 through the end of the war compared poorly with almost 10 million bales exported in the last three antebellum years. The blockade raised the price of cotton in Liverpool to several times its antebellum level, but the Southern sellers of this cotton derived little benefit from that increase, which was almost completely absorbed by skyrocketing transport and insurance costs caused by the blockade. "By toppling King Cotton from his regal perch and dealing the South a catastrophic economic loss," states a recent study, "the blockade won a victory that was surely as devastating as any particular battlefield defeat in fatally weakening the South's war-making capability."[5]

Shortages of everything that had to be imported through the blockade crippled the Confederate economy and helped cause ruinous inflation. Ironclad ships could not be completed, and worn-out rails could not be replaced because of an insufficiency of iron. An econometric analysis of the blockade found that it "raised transportation costs to high enough levels to *preclude* the shipment of many bulky products, especially railroad iron and machinery."[6] And the blockade's constriction of intracoastal trade placed a greater burden on the South's deteriorating railroads to the point of virtual breakdown in the war's later stages. The conclusion expressed by the earliest historian of the Confederate navy, who had himself served as a midshipman in that navy, seems about right. The blockade, he wrote, "shut the Confederacy out from the world, deprived it of supplies, weakened its military and naval strength."[7] And that may have been just enough to tip the balance to Union victory.

To say that the Union navy won the Civil War would state the case much too strongly. But it is accurate to say that the war could not have been won without the contributions of the navy.

Acknowledgments

As with my other books, I did most of the research for this one at Firestone Library of Princeton University, where I taught American history for forty-two years and have been an emeritus professor for eight years. The efficient interlibrary loan services of Firestone obtained several obscure but important nineteenth-century publications containing letters and diaries of naval personnel, and the Rare Books and Manuscripts Division at Firestone facilitated my research in the Blair-Lee Papers and the Roswell H. Lamson Papers. Next to Firestone, I have done more research over the past thirty-five years at the Huntington Library in San Marino, California, than anywhere else, and that remained true for this book, which has been enriched by the David Glasgow Farragut Papers and the David Dixon Porter Papers at the Huntington.

I have long been convinced that to understand—and write about—Civil War battles, one must go to the places where they occurred and walk the ground. The same is true for naval battles, where one can walk the ground of the forts and shore sites where fighting took place but must traverse the waters by ship and boat. I have been fortunate to traverse the Mississippi River from St. Louis to New Orleans, the Tennessee River from Paducah to Chattanooga, and the Cumberland River from Smithland to Nashville on the classic steamboat the *Delta Queen* as a guide on tours of the naval and land battles along these rivers. For these opportunities, I express my appreciation to the Alumni Council of Princeton University, the sponsor of the tours. I have also walked the grounds and, in some cases, sailed the waters of Charleston Harbor and its environs; Mobile Bay and the forts guarding its entrances; Fort Fisher and the Cape Fear River; the inland waterway and coastline from Wilmington, North Carolina, to Jacksonville, Florida; and Hampton Roads, where the famous clash between the CSS *Virginia* and USS *Monitor* took place. For these opportunities, I thank again the Princeton Alumni Council, HistoryAmerica Tours, and the Monitor Center of the Mariners' Museum in Newport News, Virginia.

At Newport News and at other places and times, I have learned a great deal from conversations with, lectures by, and the writings of Craig Symonds, one of America's preeminent Civil War and naval historians. Louis Masur offered helpful advice about sources and illustrations for this book. Gary Gallagher, T. Michael Parrish, and Howard Jones read the entire manuscript and offered many helpful suggestions for improvements. My wife, Patricia McPherson, served as an able research assistant for part of the project and, as always, provided a loving and warm environment as my research and writing went forward. Her coeditorship of the letters of Union naval officer Roswell H. Lamson quickened my interest in the naval history of the Civil War. And my three grandchildren—Gwynne, James, and Annie—helped provide the welcome diversions and distractions so necessary to keep an author's mind sane and healthy. For her skills in distraction, this book is dedicated to Annie.

Notes

ABBREVIATIONS

BLP   Blair and Lee Family Papers, 1764–1946, Princeton University Library, Princeton, N.J.

DFP   David G. Farragut Papers, The Huntington Library, San Marino, Calif.

DPP   David D. Porter Papers, The Huntington Library, San Marino, Calif.

OR   *War of the Rebellion: A Compilation of the Official Records of the Union and Confederate Armies,* 70 volumes in 128 serials

ORN   *Official Records of the Union and Confederate Navies,* 30 volumes in two series. Series I consists of twenty-seven volumes and Series II of three volumes. Citations indicate series, volume, and page numbers.

INTRODUCTION

1. Charles Steedman to Sally Steedman, September 30, 1864, in Steedman, *Memoir and Correspondence,* 385.

2. Grant, *Personal Memoirs of U. S. Grant,* 1:574.

3. Lincoln, *Collected Works of Lincoln,* 6:409–10.

CHAPTER 1

1. Du Pont to Foote, January 25, 1861, in Hoppin, *Life of Foote,* 148. For the orders, correspondence, and testimony concerning Armstrong, see *ORN,* I, 4:3–55.

2. Farragut, *Life . . . and Letters,* 203.

3. Martin, *Damn the Torpedoes,* 153–54; Duffy, *Lincoln's Admiral,* 40–41; Farragut to Richard P. Ashe, April 22, 1861, DFP.

4. Drayton to Lydig Hoyt, May 19 and November 30, 1861, in Drayton, *Naval Letters,* 3, 10.

5. Du Pont, *Civil War Letters,* 1:45n; Hoppin, *Life of Foote,* 148.

6. Symonds, *Confederate Admiral,* 1–3.

7. Welles, *Diary,* 1:16–19; Niven, *Welles,* 329–31; Symonds, *Lincoln and His Admirals,* 20–22.

8. *ORN,* I, 4:63, 66, 71, 74, 77, 90, 101–11, 115.

9. Fox had first suggested this plan a month before Lincoln was inaugurated. Fox to Virginia Fox, February 7, 1861, in Fox, *Confidential Correspondence,* 1:6; Fox to Winfield Scott, February 8, 1861, and Fox to Montgomery Blair, February 23, 1861, *ORN,* I, 4:223–25.

10. *ORN,* I, 4:109.

11. Ibid., 234.

12. Ibid., 111–12, 236–41; Welles, *Diary,* 1:22–26.

13. Lincoln, *Collected Works of Lincoln*, 4:323.

14. Fox's official report to Secretary of War Simon Cameron, April 19, 1861, is in *ORN*, I, 4:244–45; Lincoln to Fox, May 1, 1861, *ORN*, I, 4:251; also in Lincoln, *Collected Works of Lincoln*, 4:350–51.

15. Lincoln to Welles, May 8, 1861, in Lincoln, *Collected Works of Lincoln*, 4:363.

16. Farragut quoted in Welles, *Diary*, 2:233, entry of January 30, 1865; Du Pont to Sophie Du Pont, June 30, 1862, in Du Pont, *Civil War Letters*, 2:139. See also Hoogenboom, *Gustavus Vasa Fox*.

17. *ORN*, II, 3:97; Lincoln, *Collected Works of Lincoln*, 4:338–39.

18. Lord Lyons to Lord Russell, May 23 and August 12, 1861, in Barnes and Barnes, *American Civil War through British Eyes*, 1:94, 155. See also Stuart Anderson, "Blockade versus Closing Confederate Ports."

19. *ORN*, I, 1:818–19.

20. McPherson, *The Negro's Civil War*, 153–54; Quarles, *The Negro in the Civil War*, 32–34 (quotation on 33–34).

21. *ORN*, II, 3:104.

22. Randall, *Constitutional Problems*, 92–94; *Civil War Naval Chronology*, 6:256, 281–82.

23. Semmes's daily journal in the CSS *Sumter*, *ORN*, I, 1:708, 719, entries of September 10 and November 10, 1861.

24. Ibid., 695, entry of July 3, 1861.

25. Ibid., 621–23, 639, 663–64, 676, 680, 683–86, 715–16; Summersell, *Cruise of the Sumter*.

26. For examples, see *ORN*, I, 1:8–19, 21–31.

27. Welles to Palmer, December 13, 1861, ibid., 240.

28. Edward W. Bacon to George Bacon, October 31, 1861, in Edward W. Bacon, *Double Duty in the Civil War*, 23; Porter to Welles, August 13 and 24, 1861, *ORN*, I, 1:65, 91–92.

29. Lincoln, *Collected Works of Lincoln*, 4:346–47.

30. *ORN*, I, 1:xv–xvi; "Report of the Secretary of the Navy to a Special Session of Congress, July 4, 1861," in Moore, *Rebellion Record*, 2:235.

31. Symonds, *Lincoln and His Admirals*, 57–59; "Report of the Secretary of the Navy," December 3, 1861, 13; Lord Lyons to Lord Russell, May 2, 1861, in Barnes and Barnes, *American Civil War through British Eyes*, 1:69.

32. "Report of the Secretary of the Navy to a Special Session of Congress, July 4, 1861," in Moore, *Rebellion Record*, 2:238; Welles to Commodore Samuel L. Breese, April 17, 1861, *ORN*, I, 4:342; Lincoln, *Collected Works of Lincoln*, 4:354; "Report of the Secretary of the Navy," December 1, 1862, 43; "Report of the Secretary of the Navy," December 4, 1865, xiii; Miller, *Photographic History of the Civil War*, 10:146; Current, *Encyclopedia of the Confederacy*, 3:1123, 1131; Still, *Confederate Navy*, 135.

33. Bennett, *Union Jacks*, 1–12; Still, *Confederate Navy*, 135.

34. *ORN*, I, 4:391; Basoco, "British View of the Union Navy," 40.

35. Luraghi, *History of the Confederate Navy*, chaps. 1–4; Underwood, *Mallory*.

36. *ORN*, I, 4:274.

37. Ibid., 275–76.

38. Ibid., 277–78, 281, 288–91, 293–96, 300–302, 306; "Report of the Secretary of the Navy to a Special Session of Congress, July 4, 1861," in Moore, *Rebellion Record*, 2:236; Welles, *Diary*, 1:43–47; Mallory's Report to Jefferson Davis, July 18, 1861, *ORN*, II, 2:77.

39. Brooke to Elizabeth Brooke, August 29, 1861, in Brooke, *Ironclads and Big Guns*, 34.

CHAPTER 2

1. Lyons to Lord John Russell, May 2, 1861, in Barnes and Barnes, *American Civil War through British Eyes*, 1:72.

2. *ORN*, I, 6:5.

3. "Report of the Secretary of the Navy," December 3, 1861, 6; Boyer, *Naval Surgeon*, xix. For different figures, see Surdam, *Northern Naval Superiority*, 4–5.

4. John Sanford Barnes, "The Early Blockade and the Capture of the Hatteras Ports," 66.

5. Officer quoted in an undated letter in August 1861 in William Sewell to Gideon Welles, October 19, 1861, *ORN*, I, 12:222.

6. Wise, *Lifeline of the Confederacy*, 27.

7. W. Beversham Thompson to Warren Winslow, July 25, 1861, *ORN*, I, 6:713.

8. Lamson to Flora Lamson, August 27–29, 1861, in Lamson, *Lamson of the Gettysburg*, 32–36 (quotation on 35). For official reports of this action, see *ORN*, I, 6:119–45.

9. Brigadier General William E. Nelson to Gustavus Fox, September 25, 1861, in Fox, *Confidential Correspondence*, 1:380. For the seizure of blockade-runners, see Commander Stephen C. Rowan to Welles, September 10, 11, 13, 1861, *ORN*, I, 6:195–97, 205.

10. The best summary of the board's activities and reports is Weddle, "The Blockade Board of 1861," 123–42. See also Weddle, *Lincoln's Tragic Admiral*, 106–24. The board's "Memoirs" are in various places in the *ORN*; see especially the first report, July 5, 1861, in *ORN*, I, 12:195–98. See also Charles H. Davis to his wife, May 22, 30 and June 12, 1861, in Charles H. Davis, *Life of Charles Henry Davis*, 121, 122, 124; Gustavus Fox to Du Pont, May 22, 1861, and Du Pont to Alexander Bache, May 30, 1861, in Du Pont, *Civil War Letters*, 1:71, 73.

11. Welles, *Diary*, 1:76, entry of August 10, 1862. For the removal of Mervine from command, see Fox to Mervine, September 6, 1861, *ORN*, I, 16:660.

12. Welles to Stringham, September 14, 1861; Stringham to Welles, September 16, 1861; and Welles to Stringham, September 18, 1861, in *ORN*, I, 6:210–11, 216, 231–32.

13. Du Pont to Sophie Du Pont, September 18, 1861, in Du Pont, *Civil War Letters*, 1:150–51 and 156n. See also Du Pont to Henry Winter Davis, September 4, 1861, in ibid., 143. For the order dividing the Atlantic Squadron, see *ORN*, I, 6:193.

14. Memoir of Blockade Board, August 19, 1861, *ORN*, I, 16:629; Welles to Mervine, August 23, 1861, ibid., 644.

15. Melancton Smith to William McKean, September 22, 1861, David W. Twiggs to Leroy P. Walker, September 17, 1861, *ORN*, I, 16:677, 679.

16. Welles to Farragut, January 9, 1862, *ORN*, I, 18:5; Welles, *Diary*, 2:134–35, entry of September 22, 1864.

17. *ORN*, I, 12:195–98, 214, 259–61; Du Pont to Sophie Du Pont, October 17, 21, 24, 1861, in Du Pont, *Civil War Letters*, 1:170–71, 179, 183.

18. Lincoln, *Collected Works of Lincoln*, 4:548; *ORN*, I, 12:215.

19. *ORN*, I, 12:220.

20. John Sanford Barnes, "The Battle of Port Royal," 375, journal entry of October 8, 1861; Drayton to Lydig M. Hoyt, October 25, 1861, in Drayton, *Naval Letters*, 7–8.

21. Davis to his wife, October 28 [29] and 31, 1861, in Charles H. Davis, *Life of Charles Henry Davis*, 172, 174–75; John Sanford Barnes, "The Battle of Port Royal," 378–79, journal entry of October 30, 1861.

22. Roswell H. Lamson to Flora Lamson, November 4, 1861, in Lamson, *Lamson of the Gettysburg*, 39.

23. See the reports in *ORN*, I, 12:232–53, and Charles H. Davis to his wife, journal letter written over several days in early November 1861, in Charles H. Davis, *Life of Charles Henry Davis*, 175–78.

24. John Sanford Barnes, "The Battle of Port Royal," 384, journal entry of November 5, 1861; Lamson to Flora Lamson, November 6, 1861, in Lamson, *Lamson of the Gettysburg*, 41.

25. Roswell Lamson to Flora Lamson, November 8, 1861, in Lamson, *Lamson of the Gettysburg*, 42–43; John Sanford Barnes, "The Battle of Port Royal," 388–91, diary entry of November 9, 1861.

26. Du Pont to Dahlgren, November ?, 1861, in Dahlgren, *Memoir of John A. Dahlgren*, 29. For official reports and communications concerning the Port Royal operation, see *ORN*, I, 12:269–95. See also Du Pont to Sophie Du Pont, November 7, 1861, and May 5, 1862, in Du Pont, *Civil War Letters*, 1:222–25, 2:33.

27. Drayton to Lydig Hoyt, November 30, 1861, in Drayton, *Naval Letters*, 8–9.

28. Lee to Mildred Lee, November 15, 1861, in Robert E. Lee Jr., *Recollections and Letters of General Robert E. Lee*, 55; Merrill, *The Rebel Shore*, 44.

29. Du Pont to Morgan, December 24, 1861, Du Pont to Sophie Du Pont, December 12, 1861, in Du Pont, *Civil War Letters*, 1:285, 275.

30. Du Pont to Welles, December 24, 1861, *ORN*, I, 12:427.

31. First quotation in John Sanford Barnes, "Battle of Port Royal Ferry," 134–35; Lee to General James M. Trapier, February 19, 24, in Marchand, *Charleston Blockade*, 120–21.

32. Du Pont to Sophie Du Pont, March 4, 1862, in Du Pont, *Civil War Letters*, 1:351–55; Roswell Lamson to Flora Lamson, March 4, 1862, in Lamson, *Lamson of the Gettysburg*, 53–57.

33. *ORN*, I, 12:571–620.

34. Lamson, *Lamson of the Gettysburg*, 58–59; Lieutenant Thomas H. Stevens to Du Pont, March 28, 1862, *ORN*, I, 12:638; Silverstone, *Warships of Civil War Navies*, 144.

35. Wilkes to Welles, November 15, 16, 1861, *ORN*, I, 1:124–31; Symonds, *Lincoln and His Admirals*, 75–78.

36. Welles to Wilkes, November 30, 1861, *ORN*, I, 1:148; Symonds, *Lincoln and His Admirals*, 80–82.

37. Quoted in Symonds, *Lincoln and His Admirals*, 82.

38. Russell quoted in Symonds, *Lincoln and His Admirals*, 86. For the most recent accounts of the much-studied "Trent Affair," see Howard Jones, *Blue and Gray Diplomacy*, 83–111, and Foreman, *A World on Fire*, 172–98.

39. Symonds, *Lincoln and His Admirals*, 92–94; Donald, *Lincoln*, 323; Seward to Lord Lyons, December 26, 1861, *ORN*, I, 1:177–87.

40. Adams to Charles Francis Adams Jr., January 10, 1862, in Adams, Adams, and Adams, *A Cycle of Adams Letters*, 1:99.

41. Ephraim Douglass Adams, *Great Britain and the American Civil War*, 1:140.

42. *ORN*, II, 3:271, 299, 331; Jefferson Davis, *Jefferson Davis, Constitutionalist*, 5:401, 403.

43. Du Pont to Sophie Du Pont, January 4, 1862, in Du Pont, *Civil War Letters*, 1:308.

44. Du Pont to Welles, December 4, 1861, *ORN*, I, 12:380–81; Du Pont to Senator James W. Grimes, December 2, 1861, in Du Pont, *Civil War Letters*, 1:268.

45. Du Pont to Gustavus Fox, November 11, December 16, 1861, in Fox, *Confidential Correspondence*, 1:69, 81; Du Pont to Sophie Du Pont, May 1, 1862, in Du Pont, *Civil War Letters*, 2:23. See also Louis Goldsborough to Welles, October 3 and 4, 1861, *ORN*, I, 6:281–82, 286.

46. Du Pont to Sophie Du Pont, December 5, 1861, in Du Pont, *Civil War Letters*, 1:272 and 273n; Davis to his wife, December 2, 1861, in Charles H. Davis, *Life of Charles Henry Davis*, 193.

47. Lee to Judah P. Benjamin, December 20, 1861, *ORN*, I, 12:423.

48. Du Pont to Charles Irenée Du Pont, February 20, 1862, in Du Pont, *Civil War Letters*, 1:335–36; Du Pont to Fox, December 16, 1861, in Fox, *Confidential Correspondence*, 1:79.

49. Du Pont to Commander Enoch Parrott, February 3, 1862, *ORN*, I, 12:534.

50. Lyons to Russell, November 29, 1861, in Ephraim Douglass Adams, *Great Britain and the American Civil War*, 1:254; *ORN*, II, 3:340.

51. *Parliamentary Papers*, 1862, vol. 62, *North America*, no. 8, "Papers Relating to the Blockade of the Ports of the Confederate States," 119–20, in Du Pont, *Civil War Letters*, 1:326n. Italics added.

CHAPTER 3

1. Goldsborough to Welles, November 11, 1861, January 3, 1862, and Burnside to Goldsborough, December 12, 1861, in *ORN*, I, 6:421–22, 472–73, 496.

2. Goldsborough to Welles, January 23, 29, 1862, *ORN*, I, 6:526–28, 536–37; Goldsborough to Gustavus Fox, January 23, 30, 1862, in Fox, *Confidential Correspondence*, 1:231–33, 234–36.

3. Goldsborough to Gustavus Fox, February 9, 1862, in Fox, *Confidential Correspondence*, 1:236–40.

4. *ORN*, I, 6:605–24. For a succinct account of this campaign, see Browning, *From Cape Charles to Cape Fear*, 17–30.

5. Rowan to Goldsborough, March 20, 1862, *ORN*, I, 7:110–12.

6. Commander Samuel Lockwood to Goldsborough, April 27, 1862, ibid., 278–80.

7. Acting Rear Admiral Samuel Phillips Lee to Major General John G. Foster, April 17, 1863, *ORN*, I, 9:688–89.

8. *ORN*, I, 16:596, 598, 648, 689–90.

9. Ibid., 627.

10. *ORN*, II, 2:41–43.

11. *ORN*, I, 16:703, 705–12, 721–22, 748; Acting Master Edward F. Devens to Fox, October 28, 1861, in Fox, *Confidential Correspondence*, 1:391–96.

12. Welles to Farragut, January 9, 20, 1862, and Welles to Commander David Dixon Porter, November 18, 1861, in *ORN*, I, 18:1, 5, 8. Welles to Farragut, February 10, 1862, marked "confidential," DFP.

13. Porter to Fox, March 28, in Fox, *Confidential Correspondence*, 2:89–91. For Porter's career and personality, see Hearn, *Admiral David Dixon Porter*.

14. Farragut to Virginia Farragut, March 7 and April 11, 1862, in Farragut, *Life of Farragut*, 217–18.

15. *ORN*, I, 18:39, 57, 64–65, 67–68, 88, 109, 361.

16. Lee to Elizabeth Blair Lee, March 28, April 5, 1862, BLP.

17. *ORN*, I, 18:8.

18. Grimes to Fox, February 3, 1862, in Fox, *Confidential Correspondence*, 1:414–15.

19. Judah P. Benjamin to Lovell, January 19, 1862, *ORN*, I, 17:160–61; Lovell to George W. Randolph, April 15, 1862, *ORN*, II, 1:695–96.

20. *ORN*, II, 1:525, 687–88, 691.

21. Holton, *Cruise of the* Hartford, 10, diary entry of April 20, 1862.

22. Duncan's report in *ORN*, I, 18:266; Lee to Elizabeth Blair Lee, April 29, 1862, BLP.

23. Dufour, *The Night the War Was Lost*, 248–50; abstract of the log of USS *Itasca*, *ORN*, I, 18:812–13; Lieutenant George Bacon to Lavinia Bacon, May 1, 1862, in George B. Bacon, "Civil War Letters of George Bacon," 272–73.

24. Foltz, *Surgeon of the Seas*, 219–20, undated diary entry patched together from notes written at the time, probably April 21 or 22, 1862.

25. S. P. Lee to E. B. Lee, April 17, 1862, BLP. See also Lee to Lee, April 9, 1862, BLP.

26. Lieutenant Jonathan M. Wainwright to David D. Porter, June 1, 1862, *ORN*, I, 18:143–44.

27. Francis A. Roe diary, quoted in Dufour, *The Night the War Was Lost*, 262.

28. Bailey to Farragut, April 25, 1862, *ORN*, I, 18:171; Bailey to Montgomery Blair, May 8, 1862, BLP.

29. Log of USS *Oneida*, BLP; Theodorus Bailey to Montgomery Blair, May 8, 1862, BLP; Porter to Fox, June 2, 1862, in Fox, *Confidential Correspondence*, 1:114.

30. Lieutenant George H. Perkins to his family, April 27, 1862, *Letters of Perkins*, 119; Dufour, *The Night the War Was Lost*, 283.

31. Francis Roe, Diary, *ORN*, I, 18:768, entry of April 28, 1862.

32. Dufour, *The Night the War Was Lost*, 269–70.

33. Foltz, *Surgeon of the Seas*, 224, diary notes made on April 24.

34. Farragut to Porter, April 24, 1862, *ORN*, I, 18:142; Dufour, *The Night the War Was Lost*, 271–73.

35. Foltz, *Surgeon of the Seas*, 224.

36. Lieutenant George Bacon to Lavinia Bacon, April 25, 1862, in George B. Bacon, "Civil War Letters of George Bacon," 273–74.

37. Farragut to Virginia Farragut, April 30, 1862, in Farragut, *Life of Farragut*, 262; Dufour, *The Night the War Was Lost*, 274–75.

38. Edward Bacon to Leonard Bacon, May 5, 1862, in Edward W. Bacon, *Double Duty in the Civil War*, 39; Thomas Craven to his wife, May 16, 1862, *ORN*, II, 1:198.

39. Lovell to Adjutant General Samuel Cooper, May 22, 1862, *ORN*, I, 18:255.

40. Farragut to Welles, May 6, 1862, *ORN*, I, 18:770; Log of USS *Oneida* for April 25, 1862, BLP; Foltz, *Surgeon of the Seas*, 231, diary entry of April 26, 1862.

41. Dufour, *The Night the War Was Lost*, 290.

42. Morgan, *Civil War Diary of Sarah Morgan*, 48–49, entry of April 26, 1862.

43. *ORN*, I, 18:740–41.

44. Farragut to Virginia Farragut, April 25, 1862, DFP; Foltz, *Surgeon of the Seas*, 232, diary entry of April 25, 1862.

45. *ORN*, I, 18:741.

46. George Washington Cable, "New Orleans Before the Capture," in *Battles and Leaders*, 2:20.

47. Foltz, *Surgeon of the Seas*, 234.

48. Porter to Fox, May 24, 1862, in Fox, *Confidential Correspondence*, 2:107; Dufour, *The Night the War Was Lost*.

49. *New Orleans Delta*, April 26, 1862; *Norfolk Day Book*, April 29, 1862; *Raleigh State Journal*, May 3, 1862; *Richmond Enquirer*, April 29, 1862, quoted in McPherson, *Crossroads of Freedom*, 26; Ruffin, *Diary of Edmund Ruffin*, 3:291, entry of April 30, 1862.

50. E. B. Lee to S. P. Lee, May 7, 1862, BLP.

51. Henry Adams to Charles Francis Adams Jr., May 16, 1862, in Adams, Adams, and Adams, *A Cycle of Adams Letters*, 1:145; James Mason to Jefferson Davis, May 16, 1862, in Mason, *Public Life and Diplomatic Correspondence*, 276.

52. William M. Dayton to William H. Seward, April 17, 1862, in *Papers Relating to the Foreign Relations of the United States, 1862*, 1:333.

53. Welles to Farragut, January 20, 1862, *ORN*, I, 18:8.

54. Farragut to Welles, April 29, 1862, and Farragut to Fox, April 25 [29], 1862, in ibid., 148, 155.

55. Farragut to Welles, May 6, 1862, ibid., 159; Stone, *Brokenburn*, 100–101, diary entry of May 9, 1862.

56. James L. Autrey to S. P. Lee, May 18, 1862, *ORN*, I, 18:492. See also Lee to Farragut, May 18, 1862, and Lee to Elizabeth Blair Lee, June 10, 1862, BLP.

57. Fox to Farragut, May 12, 16, 1862, *ORN*, I, 18:245, 498; Fox to Farragut, May 17, in Fox, *Confidential Correspondence*, 1:314–15.

58. Farragut to Virginia Farragut, June 2, June ?, 1862, in Farragut, *Life of Farragut*, 269–71; Farragut to Welles, May 30, 1862, *ORN*, I, 18:519–21.

59. Farragut to Bailey, June 11, 1862, *ORN*, I, 18:551.

1. Welles to Simon Cameron, May 14, 1861, *ORN*, I, 22:277. The best study of the war on the western rivers is still Milligan, *Gunboats down the Mississippi*.

2. Welles to Joseph J. Davis, August 12, 1861, *ORN*, I, 22:299.

3. Welles to Rodgers, June 12, 1861, ibid., 284–85.

4. Foote to his wife, December 17, 1861, in Hoppin, *Life of Foote*, 189. For a modern biography, see Tucker, *Foote*.

5. Foote to Fox, January 27, 1862, Fox, *Confidential Correspondence*, 2:33.

6. Foote to Fox, March 5, 1862, ibid., 39.

7. Polk to Judah Benjamin, January 17, 1862, *ORN*, I, 22:815.

8. Fox to Foote, December 26, 1861, Henry A. Wise to Foote (quoting Lincoln), January 31, 1862, ibid., 472, 527.

9. Phelps to Foote, October 18 and 28, November 19, December 10, 1861, January 7, 1862; Halleck to Foote, January 17, 1862; Lieutenant James Shirk to Foote, January 24, 1862; and Foote to Halleck, January 28, 1862, in *ORN*, I, 22:371, 379–80, 435, 457–58, 486, 505, 521, 524.

10. For official correspondence and reports of both Union and Confederate officers, see ibid., 528–69.

11. Phelps's report to Foote, February 10, 1862, in Hoppin, *Life of Foote*, 213–14.

12. Henry A. Wise to Foote, February 10, 1862, *ORN*, I, 22:549.

13. *OR*, I, 7:325.

14. "A Confederate Private at Fort Donelson," 477–78.

15. Foote to his wife, February 16, 1862, in Hoppin, *Life of Foote*, 228.

16. Official reports and related documentation in *ORN*, I, 22:570–616.

17. Polk to Jefferson Davis, March 11, 1862, and Lieutenant Samuel Averett to Flag Officer George N. Hollins, March 26, 1862, in ibid., 654–55, 746.

18. Captain Joseph Smith to Foote, March 1, 1862, in Hoppin, *Life of Foote*, 239.

19. Foote to his wife, March 12, 19, 1862, and Foote to Welles, March 12, 1862, in Hoppin, *Life of Foote*, 262, 266, 269.

20. Foote to Welles, March 20, 1862, *ORN*, I, 22:697.

21. Pope to Henry W. Halleck, March 27, 1862, ibid., 703.

22. Foote to Halleck, April 6, 1862, ibid., 712.

23. Pope to Halleck, April 9, 1862, ibid., 724–25.

24. Grant to Nathaniel H. McLean, April 9, 1862, ibid., 766; Beauregard quoted in *Civil War Naval Chronology*, 2:45. See also *ORN*, I, 22:643–44, 647, 666–67, 762.

25. Milligan, *Gunboats down the Mississippi*, 65; Browne and Browne, *From the Fresh-Water Navy*, 71n.

26. Hiram T. Holt to Carrie Holt, April 22, 29, 1862, in Holt, "A Confederate Sergeant's Report to His Wife," 247–48, 250.

27. Foote to Welles, April 27, 1862, marked "unofficial," in Hoppin, *Life of Foote*, 306.

28. Davis to his wife, May 9, 1862, in Charles H. Davis, *Life of Charles Henry Davis*, 222–23.

29. Hoppin, *Life of Foote*, 393.

30. Symmes Browne to Fannie Bassett, May 12, 1862, in Browne and Browne, *From the Fresh-Water Navy*, 76–77.

31. Davis to Welles, May 10 and 11, 1862, *ORN*, I, 22:13, 14.

32. Montgomery to General Pierre G. T. Beauregard, May 12, 1862, *ORN*, I, 23:55–57.

33. Davis to his wife, May 24, 1862, in Charles H. Davis, *Life of Charles Henry Davis*, 232.

34. Quoted in Hearn, *Ellet's Brigade*, 9.

35. Ellet to Welles, June 21, 1861; Lorenzo Thomas to Ellet, March 14, 1862; Stanton to Ellet, March 27, 1862; and Ellet to Stanton, March 29 and 31 and April 19, 1862, in *ORN*, I, 22:288, 665, 672, 680–82, 685–86, and *ORN*, I, 23:65.

36. Charles Ellet Jr. to Lieutenant Wilson McGunnegle, April 27, 1862, *ORN*, I, 23:79. See also Currie, *Warfare along the Mississippi*, 39–40.

37. Ellet to Stanton, May 26, 1862, *ORN*, I, 23:29.

38. Davis to Ellet, May 28, 1862, ibid., 35.

39. Ellet to Davis, June 1, 1862, and Davis to Ellet, June 2, 1862, in ibid., 37, 39.

40. Ellet to Stanton, June 3, 4, 11, ibid., 42, 43–44, 132.

41. Quoted in Hearn, *Ellet's Brigade*, 31.

42. Thompson to Beauregard, June 7, 1862, *ORN*, I, 23:140.

43. Davis to Welles, June 6 (two reports), ibid., 118–20. For all of the official reports on the battle of Memphis, see ibid., 118–40.

44. Alfred Ellet to Davis, July 2, 1862, ibid., 234.

45. Farragut to his family, June 26, 1862, in Farragut, *Life of Farragut*, 273.

46. Holton, *Cruise of the* Hartford, 20, diary entry of June ?, 1862.

47. Farragut to Virginia Farragut, June 29, 1862, in Farragut, *Life of Farragut*, 276.

48. Farragut to Welles, June 28, 1862, *ORN*, I, 18:588.

49. Farragut to Halleck, June 28, 1862, and Halleck to Farragut, July 3, 1862, in ibid., 590, 593.

50. Brown to Major General Daniel Ruggles, June 4, 1862, ibid., 647.

51. Ibid., 590–91; *ORN*, I, 23:242–43.

52. S. P. Lee to Elizabeth Blair Lee, July 10, 12, 22, 1862, BLP.

53. Commander Henry H. Bell, diary, *ORN*, I, 18:714, entry of July 1, 1862; Symmes Brown to Fannie Bassett, July 27, 1862, in Browne and Browne, *From the Fresh-Water Navy*, 111.

54. Isaac N. Brown, "The Confederate Gun-Boat 'Arkansas,'" in *Battles and Leaders*, 3:576.

55. Extract from the papers of John A. Wilson, printed in *ORN*, I, 19:132–36. For all of the official reports and other documentation of this affair, see ibid., 3–75.

56. Van Dorn quoted in Milligan, *Gunboats down the Mississippi*, 85; Foltz, *Surgeon of the Seas*, 248, diary entry of July 15, 1862.

57. Farragut to Welles, July 17, 1862, and Farragut to Davis, July 16, 18, 1862, in *ORN*, I, 19:4, 8, 14.

58. Farragut to Davis, July 16, 1862, *ORN*, I, 23:236; Davis to his wife, August 18, 1862, quoted in Du Pont, *Civil War Letters*, 3:28n.

59. Davis to Farragut, July 17, 1862, *ORN*, I, 23:237; Farragut to Davis, July 19, 1862, *ORN*, I, 19:14.

60. *ORN*, I, 19:115–20; Hearn, *Ellet's Brigade*, 54–60.

61. Farragut to Virginia Farragut, July 22, 1862, DFP.

62. *ORN*, I, 19:19, 49–50, 80.

63. Campaign Diary, entry of August 1, 1862, *ORN*, I, 23:271–72; Davis to Welles, August 1, 1862, ibid., 63–64.

64. Porter to Fox, July 26, 1862, in Fox, *Confidential Correspondence*, 2:125; Welles to Davis, August 1, 1862, *ORN*, I, 23:278.

CHAPTER 5

1. Mallory to Charles M. Conrad, May 10, 1861, *ORN*, II, 2:67–69.

2. Mallory to North, May 17, 1861, and North to Mallory, August 16, 1861, in ibid., 70–72, 87.

3. Brooke, *Ironclads and Big Guns*, 22, journal entry of June 23, 1861; *ORN*, II, 1:783–84. For the origins of the Confederate ironclad program and the building of the CSS *Virginia*, see Still, *Iron Afloat*, 5–40.

4. *ORN*, I, 6:333–34, 393, 482–83, 535.

5. Quoted in Bushnell to Welles, March 9, 1877, in *Battles and Leaders*, 1:748. For modern accounts of the building of the *Monitor*, see De Kay, *Monitor*, and Fuller, *Clad in Iron*.

6. Quoted in William C. Davis, *Duel between First Ironclads*, 21.

7. Smith to Worden, January 11, 1862, *ORN*, I, 6:515; William F. Keeler to Anna Keeler, March ?, 1862, in Keeler, *Aboard the USS* Monitor, 40–51.

8. Mallory to Buchanan, February 24, 1862, *ORN*, I, 6:776–77.

9. Quoted in William C. Davis, *Duel between First Ironclads*, 89.

10. John V. Quarstein, "Sink before Surrender: The Story of the CSS *Virginia*," in Holzer and Mulligan, *The Battle of Hampton Roads*, 72.

11. Charles H. Davis to Samuel F. Du Pont, April 9, 1862, in Charles H. Davis, *Life of Charles Henry Davis*, 212.

12. Foote, *The Civil War*, 1:260.

13. Keeler to Anna Keeler, March 6–8, 1862, in Keeler, *Aboard the USS* Monitor, 28–30.

14. Keeler to Anna Keeler, journal letter started on March 6 and continued for several days, in ibid., 40.

15. Greene to his parents, March 14, in "I Fired the First Shot," 102–3; Keeler to Anna Keeler, Journal letter begun on March 6, in Keeler, *Aboard the USS* Monitor, 35.

16. Stimers to Ericsson, March 9, 1862, *ORN*, I, 7:27. For reports, correspondence, telegrams, and other documentation of this historic battle, see ibid., 3–96.

17. Sinclair to John M. Brooke, March 11, 1862, in Brooke, *Ironclads and Big Guns*, 74–75.

18. Captain Gershom J. Van Brunt's report, March 10, 1862, *ORN*, I, 7:11–12.

19. Sinclair to John M. Brooke, March 11, 1863, and Maury to Captain De la Marcha, March 15, 1862, in Brooke, *Ironclads and Big Guns*, 75, 232n.

20. Welles to Goldsborough, March 10, 1862, in Keeler, *Aboard the USS* Monitor, 75n.

21. William F. Keeler to Anna Keeler, March 30, 1862, in ibid., 63.

22. "The Monitor Boys to Lieutenant John L. Worden," April 24, 1862, *ORN*, I, 7:40.

23. Fox to Goldsborough, March 24, 1862, ibid., 167–68.

24. Missroon to McClellan, April 6 and 8, 1862, ibid., 206–7, 208–10.

25. McClellan to Fox, April 14, 1862, in Fox, *Confidential Correspondence*, 2:288.

26. Welles to Goldsborough, April 17, 1862, and Goldsborough to McClellan, April 6, 1862, in *ORN*, I, 7:244, 206. See also Goldsborough to Fox, April 21, 1862, in Fox, *Confidential Correspondence*, 1:259–61.

27. Fox to Goldsborough, May 7, 1862, *ORN*, I, 7:327–28.

28. Lincoln to Goldsborough, May 7, 10, 1862, in Lincoln, *Collected Works of Lincoln*, 5:207, 209; William F. Keeler to Anna Keeler, May 9, 1862, in Keeler, *Aboard the USS* Monitor, 113, 115.

29. *ORN*, I, 7:357–60, 362, 369–70; Keeler to Anna Keeler, journal letter dated May 12–19, 1862, in Keeler, *Aboard the USS* Monitor, 126–32.

30. Mallory to his wife, May 27 and July 21, 1862, in Brooke, *Ironclads and Big Guns*, 240n, 104.

31. Fox to Goldsborough, May 17, 1862, and Goldsborough to Fox, May 21, 1862, in Fox, *Confidential Correspondence*, 1:269–71.

32. Welles to Andrew H. Foote, July 24, 1862, marked "personal," in Hoppin, *Life of Foote*, 344–45.

33. William F. Keeler to Anna Keeler, June 14, 1862, in Keeler, *Aboard the USS* Monitor, 154–55.

34. Welles to Wilkes, July 6, 1862; Goldsborough to Welles, July 10, 11, 15, 1862; and Welles to Goldsborough, July 21, 1862, in *ORN*, I, 7:548, 563–64, 566, 573–74.

35. Welles, *Diary*, 1:73, 87, entries of August 10 and 18, 1862.

36. *ORN*, I, 7:629–31, 655–56, 674.

37. Welles, *Diary*, 1:109, entry of September 4, 1862; Welles to Wilkes, September 8, 1862, *ORN*, I, 1:470–71.

38. Welles to Wilkes, December 15, 1862, *ORN*, I, 1:587–88.

39. Mallory to Bulloch, May 9, 1861, *ORN*, II, 1:364–65.

40. Bulloch, *Secret Service*.

41. Moran, *Journal*, 2:984, entry of April 25, 1862.

42. *ORN*, I, 1:363, 364, 397–98, 399–400. See also Milton, *Lincoln's Spymaster*, 34–37.

43. Maffitt's journal in Maffitt, *Life and Services*, 252–53.

44. Ibid., 254; Preble to Farragut, September 4, 1862, *ORN*, I, 1:432.

45. Farragut to Preble, September 5, 1862, and Preble to Farragut, September 6, 1862, in ibid., 433–34.

46. Welles, *Diary*, 1:140–42, entries of September 19 and 20, 1862; Welles to Preble, September 20, 1862, *ORN*, I, 1:434.

47. *ORN*, I, 1:434–68 (quotation on 455).

48. Bulloch to Mallory, August 3, 1862, ibid., 775. See also Milton, *Lincoln's Spymaster*, 39–46.

49. Bulloch to Mallory, August 3 and September 10, 1862, and Semmes to Mallory, January 24, 1863, in *ORN*, I, 1:775–80. See also Howard Jones, *Blue and Gray Diplomacy*, 192–99.

50. Edward Maffitt Anderson to his father, November 18, 1862, in Edward Maffitt Anderson, "Letters from a Georgia Midshipman," 418.

51. Welles, *Diary*, 1:109, entry of September 4, 1862.

52. Du Pont to Sophie Du Pont, November 10–11, 1862, in Du Pont, *Civil War Letters*, 2:283. The David D. Porter Papers at the Huntington Library contain many telegrams from Welles to commanders of navy yards to send out ships to find the *Alabama*.

53. Edward M. Anderson to his father, November 18, 1862, in Edward Maffitt Anderson, "Letters from a Georgia Midshipman," 420–21.

54. *ORN*, I, 1:416–17, 480, 490, 517–33, 549–50; Fox to George W. Blunt, December 30, 1862, in Fox, *Confidential Correspondence*, 2:486.

55. Dalzell, *Flight from the Flag*. A substantial portion of *ORN*, I, volume 1 details the cruises of the *Alabama* and Semmes's judgments on the ownership of ships and cargoes. There are many books about the *Alabama*; one of the best is Stephen Fox, *Wolf of the Deep*.

CHAPTER 6

1. Welles's endorsement on a communication from Louis Goldsborough, July 12, 1862, *ORN*, I, 7:568.

2. Febiger to Farragut, April 11, 1862, *ORN*, I, 18:116–17.

3. Carse, *Blockade*, 41.

4. Quoted in Josiah Gorgas to James A. Seddon, December 5, 1862, *OR*, IV, 2:227–28.

5. Captain A. Ludlow Case to Samuel Phillips Lee, March 12, 26, 1863, *ORN*, I, 8:599, 631; Case to Lee, March 23, 1863, BLP, Letterbook 6, 146–47; Lee to Welles, March 15, 1863, *ORN*, I, 8:592.

6. William Keeler to Anna Keeler, April 11, 1863, in Keeler, *Aboard the USS Florida*, 20.

7. Walker, *Private Journal*, 39–40, undated entry, Spring 1863.

8. Du Pont to Welles, April 23, 1862, *ORN*, I, 12:771–73.

9. Marchand, *Charleston Blockade*, 139–40; Du Pont to Welles, May 9, 1862, *ORN*, I, 12:804.

10. Marchand, *Charleston Blockade*, 152, journal entry of April 28, 1862.

11. *New York Times*, May 26, 1862; Du Pont to Sophie Du Pont, June 4, 1862, in Du Pont, *Civil War Letters*, 2:103.

12. General William H. C. Whiting to Secretary of War George Randolph, November 14, 1862, *ORN*, I, 8:846.

13. Du Pont to Sophie Du Pont, August 29, 1862, in Du Pont, *Civil War Letters*, 2:206–7; Commander Charles Steedman to Du Pont, August 25, 1862, *ORN*, I, 13:288–89.

14. Captain Charles S. Boggs to S. P. Lee, May 28, 1863, and Captain Benjamin F. Sands to Lee, December 23, 1862, in *ORN*, I, 9:51, and *ORN*, I, 8:313–14.

15. Du Pont to Sophie Du Pont, May 1, July 8, and August 24, 1862, in Du Pont, *Civil War Letters*, 2:23, 155, 197–98; Du Pont to Gustavus Fox, August 21, 1862, *ORN*,

I, 13:269; Charles Steedman to Sally Steedman, August 18, 1862, in Steedman, *Memoir and Correspondence*, 322.

16. Farragut to Welles, August 3, 1862, and Fox to Farragut, September 9, 1862, in *ORN*, I, 19:110, 184.

17. Boyer, *Naval Surgeon*, 28, 49, 107, 112, 113–14.

18. Du Pont to Welles, January 31, 1863, *ORN*, I, 13:551–52; Du Pont to Benjamin Gerhard, January 31, 1863, and Du Pont to Sophie Du Pont, February 2, 1863, in Du Pont, *Civil War Letters*, 2:396–97, 409.

19. For reports and other documentation of this affair, see *ORN*, I, 13:577–623.

20. Caleb Huse to Josiah Gorgas, August 4, 1862, in Vandiver, *Confederate Blockade Running through Bermuda*, xxi. For reports of numerous captures of runners near the Bahamas in 1862, see *ORN*, I, 17:221, 230–31, 289, 296, 309–10, 312.

21. Farragut to Welles, July 29, August 11 and 15, 1862; Welles to Farragut, August 19, 1862; Fox to Farragut, September 9, 1862; Farragut to Welles, September 30, 1862; and Farragut to Benjamin Butler, October 23, 1862, in *ORN*, I, 19:96–98, 146–47, 161–63, 185, 242, 313.

22. Farragut to Fox, December 23, 1862, in Fox, *Confidential Correspondence*, 1:322.

23. Acting Master Frederick Crocker to Farragut, October 2, 1862, and Farragut to Welles, October 9, 1862, in *ORN*, I, 19:217–18, 289.

24. Farragut to Commander William B. Renshaw, October 14, 1862, ibid., 260.

25. French to Farragut, September 8 and 18, 1862, ibid., 180, 291–92; Daddysman, *The Matamoros Trade*, 160–61.

26. Farragut to French, August 25, 1862, *ORN*, I, 19:169.

27. Welles to William W. McKean, November 25, 1862, and Welles to James L. Lardner, August 29, 1862, in *ORN*, I, 16:789, and *ORN*, I, 17:303–4.

28. Bernath, *Squall across the Atlantic*, 63–84.

29. Farragut to George F. Denison, December 10, 1862, *ORN*, I, 19:400.

30. George Cupples to his wife, January 1–2, 1863, in Cupples, "Two Battles of Galveston," 253.

31. *ORN*, I, 19:437–77.

32. Farragut to Welles, January 21, 1863, and Fox to David D. Porter, February 6, 1863, in *ORN*, I, 19:553, and *ORN*, I, 24:242–43.

33. Farragut to Captain James Alden, January 5, 1863, *ORN*, I, 19:489; Farragut to Bell, January 6, 1863, DFP.

34. Farragut to Welles, January 15, 1863, *ORN*, I, 19:506. See also ibid., 507, 737. For Semmes's report to Confederate naval secretary Stephen Mallory, see *ORN*, I, 2:683–84. Two other Confederate accounts are Low, *Logs of the* Alabama, 33–34, and Fullam, *Journal of Fullam*, 71–72.

35. Commodore Robert B. Hitchcock to Farragut, January 16, 1863; Captain John Maffitt to Mallory, January 27 and May 11, 1863; and Farragut to Welles, January 19, 1863, in *ORN*, I, 2:27–28, 639–40, and *ORN*, I, 19:528.

36. Reports and other documentation in *ORN*, I, 19:553–73, 586.

37. Farragut to James Alden, January 27, 1863, ibid., 584; Farragut to Virginia Farragut, January 18, 1863, DFP.

38. *ORN*, I, 24:9–10; 25:559; 23:348–52, 388.

39. Welles, *Diary*, 1:157–58, 167, entries of October 1, 10, 1862.

40. Porter to Welles, December 17, 1862, *ORN*, I, 23:545. See also ibid., 397–98, 544–46.

41. Porter to Andrew H. Foote, January 3, 1863, in Hoppin, *Life of Foote*, 359–60.

42. Fox to Lee, December 15, 1862, BLP.

43. *ORN*, I, 8:237, 243, 298–99, 310–12, 318–19, 320–21, 323, 324, 327, 362, 388–89, 399–400, 414, 418, 855, 857; Fox, *Confidential Correspondence*, 2:217, 230, 232–34, 236, 245–46, 248; Welles, *Diary*, 1:216, entry of January 5, 1863. See also Lee's correspondence with Fox and Welles in the BLP, Box 67, Letterbook 7, 14–17, 19, 33–36, 37.

44. William Keeler to Anna Keeler, January 4 and 6, 1863, in Keeler, *Aboard the USS* Monitor, 252–56; George Geer to Gilbert Geer, January 13, 1863, in Geer, Monitor *Chronicles*, 235–36. See also *ORN*, I, 8:339–59.

CHAPTER 7

1. Drayton to Lydig Hoyt, November 30, 1861, in Drayton, *Naval Letters*, 8–9.

2. Welles to Flag Officer William Mervine, July 22, 1861, *ORN*, I, 16:593. See also Welles to Flag Officer Silas Stringham, July 22, 1861, *ORN*, I, 6:10.

3. Welles to Captain Thomas T. Craven, September 25, 1861, and Welles to Davis, April 30, 1862, in *ORN*, I, 4:692, and *ORN*, I, 23:81. For full-scale studies of these policies, see Tomblin, *Bluejackets and Contrabands*, and Ramold, *Slaves, Sailors, Citizens*.

4. Porter to Andrew H. Foote, January 3, 1863, *ORN*, I, 23:603; Porter to Gustavus V. Fox, January 16, 1863, in Fox, *Confidential Correspondence*, 2:155.

5. Reigand V. Lowry to Welles, May 19, 1863, *ORN*, I, 27:499.

6. Du Pont to James Stokes Biddle, December 17, 1861, and Du Pont to Titus Coan, February 8, 1863, in Du Pont, *Civil War Letters*, 1:181, 2:422–23.

7. Du Pont to Sophie Du Pont, April 10, 1862, in ibid., 1:413.

8. Du Pont to Benjamin Gerhard, May 27, 1862, in ibid., 2:75–76.

9. Du Pont to Sophie Du Pont, May 1, 1862, in ibid., 2:23; Marchand, *Charleston Blockade*, 152–53, journal entry of April 28, 1862.

10. *ORN*, I, 12:820–26; McPherson, *The Negro's Civil War*, 154–57; Roswell H. Lamson to Flora Lamson, May 18, 1862, in Lamson, *Lamson of the Gettysburg*, 62–63.

11. Du Pont to Sophie Du Pont, May 1, 1862, in Du Pont, *Civil War Letters*, 2:23; Du Pont to Sophie Du Pont, July 14, 1862, quoted in John Sanford Barnes, "The Battle of Port Royal Ferry," 120n.

12. Marchand, *Charleston Blockade*, 176–83, journal entries of May 21, 22, 24, 1862.

13. Percival Drayton to Du Pont, July 2, 1863, enclosed in a letter from Du Pont to Gustavus Fox, July 9, 1862, in Fox, *Confidential Correspondence*, 1:136.

14. Bankhead to Fox, June 29, 1862, and Du Pont to Fox, August 13, 1862, in ibid., 2:317–19, 1:149; Charles Steedman to Sally Steedman, July 4, 1862, in Steedman, *Memoir and Correspondence*, 308.

15. Fox to Du Pont, April 3, May 12, June 3, 1862, in Fox, *Confidential Correspondence*, 1:114–15; Du Pont, *Civil War Letters*, 2:91n, 96–97.

16. Du Pont to Fox, September 20, 1862, in Fox, *Confidential Correspondence*, 1:156.

Du Pont to Fox, May 31, 1862, and Du Pont to Sophie Du Pont, June 13 and 22, 1862, in Du Pont, *Civil War Letters*, 2:91–92, 113, 129.

17. Du Pont to Commodore Theodorus Bailey, October 30, 1862, and Du Pont to Captain Henry A. Wise, January 16, 1863, in *ORN*, I, 13:423, 513; Du Pont to Henry Winter Davis, October 25, 1862, in Du Pont, *Civil War Letters*, 2:259n.

18. Du Pont to Sophie Du Pont, December 17, 1862, and Du Pont to Charles H. Davis, January 4, 1863, in Du Pont, *Civil War Letters*, 2:324, 340.

19. Fox to Du Pont, February 16, 1862, in Du Pont, *Civil War Letters*, 2:443–44.

20. Fox to Du Pont, February 26, March 3, 1863, in Fox, *Confidential Correspondence*, 1:184, 188; Welles to Du Pont, January 6 and 31, 1863, *ORN*, I, 13:503, 571.

21. Welles to Du Pont, January 6, 1863, *ORN*, I, 13:503; Fox to Du Pont, February 20, 1863, in Du Pont, *Civil War Letters*, 2:450.

22. Du Pont to Sophie Du Pont, March 2, 1863, in Du Pont, *Civil War Letters*, 2:461.

23. Du Pont to Fox, March 2, 1863; Du Pont to Davis, April 1, 1863 in Du Pont, *Civil War Letters*, 2:464, 534.

24. Du Pont to Welles, January 28, 1863, *ORN*, I, 13:543; Du Pont to Benjamin Gerhard, January 30, 1863, in Du Pont, *Civil War Letters*, 2:394. See also John Worden to Du Pont, January 31 and February 2, 1863, *ORN*, I, 13:576, 626–28.

25. Worden to Du Pont, February 28, 1863, and Du Pont to Welles, March 2, 1863, in *ORN*, I, 13:696–98; Du Pont to Sophie Du Pont, March 1, 1863, in Du Pont, *Civil War Letters*, 2:458–59.

26. Du Pont to Welles, March 6, 1863, and Percival Drayton to Du Pont, March 4, 1863, in *ORN*, I, 13:716, 717.

27. Major D. B. Harris to Brigadier General Thomas Jordan, March 9, 1863, *ORN*, I, 13:730.

28. Du Pont to James Biddle, March 26, 1863, in Du Pont, *Civil War Letters*, 2:510.

29. Charles Steedman to Sally Steedman, April 3, 1863, in Steedman, *Memoir and Correspondence*, 366–67; Drayton to Alexander Hamilton Jr., February 11, 1863, in Drayton, *Naval Letters*, 26–27.

30. Du Pont to Sophie Du Pont, April 4, 1863, in Du Pont, *Civil War Letters*, 2:544.

31. Welles, *Diary*, 1:237, 247, entries of February 16 and March 12, 1863.

32. Du Pont to Welles, April 8, 1863, *ORN*, I, 14:3–4. The reports and other documentation of the battle are in ibid., 3–112.

33. Cornelius L. Burkmyer to C. Rebecca Burkmyer, April 17, 1863, in Burkmyer, *Burkmyer Letters*, 49.

34. Du Pont to Senator James W. Grimes, August 8, 1863, in Du Pont, *Civil War Letters*, 3:220.

35. Du Pont to Sophie Du Pont, April 8 and May 2, 1863, in ibid., 3:3, 74.

36. Reprinted in *ORN*, I, 14:57–59.

37. Du Pont to David Hunter, April 8, 1863, *ORN*, I, 14:31. For the aftermath of the battle and the criticisms of Du Pont, see Weddle, *Lincoln's Tragic Admiral*, 195–207.

38. Drayton to Alexander Hamilton Jr., April 15, 1863, in Drayton, *Naval Letters*, 34–35; Rodgers to Welles, May 2, 1863, in Du Pont, *Naval Letters*, 1:lxxxviii. The captains' official reports to Welles, April 24, 1863, are in *ORN*, I, 14:45–48.

39. Welles, *Diary*, 1:295–96, 302, entries of May 8 and 14, 1863.

40. Ibid., 228, 309, entries of April 30 and May 23, 1863.

41. Dahlgren's requests and Welles's responses can be followed in *ORN*, I, 13:353–54, 376–78, 390, 416, 426; in Dahlgren's diary, *Memoir of John A. Dahlgren*, 360, 374, 376, 381; and in Welles, *Diary*, 1:158, 160, 163–64.

42. Welles, *Diary*, 1:238–39, entries of February 19 and 22, 1863.

43. Farragut to Du Pont, April 20, 1863, in Du Pont, *Civil War Letters*, 3:49.

44. *ORN*, I, 14:230, 240–41, 295; Dahlgren, *Memoir of John A. Dahlgren*, 391–93, 395, entries of May 28, June 3 and 21, 1863; Welles, *Diary*, 1:337–38, entry of June 21, 1863.

45. Webb to Mallory, June 10, 1863, *ORN*, I, 14:710–11.

46. Du Pont to Welles, June 17, 1863; John Rodgers to Du Pont, June 17, 1863; Welles to Du Pont, June 26, 1863; and Welles to Rodgers, June 25, 1863, in *ORN*, I, 14:263, 265–66, 282–84.

47. *Boston Herald*, June 25, 1863, quoted in Weddle, *Lincoln's Tragic Admiral*, 204.

48. Welles, *Diary*, 1:110, entry of September 5, 1862.

49. Welles, *Diary*, 1:304, 316, entries of May 16 and 29, 1863; Welles to Commodore James Lardner, June 1, 1863, *ORN*, I, 2:250–53; Symonds, *Lincoln and His Admirals*, 223–26, 254–55.

50. Roswell H. Lamson to Flora Lamson, June 30, 1863, in Lamson, *Lamson of the Gettysburg*, 114. For Read and his exploits, consult Shaw, *Sea Wolf of the Confederacy*.

51. *ORN*, I, 2:273–332, 380, 614, 645; Welles, *Diary*, 1:327, entry of June 13, 1863. The originals of many Navy Department telegrams to commanders of navy yards are in the DPP.

CHAPTER 8

1. J. Wainwright to Gustavus Fox, July 29, 1862, in Fox, *Confidential Correspondence*, 2:338–39.

2. *ORN*, I, 23:394, 444, 466, 477, 500; Porter to Fox, October 17, 1862, in Fox, *Confidential Correspondence*, 2:141; Silverstone, *Warships of Civil War Navies*, 164–80.

3. *ORN*, I, 23:396, 418, 428–31, 469; Lincoln to Alfred Ellet, November 7, 1862, in Lincoln, *Collected Works of Lincoln*, 5:490; Hearn, *Ellet's Brigade*, 69–79.

4. *ORN*, I, 23:240–41.

5. Symmes Brown to Fannie Bassett, December 20, 1862, in Browne and Browne, *From the Fresh-Water Navy*, 123–24.

6. Porter to Fox, November 10, 1862, in Fox, *Confidential Correspondence*, 2:149.

7. Undated order, mid-February 1863, *ORN*, I, 24:365.

8. Porter to Major General Carter L. Stevenson, March 2, 1863, ibid., 366–67.

9. Lieutenant Commander George M. Ransom to Farragut, October 7, 1862, *ORN*, I, 19:247–49.

10. Grant to Henry W. Halleck, January 11, 1863, *ORN*, I, 24:106.

11. Samuel Bartlett to Mary Bartlett, January 16, 1863, in Bartlett, "A Union Volunteer with the Mississippi Ram Fleet," 189–90. For official reports of this action, see *ORN*, I, 24:98–115.

12. Porter to Welles, January 12, 1863, *ORN*, I, 24:116, which Welles forwarded to other fleet commanders in a circular dated January 28, 1863, *ORN*, I, 8:483–84; Samuel Francis Du Pont to Sophie Du Pont, March 10, 1863, in Du Pont, *Civil War Letters*, 2:479; Lieutenant Commander Charles C. Carpenter to his wife, April ?, 1863, in Carpenter, "'Such a Fire I Never Saw,'" 13.

13. Halleck to Banks, November 9, 1862, *OR*, I, 15:590–91; Lincoln quoted by William M. Strong to Samuel R. Curtis, December 23, 1862, in Lincoln, *Recollected Words of Lincoln*, 431.

14. Halleck to Grant, March 25, 1863, *OR*, I, 24, part 1, 22.

15. Porter to Welles, February 2, 1863, *ORN*, I, 24:217–18.

16. Ibid., 222–23, 321, 424, 382–87.

17. Ibid., 375–419, for reports and other documentation.

18. Porter to Welles, February 27, 1863, ibid., 390–91.

19. Colonel Wirt Alexander to Major J. J. Reeve, March 1, 1863, ibid., 411.

20. Foote, *The Civil War*, vol. 2, *Fredericksburg to Meridian*, 201; *Vicksburg Whig* quoted in *ORN*, I, 24:397. See also *Civil War Naval Chronology*, 3:34–35.

21. Farragut to Commodore Henry H. Bell, March 5, 1863, DFP.

22. Foltz, *Surgeon of the Seas*, 262, diary entry of March 16, 1863.

23. Extract from the Journal of the USS *Richmond*, *ORN*, I, 19:769, entry of March 14, 1863.

24. For reports and other documentation, see ibid., 665–704.

25. Farragut to Welles, March 16, 1863, ibid., 665.

26. Fox to Farragut, April 2, 1863, in Fox, *Confidential Correspondence*, 1:331.

27. Extract from the diary of Acting Third Assistant Engineer George W. Baird of the *Calhoun*, *ORN*, I, 20:137, entry of April 14, 1863.

28. Farragut to Virginia Farragut, July 15, 1863, in Farragut, *Life of Farragut*, 381.

29. Porter to Fox, April 16, 1863, in Fox, *Confidential Correspondence*, 2:166–67. For official reports and dispatches concerning this expedition, see *ORN*, I, 24:243–304. See also Grant to Porter, February 14, 1863, DPP.

30. Carter, *Final Fortress*, 147.

31. *ORN*, I, 24:478–79. For all of the reports and dispatches concerning this operation, see ibid., 474–501.

32. Grant to William T. Sherman, March 22, 1863, *ORN*, I, 24:489; Fox to Farragut, April 2, 1863, in Fox, *Confidential Correspondence*, 1:331; Dahlgren, *Memoir of Dahlgren*, 389, diary entry of March 29, 1863.

33. Porter to Welles, March 26, 1863, *ORN*, I, 24:479.

34. Porter to Grant, March 29, 1863, and Welles to Porter, April 2, 1863, in *ORN*, I, 24:518, 522; Porter to Fox, April 25, 1863, in Fox, *Confidential Correspondence*, 2:172.

35. *ORN*, I, 24:552–68, 604–5; Charles H. Gulick to editor of the *Peoria Mail*, printed in the issue of April 30, 1863, in Gulick, "War on the River," 26; Porter to Fox, April 17, 1863, in Fox, *Confidential Correspondence*, 2:169–70.

36. Porter to Welles, April 29, 1863, *ORN*, I, 24:611.

37. *ORN*, I, 23:413–14, 24:610–34.

38. Grant, *Personal Memoirs*, 1:480–81.

39. *ORN*, I, 20:212, 214, 221, 234, 367; 24:645–47.

40. Charles H. Gulick to editor of the *Peoria Mail*, May 24, 1863, in Gulick, "War on the River," 29–31.

41. *ORN*, I, 25:38.

42. Porter to Welles, June 9, 1863, ibid., 162.

43. Ibid., 25:133, 282–85.

44. Porter to Welles, July 4, 1863, ibid., 103–4. For all reports and dispatches relating to the siege, see ibid., 21–124.

45. Welles, *Diary*, 1:364, entry of July 7, 1863.

46. Welles to Porter, July 13, 1863, and Farragut to Porter, July 15, August 1, 1863, in *ORN*, I, 25:11, 393, 432.

CHAPTER 9

1. Lincoln to Grant, August 9, 1863, in Lincoln, *Collected Works of Lincoln*, 6:374; Welles, *Diary*, 1:389–91, entry of July 30, 1863. For the tangled story of French intervention in Mexico and Franco-Confederate and Franco-American relations, see Case and Spencer, *The United States and France*, especially chaps. 15–16, and Howard Jones, *Blue and Gray Diplomacy*, especially chap. 9.

2. Farragut to Welles, July 30, 1863, *ORN*, I, 20:428–29.

3. Banks to Halleck, September 13, 1863, ibid., 532.

4. Welles, *Diary*, 1:441–42, entry of September 23, 1863.

5. *ORN*, I, 20:515–63.

6. Ibid., 643–45, 648, 679–80, 694, 702–3, 741–42; *ORN* I, 21:183.

7. *ORN*, I, 14:355–73; Charles C. Carpenter to Mrs. Carpenter, July 12, 1863, in Carpenter, "'Such a Fire I Never Saw,'" 17.

8. Beauregard to Tucker, July 12, 18, 1863, *ORN*, I, 14:725, 728.

9. Dahlgren, *Memoir of Dahlgren*, 402–3, diary entry of July 18, 1863.

10. Welles to Dahlgren, July 24, 28, 1863, *ORN*, I, 14:395, 401.

11. Welles, *Diary*, 1:382–84, entry of July 26, 1863; Wise, *Gate of Hell*, 137–38.

12. Dahlgren, *Memoir of Dahlgren*, 411.

13. *ORN*, I, 14:596.

14. Colonel Lawrence M. Keitt to "Captain Nance," September 5, 1863, and Beauregard to General Samuel Cooper, September 6, 1863, in ibid., 572–73.

15. Dahlgren to Welles, January 28, 1864, ibid., 600.

16. Cornelius L. Burkmyer to his wife, August 31, 1863, in Burkmyer, *Burkmyer Letters*, 165.

17. Official reports and communications regarding this affair are in *ORN*, I, 14:606–40.

18. Dahlgren, *Memoir of Dahlgren*, 416, diary entry of September 27, 1863.

19. Welles, *Diary*, 1:464, 474–75, entries of October 3, 24, 1863; Dahlgren, *Memoir of Dahlgren*, 433–34, entries of December 31, 1863, and January 1, 1864.

20. *ORN*, I, 15:10–11, 16–17, 431, 439.

21. Ibid., 226, 229, 238–39.

22. Perry, *Infernal Machines*, 94–108; Luraghi, *History of the Confederate Navy*,

250–64; Ragan, *Union and Confederate Submarine Warfare*, 105–206; Hoyt, *Voyage of the* Hunley; Chaffin, *The* H. L. Hunley.

23. *ORN*, I, 15:327–28.

24. Dahlgren to Fox, October 18, 1863, *ORN*, I, 15:50; Dahlgren, *Memoir of Dahlgren*, 419, diary entry of October 22, 1863.

25. Welles to Dahlgren, October 9, 1863, *ORN*, I, 15:26–27.

26. Dahlgren, *Memoir of Dahlgren*, 443, diary entry of March 4, 1864.

27. Du Pont to Sophie Du Pont, February 17, 1863, in Du Pont, *Civil War Letters*, 2:349.

28. Perry, *Infernal Machines*, 84, 117.

29. Dahlgren, *Memoir of Dahlgren*, 418, diary entry of unknown date, probably in October 1863; Perry, *Infernal Machines*, 122.

30. Cornish and Laas, *Lincoln's Lee*, 122.

31. Post, "A Diary on the Blockade in 1863," 2580, entry of June 11, 1863.

32. John T. Bourne to Charles Williams and Wentworth Gray, October 12, 1863, and Bourne to Osley and Company, November 19, 1863, in Vandiver, *Blockade Running through Bermuda*, 48, 50.

33. Walker, *Private Journal*, 47, 54, entries of November ? and December 15, 1863.

34. Hotze to Benjamin, January 10, 1864, *ORN*, II, 3:1001.

35. Welles to Lee, July 2, 1864, *ORN*, I, 10:224.

36. Acting Master W. R. Browne to Flag Officer Theodorus Bailey, December 20, 1863, and Bailey to Welles, March 6, 1864, in *ORN*, 17:600, 648–49. The *ORN* contains many similar reports of the destruction of saltworks.

37. Lonn, "The Extent and Importance of Federal Raids on Salt Making," 167–84. See also Lonn, *Salt as a Factor in the Confederacy*.

38. Stephen R. Mallory to Commander James W. Cooke, January 15, 1864, and J. Taylor Wood to Commander Catesby ap R. Jones, February 26, 1864, in *ORN*, I, 9:799–801.

39. Ibid., 552, 556, 569, 586–87, 592–604, 638–58.

40. Sayres Ogden Nichols to his mother, April 19, 1864, in Nichols, "Fighting in North Carolina Waters," 79.

41. General Pierre G. T. Beauregard to General Richard F. Hoke, May 1, 1864, *ORN*, I, 9:810.

42. Reports in ibid., 732–70, and *ORN*, I, 10:627. See also Sayres Ogden Nichols to his father, May 6, 1864, in Nichols, "Fighting in North Carolina Waters," 83–84, and Josselyn, "A Gunboat Captain's Diary," 121.

43. Brigadier General Lawrence S. Baker to Maffitt, July 6, 1864, and Baker to Captain John M. Otey, July 8, 1864, in *ORN*, 10:718, 719.

44. Lee to Welles, July 9, 1864, *ORN*, I, 10:247–48.

45. Cushing to Lee, August 25, 1863, March 5 and July 2, 1864; General William H. C. Whiting to W. F. Lynch, March 2, 1864; Whiting to General Samuel Cooper, July 4, 1864; and Gideon Welles to Cushing, July 14, 1864, in *ORN*, I, 9:177–78, 511, 513, and *ORN*, I, 10:202–4, 205, 714. For these and other exploits by Cushing, see Roske and Van Doren, *Lincoln's Commando*.

46. Cushing to Rear Admiral David D. Porter, October 30, 1864, *ORN*, I, 10:611–12. For all of the reports and other documentation, see ibid., 610–24.

1. Porter to Welles, December 26, 1863, *ORN*, I, 25:660–61. See also Porter to Welles, October 1, 1863, ibid., 441; Acting Volunteer Lieutenant A. Frank O'Neill to Porter, December 19, 1863, DPP; and Lieutenant Commander James M. Pritchett to Porter, February 28, 1864, DPP.

2. De Witt C. Morse to Archibald Beal, May 30, 1864, in Morse, "A Fighting Sailor on the Western Rivers," 270–71.

3. John Swift to Sophie Swift, June 6, 1864, and John Swift to unspecified recipient, July 2, 1864, in Swift, "Letters from a Sailor on a Tinclad," 56, 59.

4. Lieutenant-Colonel George E. Currie to "Dear Sir," September 10, 1863, in Currie, *Warfare along the Mississippi*, 97–100.

5. *ORN*, I, 25:293–301, 524, 642, 693–94, 723; *ORN*, I, 26:481; Lieutenant Commander James A. Greer to David D. Porter, December 21, 1863, DPP; Hearn, *Ellet's Brigade*, 231–69; Currie, *Warfare along the Mississippi*, passim, quotation from 101.

6. *ORN*, I, 24:1–78, passim, quotations from ibid., 443, and *ORN*, I, 23:312.

7. Lieutenant Commander Le Roy Fitch to Fleet Captain Alexander M. Pennock, February 4, 1863, *ORN*, I, 24:25–37; quotation from Fitch to Porter, November 5, 1863, *ORN*, I, 23:313–14.

8. *ORN*, I, 25:474, 476, 480, 546–47, 608–9; quotation from 474.

9. Ibid., 387, 671, 783–85.

10. *ORN*, I, 25:238–59; quotations from Le Roy Fitch's report, ibid., 243, and from Major General Jacob D. Cox to David D. Porter, July 31, 1863, ibid., 257.

11. Herbert Saunders to his mother, March 28, April 3, 1864, in Saunders, "Civil War Letters," 22–24. See also *ORN*, I, 26:196–204.

12. *ORN*, I, 26:19–26. Of the large literature on the Fort Pillow massacre, see especially Cimprich, *Fort Pillow*, and Ward, *River Run Red*.

13. Porter to Thomas H. Yeatman, December 3, 1862, *ORN*, I, 23:528–29; and Le Roy Fitch to Porter, February 17, 1864, DPP.

14. Porter to Grant, February 14, 1863, ORN, I, 24:341. See also ibid., 334–54, 428, 435–36, 443.

15. Porter to Welles, May 18, 31, 1864, and Porter to Charles Eames, June 24, 1864, in ORN, I, 26:308, 342, 412; Elias K. Owen to Porter, February 21, 1864, DPP.

16. Halleck to Grant, January 18, 1864, *OR*, I, 32, part 2, 40–42.

17. Sherman to Porter, January 26, 1864, and Porter to Lieutenant Commander James A. Greer, February 13, 1864, in *ORN*, I, 25:716, 748.

18. Porter to Welles, March 16, 1864, *ORN*, I, 26:29. See also S. Ledyard Phelps to Porter, March 16 and 30, April 2, 1864, DPP.

19. Porter to Sherman, April 14, 1864, *ORN*, I, 26:56.

20. Selfridge to Porter, April 16, 1864, ibid., 49.

21. Porter to Welles, April 23, 1864, ibid., 68–70.

22. Porter to Welles, May 16, 1864, ibid., 130–35.

23. Symmes Browne to Fannie Bassett Browne, May 6, 1864, in Browne and Browne, *From the Fresh-Water Navy*, 272–74.

24. Joiner, *One Damn Blunder from Beginning to End*, xix. See also Joiner, *Through the Howling Wilderness*, and Johnson, *Red River Campaign*.

25. Lee to Welles, April 14, 1863, Box 69, Letterbook 8, 146, BLP.

26. Longstreet to Secretary of War James A. Seddon, April 22, 1863, *ORN*, I, 8:870.

27. For reports, dispatches, orders, and other documentation of these events, see ibid., 712–69. Lamson's letters to his fiancée are in *Lamson of the Gettysburg*, 91–109, and Lee's reports and dispatches are in Box 69, Letterbooks 8, 9, and 10, BLP.

28. *ORN*, I, 10:9, 15, 27–28.

29. Ibid., 49; Lamson to Kate Buckingham, May 12, 1864, in Lamson, *Lamson of the Gettysburg*, 160.

30. Lamson to Kate Buckingham, May 14, 1864, in Lamson, *Lamson of the Gettysburg*, 162.

31. Lamson to Flora Lamson, June 12, 1864, and Lamson to Kate Buckingham, June 12, 1864, in Lamson, *Lamson of the Gettysburg*, 173, 177.

32. Lee to Welles, June 1, 1864, *ORN*, I, 10:113.

33. Ibid., 634–94.

34. Lee to Welles, June 7, 1864; Lee to Butler, June 2, 1864; Butler to Lee, June 2, 1864; and Lee to Butler, June 7, 1864, in ibid., 129, 131, 133.

35. Lee to Welles, June 15, 1864, and Lee to Gustavus Fox, June 25, 1864, in ibid., 149, 207–8; Roswell Lamson to Kate Buckingham, June 14, 1864, in Lamson, *Lamson of the Gettysburg*, 178; *New York Herald*, June 23 and 25, 1864; Elizabeth Blair Lee to S. P. Lee, June 25, 1864, BLP.

36. *ORN*, I, 3:137–84.

37. *ORN*, I, 10:414–15, 420, 432–33, 441–44, 454–55, 502–3.

38. Whiting to Stephen Mallory, September 27, October 6, 1864, ibid., 751–52, 755; Foreman, *A World on Fire*, 649.

39. Mallory to Bulloch, April 30, 1862, and Bulloch to Mallory, July 4, 1862, in *ORN*, II, 2:186–87, 212, 222–26.

40. Foreman, *A World on Fire*, 409–10.

41. John R. Hamilton to James North, April 23, 1863, *ORN*, II, 2:409; Merli, *Great Britain and the Confederate Navy*, 160–77.

42. Merli, *Great Britain and the Confederate Navy*, 178–217; Bulloch to Stephen Mallory, December 2, 1862, and June 30, September 1, and October 20, 1863, *ORN*, II, 2:307, 445–46, 488, 507–11.

43. *ORN*, II, 2:185, 330, 361, 413, 439, 566, 581; quotation from Bulloch to Mallory, November 25, 1863, ibid., 524.

44. Bulloch to Mallory, June 10, 1864, ibid., 665–68, quotation from 666.

45. Slidell to Benjamin, June 2 and August 8, 1864, ibid., 1139, 1187. See also ibid., 423, 468, 526, 655, 692, 1148.

46. Bulloch to Mallory, February 17, 1864, ibid., 585.

47. Ibid., 477, 502, 574, 578, 625, 658, 662, 684, 703, 718, 720.

48. Semmes to Barron, June 14, 1864, and Semmes's daily journal, June 15, 1864, ibid., I, 3:651, 677.

49. Winslow to Thomas A. Dudley, June 24, 1864, in Dillon, "Documents," 127.

50. *ORN*, I, 3:665. For reports of the battle, see ibid., 50, 61, 651, 663.

51. *ORN*, I, 3:252–69, 631–42.

52. Hoogenboom, *Gustavus Vasa Fox*, 161–62, 190–91; Welles, *Diary*, 2:52–53, 81–82, 108, 241–42, entries of June 10, July 19, and August 17, 1864, February 21, 1865; Silverstone, *Warships of Civil War Navies*, 12–14.

CHAPTER 11

1. Farragut to Loyall Farragut, February 21, 1864, DFP.

2. Quotation from Farragut to Virginia Farragut, June 21, 1864, in Farragut, *Life of Farragut*, 402. See also Farragut to Welles, May 8, 1864; Welles to Farragut, June 25, 1864; and David D. Porter to Edward R. S. Canby, July 1, 1864, in *ORN*, I, 21:267–68, 344, 368.

3. Ely, "This Filthy Ironpot," 47–48.

4. Hults, "Aboard the *Galena* at Mobile," 21, diary entry of August 4, 1864.

5. Brother, "Journal of Charles Brother," *Civil War Naval Chronology*, 6:51.

6. Drayton to Samuel Francis Du Pont, September 18, 1864, in Du Pont, *Civil War Letters*, 3:383.

7. Brother, "Journal of Charles Brother," *Civil War Naval Chronology*, 6:51, John O'Connell statement.

8. For all of the reports, dispatches, and other documentation of the battle, see *ORN*, I, 21:397–600. See also Farragut to General Benjamin Butler, August ?, 1864, DFP.

9. Purnell F. Harrington to his father, August 7, 1864, in Harrington, "Storming of Mobile Bay," 16.

10. Ely, "This Filthy Ironpot," 100, diary entry of August 5, 1864.

11. Brother, "Journal of Charles Brother," *Civil War Naval Chronology*, 6:81–83, entry of August 5, 1864.

12. John William Draper to Farragut, August 29, 1864, DFP. For Lincoln's blind memorandum, see Lincoln, *Collected Works of Lincoln*, 7:514–15.

13. Farragut to Welles, August 27, 1864, *ORN*, I, 21:612.

14. Welles, *Diary*, 2:127, entry of August 30, 1864.

15. Welles to Farragut, September 5 and 22 and October 1, 1864; Welles to Lee, September 17, 1864; and Welles to Porter, September 22, 1864, in *ORN*, I, 10:430–31, 467, 473–74, and *ORN*, I, 21:655–56, 668–69. Quotation from Welles, *Diary*, 2:146–47, entry of September 15, 1864.

16. *ORN*, I, 11:215–17. See also ibid., 68, 78–79, 90, 119, 207–15.

17. Porter to Rhind, December 17, 1864, ibid., 222–23.

18. Rhind to Porter, December 26, 1864, ibid., 226–27; Gragg, *Confederate Goliath*, 50–52.

19. Porter to Welles, December 24, 27, 29, *ORN*, I, 11:253, 261–62, 264.

20. Lamb to Major James H. Hill, December 27, 1864, ibid., 366–69; extract of Whiting's report, February 19, 1865, ibid., 593.

21. "Special Orders No. 8," January 3, 1865, ibid., 427.

22. Porter to Fox, January 7, 1865, in Porter, "Fort Fisher and Wilmington Campaign," 467; "General Orders No. 81," January 4, 1865, *ORN*, I, 11:427.

23. Porter to Welles, January 15, 1865, *ORN*, I, 11:434–35.

24. Two good modern accounts are Fonvielle, *The Wilmington Campaign*, and Gragg, *Confederate Goliath*.

25. Porter to Fox, January 20, 1865, in Porter, "Fort Fisher and Wilmington Campaign," 470.

26. Stephens, *Constitutional View of the War between the States*, 2:619.

27. Mallory to Mitchell, January 16 and 21, 1865, *ORN*, I, 11:797–98, 803.

28. Ibid., 635–41, 644–45, 650–51, 655–56, 658.

29. Ibid., 662–63.

30. *ORN*, I, 12:184–85.

31. *ORN*, I, 26:598–630, 683.

32. Ibid., 670, 678–79; *ORN*, I, 27:10–12, 153.

33. *ORN*, I, 27:154 and passim.

34. Mallory to Bulloch, November 17 and December 16, 1864, *ORN*, II, 2:767, 779.

35. *ORN*, I, 3:749–55; *ORN*, II, 2:701, 708, 713, 717, 731–32; Chaffin, *Sea of Gray*.

36. Barron to Captain Thomas J. Page, December 17, 1864, *ORN*, I, 3:719–20.

37. Craven to Welles, March 29, 1865, ibid., 461–62.

38. Page to Bulloch, March 25, 1865, ibid., 742.

39. Ibid., 467–70.

CONCLUSION

1. Surdam, *Northern Naval Superiority*, 206.

2. "Report of the Secretary of the Navy," December 5, 1864, xxiii; "Report of the Secretary of the Navy," December 5, 1865, xiii.

3. Silverstone, *Warships of Civil War Navies*, 200–249.

4. Owsley, *King Cotton Diplomacy*, 250–90; Wise, *Lifeline of the Confederacy*, 221 and passim.

5. Surdam, *Northern Naval Superiority*, 162.

6. Ibid., 6.

7. Scharf, *History of the Confederate States Navy*, v.

Bibliography

MANUSCRIPT COLLECTIONS

Princeton, N.J.
> Princeton University Library
>> Roswell H. Lamson Papers
>> Samuel Phillips Lee, Letters, Blair and Lee Family
>> Papers, 1764–1946

San Marino, Calif.
> The Huntington Library
>> David G. Farragut Papers
>> David D. Porter Papers

PRIMARY SOURCES

Adams, Charles Francis, Charles Francis Adams Jr., and Henry Adams. *A Cycle of Adams Letters, 1861–1865.* Edited by Worthington Chauncey Ford. 2 vols. Boston: Houghton Mifflin Company, 1920. Reprint, New York: Kraus Reprint Co., 1969.

Anderson, Edward Maffitt. "Letters from a Georgia Midshipman on the C.S.S. *Alabama.*" Edited by W. Stanley Hoole. *Georgia Historical Quarterly* 59 (1975): 416–32.

Arnold, George E. "A Blue Jacket's Letters Home, 1863–1864." Edited by Arthur M. Schlesinger. *New England Quarterly* 1 (1928): 554–67.

Bacon, Edward W. *Double Duty in the Civil War: The Letters of Sailor and Soldier Edward W. Bacon.* Edited by George S. Burkhardt. Carbondale: Southern Illinois University Press, 2009.

Bacon, George B. "The Civil War Letters of Lieutenant-Commander George B. Bacon." Edited by John K. Mahon. *American Neptune* 12 (1952): 271–81.

Barnes, James J., and Patience P. Barnes, eds. *The American Civil War through British Eyes.* 3 vols. Kent, Ohio: Kent State University Press, 2005.

Barnes, James S. *Submarine Warfare Offensive and Defensive.* New York: D. Van Nostrand, 1869.

Barnes, John Sanford. "The Battle of Port Royal Ferry, South Carolina: With the Entry for New Year's Eve and Day, 1862, from the Journal of John S. Barnes." Edited by John D. Hayes and Lillian O'Brien. *New York Historical Society Quarterly* 47 (1963): 109–36.

———. "The Battle of Port Royal, S.C." Edited by John D. Hayes. *New York Historical Society Quarterly* 45 (1961): 365–95.

———. "The Early Blockade and the Capture of the Hatteras Ports." Edited by John D. Hayes and Lillian O'Brien. *New York Historical Society Quarterly* 46 (1962): 61–85.

Bartlet, Samuel J. "A Union Volunteer with the Mississippi Ram Fleet." Edited by L. Moody Simms Jr. *Lincoln Herald* 70 (1968): 189–92.

Bartlett, Stephen C. "The Letters of Stephen Chandler Bartlett aboard U.S.S. 'Lenapee,' January to August 1865." Edited by Paul Murray and Stephen Russell Bartlett Jr. *North Carolina Historical Review* 33 (1956): 66–92.

Basoco, Richard W., William E. Geoghogan, and Frank J. Merli, eds. "A British View of the Union Navy, 1864; a Report Addressed to Her Majesty's Minister at Washington." *American Neptune* 27 (1967): 30–45.

Battles and Leaders of the Civil War. Edited by Robert U. Johnson and Clarence C. Buel. 4 vols. New York: The Century Co., 1888. Reprint, Secaucus, N.J.: Castle, 1982.

Boyer, Samuel P. *Naval Surgeon: The Diary of Dr. Samuel Pellman Boyer.* Edited by Elinor Barnes and James A. Barnes. 2 vols. Bloomington: Indiana University Press, 1963.

Brooke, John M. *Ironclads and Big Guns of the Confederacy: The Journals and Letters of John M. Brooke.* Edited by George M. Brooke. Columbia: University of South Carolina Press, 2002.

Brother, Charles. "The Journal of Private Charles Brother." In *Civil War Naval Chronology*, vol. 6, compiled by Naval History Division, Navy Department, 47–83. Washington, D.C.: Government Printing Office, 1971. Also published in *Two Naval Journals: 1864, at the Battle of Mobile Bay*, edited by C. Carter Smith, 1–17. Chicago: Wyvern Press, 1964.

Browne, Henry R., and Symmes E. Browne. *From the Fresh-Water Navy, 1862–1864: The Letters of Acting Master's Mate Henry R. Browne and Acting Ensign Symmes E. Browne.* Edited by John D. Milligan. Annapolis: Naval Institute Press, 1970.

Bulloch, James Dunwoody. *The Secret Service of the Confederate States in Europe.* 2 vols. New York: Putnam, 1884. Reprint, New York: Yoseloff, 1959.

Burkmyer, Cornelius L. *Burkmyer Letters, March 1863–June 1865.* Edited by Charlotte R. Holmes. Columbia, S.C.: The State Co., 1926.

Carpenter, Charles C. "'Such a Fire I Never Saw' (Letters of Lt. Commander Charles C. Carpenter)." Edited by Wallace Shugg. *Civil War Times* 10 (July 1971): 13–22.

Cary, Clarence Fairfax. "The War Journal of Midshipman Cary." Edited by Brooks Thompson and Frank Lawrence Owsley Jr. *Civil War History* 9 (June 1963): 187–202.

Church, Frank Linnarus. *Civil War Marine: A Diary of the Red River Expedition, 1864.* Edited by James P. Jones and Edward F. Keuchel. Washington, D.C.: U.S. Government Printing Office, 1975.

Collins, James, and Joseph Collins. "Two New Yorkers in the Union Navy." Edited by James J. Heslin. *New York Historical Society Quarterly* 43 (1959): 161–201.

Cupples, George. "Two Battles of Galveston Letters." Edited by Dorman H. Winfrey. *Southwestern Historical Quarterly* 65 (1961): 251–57.

Currie, George E. *Warfare along the Mississippi: The Letters of Lt. George E. Currie.*

Edited by Norman E. Clark. Mt. Pleasant: Central Michigan University Press, 1961.

Dahlgren, Madeleine V. *Memoir of John A. Dahlgren, Rear Admiral, U.S. Navy.* Boston: J. R. Osgood, 1882. Includes Dahlgren's diary and some letters.

Davis, Charles H., Jr. *Life of Charles Henry Davis, Rear Admiral, 1807–1877.* Boston: Houghton Mifflin, 1899. Includes letters.

Davis, Jefferson. *Jefferson Davis, Constitutionalist: His Letters, Papers, and Speeches.* Edited by Dunbar Rowland. 10 vols. Jackson: Mississippi Department of Archives and History, 1923.

Dickson, James. *High Seas and Yankee Gunboats: A Blockade-Running Adventure from the Diary of James Dickson.* Edited by Roger S. Durham. Columbia: University of South Carolina Press, 2005.

Dillon, Richard H. "Documents." *American Neptune* 19 (1959): 126–28. Letters of John A. Winslow and Thomas H. Dudley regarding the sinking of CSS *Alabama.*

Drayton, Percival. *Naval Letters from Captain Percival Drayton, 1861–1865.* New York: New York Public Library, 1906.

Du Pont, Samuel Francis. *Samuel Francis Du Pont: A Selection from His Civil War Letters.* Edited by John D. Hayes. 3 vols. Ithaca: Cornell University Press, 1969.

Ely, Robert B. "This Filthy Ironpot." *American Heritage* 19 (February 1968): 46–51, 108–11. Diary of officer on the USS *Manhattan.*

Farragut, Loyall. *The Life of David Glasgow Farragut, First Admiral of the United States Navy, Embodying His Journal and Letters.* New York: D. Appleton and Co., 1879.

Foltz, Jonathan M. *Surgeon of the Seas: The Adventurous Life of Surgeon General Jonathan M. Foltz in the Days of Wooden Ships.* Edited by Charles S. Foltz. Indianapolis: Bobbs-Merrill, 1931.

Forrest, Douglas French, *Odyssey in Gray: A Diary of Confederate Service, 1863–1865.* Edited by William N. Still Jr. Richmond: Virginia State Library, 1979.

Fox, Gustavus V. *Confidential Correspondence of Gustavus Vasa Fox, Assistant Secretary of the Navy, 1861–1865.* Edited by Robert M. Thompson and Richard Wainwright. 2 vols. New York: Naval History Society, 1918–19.

Fullam, George Townley. *The Journal of George Townley Fullam, Boarding Officer of the Confederate Sea Raider Alabama.* Edited by Charles G. Summersell. University, Ala.: University of Alabama Press, 1973.

Geer, George. *The* Monitor *Chronicles: One Sailor's Account.* Edited by William Marvel. New York: Simon & Schuster, 2000.

Gould, William B. *Diary of a Contraband: The Civil War Passage of a Black Sailor.* Edited by William B. Gould IV. Stanford: Stanford University Press, 2002.

Grant, Ulysses S. *Personal Memoirs of U. S. Grant.* 2 vols. New York: Charles L. Webster and Company, 1885–86.

Grattan, John W. *Under the Blue Pennant: Or Notes of a Naval Officer, 1863–1865.* Edited by Robert J. Schellner Jr. New York: Wiley, 1999.

Greene, S. Dana. "I Fired the First Gun and Thus Commenced the Great Battle." *American Heritage* 8 (June 1957): 10–13, 102–5.

Gulick, Charles Heckman. "War on the River: A River Pilot's Mail." Edited by Stan Hamper. *Civil War Times* 21 (October 1982): 24–31.

Harrington, Purnell Frederick. "The Storming of Mobile Bay." Edited by Richard R. Duncan. *Alabama Historical Quarterly* 40 (1978): 6–19.

Holt, Hiram Talbert. "A Confederate Sergeant's Report to His Wife during the Bombardment of Fort Pillow." Edited by Robert Partin. *Tennessee Historical Quarterly* 15 (1956): 243–52.

Holton, William C. *Cruise of the U.S. Flag-ship* Hartford . . . *from the Private Journal of William C. Holton*. Edited by B. S. Osbon. New York: L. W. Paine, 1863.

Hoppin, James M. *Life of Andrew Hull Foote, Rear-Admiral United States Navy*. New York: Harper, 1874. Includes Foote's letters.

Hults, Ellsworth H. "Aboard the *Galena* at Mobile." *Civil War Times* 10 (April 1971): 13–21; *Civil War Times* 10 (May 1971): 29–38.

Hunter, Alvah Folsom. *A Year on a Monitor and the Destruction of Fort Sumter*. Edited by Craig Symonds. Columbia: University of South Carolina Press, 1987.

Josselyn, Francis. "Francis Josselyn: A Gunboat Captain's Diary." Edited by John M. Taylor. *Manuscripts* 33 (1981): 113–22.

Keeler, William F. *Aboard the USS* Florida, *1863–1865: The Letters of Paymaster William Frederick Keeler, U.S. Navy*. Edited by Robert W. Daly. Annapolis: U.S. Naval Institute Press, 1968.

———. *Aboard the USS* Monitor, *1862: The Letters of Acting Paymaster William Frederick Keeler*. Edited by Robert W. Daly. Annapolis: Naval Institute Press, 1964.

Lamson, Roswell H. *Lamson of the Gettysburg: The Civil War Letters of Lieutenant Roswell H. Lamson, U.S. Navy*. Edited by James M. McPherson and Patricia R. McPherson. New York: Oxford University Press, 1997.

Lee, Elizabeth Blair. *Wartime Washington: The Civil War Letters of Elizabeth Blair Lee*. Edited by Virginia Jeans Laas. Urbana: University of Illinois Press, 1991.

Lee, Robert E., Jr. *Recollections and Letters of General Robert E. Lee*. New York: Doubleday, 1905.

Lincoln, Abraham. *The Collected Works of Abraham Lincoln*. Edited by Roy B. Basler. 9 vols. New Brunswick, N.J.: Rutgers University Press, 1953–55.

———. *Recollected Words of Abraham Lincoln*. Edited by Don E. Fehrenbacher and Virginia Fehrenbacher. Stanford: Stanford University Press, 1996.

Low, John. *The Logs of the CSS* Alabama *and the CSS* Tuscaloosa, *1862–1863*. Edited by W. S. Hoole. University, Ala.: Confederate Publishing Co., 1972.

Maffitt, Emma. *The Life and Services of John Newland Maffitt*. New York: Neale Pub. Co., 1906. Includes letters and diary entries.

Manigault, Edward. *Siege Train: The Journal of a Confederate Artilleryman in the Defense of Charleston*. Edited by Warren Ripley. Columbia: University of South Carolina Press, 1986.

Marchand, John B. *Charleston Blockade: The Journals of John B. Marchand, U.S. Navy, 1861–62*. Edited by Craig L. Symonds. Newport: Naval War College Press, 1976.

Mason, Virginia. *The Public Life and Diplomatic Correspondence of James M. Mason*. New York: The Neale Publishing Company, 1906.

McPherson, James M. *The Negro's Civil War*. New York: Pantheon Books, 1965.

Mervine, Charles K. "Jottings by the Navy: A Sailor's Log—1862 to 1864." Edited by Kent Packard. *Pennsylvania Magazine of History and Biography* 71 (April 1947): 121–51; (July 1947): 242–82.

Moore, Frank, ed. *The Rebellion Record: A Diary of American Events*. 12 vols. Reprint edition, New York: Arno Press, 1977.

Moran, Benjamin. *The Journal of Benjamin Moran, 1857–1865*. Edited by Sarah H. Wallace and Francis E. Gillespie. 2 vols. Chicago: University of Chicago Press, 1949.

Morgan, Sarah. *The Civil War Diary of Sarah Morgan*. Edited by Charles East. Athens: University of Georgia Press, 1991.

Morrow, Leslie G. *Journal of Leslie G. Morrow, Captain's Clerk of the U.S.S. Galena*. Edited by Albert P. Morrow. Yorba Linda, Calif.: Specialty Services Co., 1988.

Morse, DeWitt C. "A Fighting Sailor on the Western Rivers: The Civil War Letters of 'Gunboat.'" Edited by Jeffrey L. Patrick. *Journal of Mississippi History* 58 (1996): 255–83.

Nichols, Sayres O. "Fighting in North Carolina Waters." Edited by Roy F. Nichols. *North Carolina Historical Review* 40 (1963): 75–84.

Official Records of the Union and Confederate Navies in the War of the Rebellion. 30 vols. Washington, D.C.: Government Printing Office, 1894–1922.

Papers Relating to the Foreign Relations of the United States, 1862. Washington, D.C.: Government Printing Office, 1863.

Perkins, George H. *Letters of Captain Geo. Hamilton Perkins, U.S.N.* Edited by George E. Belknap. Concord, N.H.: The Rumford Press, 1901.

Porter, David D. "The Fort Fisher and Wilmington Campaign: Letters from Rear Admiral David D. Porter." Edited by James M. Merrill. *North Carolina Historical Review* 35 (1958): 461–75.

Post, Charles A. "A Diary on the Blockade in 1863." *U.S. Naval Institute Proceedings* 44 (1918): 2333–50, 2567–94.

Ramseur, Stephen Dodson. "'The Fight between the Two Iron Monsters': The *Monitor* vs. the *Virginia*, as Described by Major Stephen Dodson Ramseur, C.S.A." Edited by Gary W. Gallagher. *Civil War History* 30 (1984): 268–71.

"Report of the Secretary of the Navy." Senate Doc. no. 1, vol. 3. 37th Cong., 2d Sess. December 3, 1861.

"Report of the Sec. of the Navy." House Exec. Doc. no. 1, vol. 3. 37th Cong., 34d Sess. December 1, 1862.

"Report of the Secretary of the Navy." House Exec. Doc. no. 1, vol. 5. 38th Cong., 1st Sess. December 5, 1863.

"Report of the Sec. of the Navy." House Exec. Doc. no. 1, pt. 6, vol. 6. 38th Cong., 2d Sess. December 5, 1864.

"Report of the Sec. of the Navy." House Exec. Doc. no. 1, vol. 6. 39th Cong., 1st Sess. December 4, 1865.

Ruffin, Edmund. *The Diary of Edmund Ruffin*. Edited by William K. Scarborough. 3 vols. Baton Rouge: Louisiana State University Press, 1989.

Saunders, Herbert. "The Civil War Letters of Herbert Saunders." Edited by Ronald K. Huch. *Register of the Kentucky Historical Society* 69 (1971): 17–29.

Semmes, Raphael. "Admiral on Horseback: The Diary of Brigadier General Raphael Semmes, Feb.–May 1865." Edited by W. Stanley Hoole. *Alabama Review* 28 (1975): 129–50.

———. *Memoirs of Service Afloat during the War between the States*. Baltimore: Kelly, Piet, & Co., 1869. Reprint, Secaucus, N.J.: Blue and Gray Press, 1987.

Steedman, Charles. *Memoir and Correspondence of Charles Steedman, Rear Admiral, United States Navy*. Edited by Amos Lawrence Mason. Cambridge, Mass.: Riverside Press, 1912.

Stephens, Alexander H. *A Constitutional View of the Late War between the States*. 2 vols. Philadelphia: National Publishing Co., 1868–70.

Stone, Kate. *Brokenburn: The Journal of Kate Stone, 1861–1865*. Edited by John Q. Anderson. Baton Rouge: Louisiana State University Press, 1972.

Swift, John. "Letters from a Sailor on a Tinclad." Edited by Lester L. Swift. *Civil War History* 7 (1961): 48–62.

Tipton, William. *Dearest Carrie: Civil War Letters Home*. Lawrenceville, Va.: Brunswick Publishing Corp., 1895.

Vandiver, Frank E., ed. *Confederate Blockade Running through Bermuda: Letters and Cargo Manifests*. Houston: University of Texas Press, 1946.

Walker, Georgiana G. *The Private Journal of Georgiana Gholson Walker, 1862–1865*. Tuscaloosa, Ala.: Confederate Publishing Co., 1963.

War of the Rebellion . . . Official Records of the Union and Confederate Armies. 128 vols. Washington, D.C.: Government Printing Office, 1880–1901.

Watson, Robert. *Southern Service on Land and Sea: The Wartime Journal of Robert Watson, CSA/CSN*. Knoxville: University of Tennessee Press, 2002.

Welles, Gideon. *Civil War and Reconstruction: Selected Essays*. Edited by Albert Mordell. New York: Twayne Publishers, 1959.

———. *Diary of Gideon Welles*. Edited by Howard K. Beale. 3 vols. New York: W. W. Norton & Company, 1960.

SECONDARY SOURCES

Adams, Ephraim Douglass. *Great Britain and the American Civil War*. 2 vols. New York: Russell & Russell, 1925.

Allard, Dean C. "Naval Technology during the American Civil War." *American Neptune* 49 (Spring 1984): 114–22.

Ammen, Daniel. *Campaigns of the Civil War: The Atlantic Coast*. New York: Scribner, 1883.

Anderson, Bern. *By Sea and by River: The Naval History of the Civil War*. New York: Knopf, 1962.

Anderson, Stuart. "Blockade versus Closing the Confederate Ports." *Military Affairs* 41 (1977): 190–93.

Arnold, James R. *Grant Wins the War: Decision at Vicksburg*. New York: Crown, 2007.

Ballard, Michael B. *Vicksburg: The Campaign That Opened the Mississippi*. Chapel Hill: University of North Carolina Press, 2004.

Barrett, John G. *The Civil War in North Carolina*. Chapel Hill: University of North Carolina Press, 1963.

Bearss, Edwin C. "A Federal Raid up the Tennessee River." *Alabama Review* 17 (1964): 261–70.

———. "The Fiasco at the Head of the Passes." *Louisiana History* 4 (1963): 301–11.

———. *Hardluck Ironclad: The Sinking and Salvage of the* Cairo. Baton Rouge: Louisiana State University Press, 1966.

Bennett, Michael J. *Union Jacks: Yankee Sailors in the Civil War*. Chapel Hill: University of North Carolina Press, 2004.

Bernath, Stuart L. *Squall across the Atlantic: American Civil War Prize Cases and Diplomacy*. Berkeley: University of California Press, 1970.

Bigelow, John. *France and the Confederate Navy, 1862–1865*. New York: Harper & Brothers, 1888. Reprint, New York: Bergman, 1968.

Bolster, Jeffrey W. *Black Jacks: African-American Seamen in the Age of Sail*. Cambridge: Harvard University Press, 1997.

Bonner, M. Brem, and Peter McCord. "Reassessment of the Union Blockade's Effectiveness in the Civil War." *North Carolina Historical Review* 88 (October 2011): 375–98.

Boykin, Edward C. *Ghost Ship of the Confederacy: The Story of the* Alabama *and Her Captain, Raphael Semmes*. New York: Funk and Wagnalls, 1957.

———. *Sea Devil of the Confederacy: The Story of the* Florida *and Her Captain, John Newland Maffitt*. New York: Funk and Wagnalls, 1959.

Boynton, Charles B. *The History of the Navy during the Rebellion*. 2 vols. New York: D. Appleton & Co., 1867–68.

Browning, Robert M., Jr. *From Cape Charles to Cape Fear: The North Atlantic Blockading Squadron in the Civil War*. Tuscaloosa: University of Alabama Press, 1993.

———. *Success Is All That Was Expected: The South Atlantic Blockading Squadron during the Civil War*. Dulles, Va.: Brassey, 2002.

Buker, George E. *Blockaders, Refugees, and Contrabands: Civil War on Florida's Gulf Coast, 1861–1865*. Tuscaloosa: University of Alabama Press, 1993.

Burton, E. Milby. *The Siege of Charleston, 1861–1865*. Columbia: University of South Carolina Press, 1970.

Callahan, Edward W. *List of Officers of the Navy of the United States and of the Marine Corps from 1775 to 1900*. New York, 1901.

Campbell, R. Thomas. *Confederate Naval Forces on Western Waters: The Defense of the Mississippi River and Its Tributaries*. Jefferson, N.C.: McFarland, 2005.

Canfield, Eugene B. *Notes on Naval Ordnance of the American Civil War*. Washington, D.C.: Am. Ordnance Assoc., 1960.

Canney, Donald L. *Lincoln's Navy: The Ships, Men, and Organization, 1861–1865*. Annapolis: Naval Institute Press, 1998.

Carse, Robert. *Blockade: The Civil War at Sea*. New York: Rinehart, 1958.

Carter, Samuel, III. *The Final Fortress: The Campaign for Vicksburg*. New York: St. Martin's Press, 1980.

Case, Lynn M., and Warren G. Spencer. *The United States and France: Civil War Diplomacy*. Philadelphia: University of Pennsylvania Press, 1970.

Chaffin, Tom. *The H. L. Hunley: The Secret Hope of the Confederacy*. New York: Hill and Wang, 2008.

———. *Sea of Gray: The Around-the-World Odyssey of the Confederate Raider Shenandoah*. New York: Hill and Wang, 2006.

Cimprich, John. *Fort Pillow, a Civil War Massacre and Public Memory*. Baton Rouge: Louisiana State University Press, 2005.

Cochran, Hamilton. *Blockade Runners of the Confederacy*. Indianapolis: Bobbs-Merrill, 1958.

Coddington, Edwin B. "The Civil War Blockade Reconsidered." In *Essays in History and International Relations in Honor of George Hubbard Blakeslee*, edited by Dwight E. Lee and George E. McReynolds, 284–305. Worcester, Mass.: Clark University Press, 1949.

Coletta, Paola E. "A Selectively Annotated Bibliography of Naval Power in the American Civil War." *Civil War History* 42 (March 1996): 32–63.

Cook, Adrian. *The Alabama Claims: American Politics and Anglo-American Relations, 1865–1873*. Ithaca: Cornell University Press, 1975.

Cooling, Benjamin Franklin. *Forts Henry and Donelson: The Key to the Confederate Heartland*. Knoxville: University of Tennessee Press, 1987.

Coombe, Jack D. *Thunder along the Mississippi: The River Battles That Split the Confederacy*. New York: Sarpedon, 1996.

Coski, John M. *Capital Navy: The Men, Ships, and Operations of the James River Squadron*. Campbell, Calif.: Savas, 1996.

Cotham, Edward T. *Battle on the Bay: The Civil War Struggle for Galveston*. Austin: University of Texas Press, 1998.

Cross, Coy F. *Lincoln's Man in Liverpool: Consul Dudley and the Legal Battle to Stop Confederate Warships*. De Kalb: Northern Illinois Press, 2007.

Cunningham, Edward. *The Port Hudson Campaign, 1862–1863*. Baton Rouge: Louisiana State University Press, 1963.

Current, Richard N., ed. *Encyclopedia of the Confederacy*. 4 vols. New York: Simon & Schuster, 1993.

Daddysman, James W. *The Matamoros Trade: Confederate Commerce, Diplomacy, and Intrigue*. Newark: University of Delaware Press, 1984.

Daly, Robert W. *How the Merrimac Won: The Strategic Story of the C.S.S. Virginia*. New York: Thomas Y. Crowell, 1957.

Dalzell, George W. *The Flight from the Flag: The Continuing Effect of the Civil War upon the American Carrying Trade*. Chapel Hill: University of North Carolina Press, 1940.

Daniel, Larry J., and Lynn N. Bock. *Island No. 10: Struggles for the Mississippi Valley*. Tuscaloosa: University of Alabama Press, 1996.

Davis, William C. *Duel between the First Ironclads*. Garden City, N.Y.: Doubleday, 1975.

De Kay, James Tertius. Monitor: *The Story of the Legendary Civil War Ironclad and the Man Whose Invention Changed the Course of History*. New York: Walker and Company, 1997.

———. *The Rebel Raiders: The Astonishing History of the Confederacy's Secret Navy*. New York: Ballantine Books, 2002.

Delaney, Robert W. "Matamoros: Port for Texas during the Civil War." *Southwestern Historical Quarterly* 58 (1955): 473–87.

Dougherty, Kevin. *Strangling the Confederacy: Coastal Operations in the Civil War*. Havertown, Pa.: Casemate, 2010.

Dufour, Charles E. *The Night the War Was Lost*. Garden City: Doubleday, 1960.

Elliott, Robert G. *Ironclad of the Roanoke: Gilbert Elliott's Albemarle*. Shippensburg, Pa.: White Mane Books, 1999.

Ferris, Norman B. *The Trent Affair: A Diplomatic Crisis*. Knoxville: University of Tennessee Press, 1977.

Fonvielle, Chris E., Jr. *The Wilmington Campaign: Last Rays of Departing Hope*. Mechanicsville, Pa.: Stackpole Books, 1997.

Foote, Shelby. *The Civil War: A Narrative*. 3 vols. New York: Random House, 1958–1974.

Foreman, Amanda. *A World on Fire: Britain's Crucial Role in the American Civil War*. New York: Random House, 2010.

Fowler, William N., Jr. *Under Two Flags: The American Navy in the Civil War*. New York: Norton, 1990.

Fox, Stephen. *Wolf of the Deep: Raphael Semmes and the Notorious Confederate Raider CSS Alabama*. New York: Alfred A. Knopf, 2007.

Friend, Jack. *West Wind, Flood Tide: The Battle of Mobile Bay*. Annapolis: Naval Institute Press, 2004.

Fuller, Howard J. *Clad in Iron: The American Civil War and the Challenge of British Naval Power*. Westport, Conn.: Praeger, 2008.

Gaines, W. Craig. *Encyclopedia of Civil War Shipwrecks*. Baton Rouge: Louisiana State University Press, 2008.

Gosnell, H. Allen. *Guns on the Western Waters*. Baton Rouge: Louisiana State University Press, 1949.

Gragg, Rod. *Confederate Goliath: The Battle of Fort Fisher*. New York: HarperCollins, 1991.

Hearn, Chester G. *The Capture of New Orleans, 1862*. Baton Rouge: Louisiana State University Press, 1995.

———. *Ellet's Brigade: The Strangest Outfit of All*. Baton Rouge: Louisiana State University Press, 2000.

———. *Gray Raiders of the Sea: How Eight Confederate Warships Destroyed the Union's High Seas Commerce*. Camden, Maine: International Marine Publishing, 1992.

———. *Mobile Bay and the Mobile Campaign: The Last Great Battle of the Civil War*. Jefferson, N.C.: McFarland, 1993.

Hewitt, Lawrence Lee. *Port Hudson: Confederate Bastion on the Mississippi*. Baton Rouge: Louisiana State University Press, 1987.

Hinds, John W. *The Hunt for the* Albemarle: *Anatomy of a Gunboat War.* Shippensburg, Pa.: Burd Street Press, 2001.

Holzer, Harold, and Tim Mulligan, eds. *The Battle of Hampton Roads.* New York: Fordham University Press, 2006.

Hoyt, Edwin P. *The Voyage of the* Hunley. Short Hills, N.J.: Burford Books, 2002.

Johnson, Ludwell H. *Red River Campaign: Politics and Cotton in the Civil War.* Baltimore: Johns Hopkins University Press, 1958.

Joiner, Gary D. *Mr. Lincoln's Brown Water Navy: The Mississippi Squadron.* Lanham, Md.: Rowman and Littlefield, 2007.

———. *One Damn Blunder from Beginning to End: The Red River Campaign of 1864.* Lanham, Md.: SR Books, 2003.

———. *Through the Howling Wilderness: The 1864 Red River Campaign and Union Failure in the West.* Knoxville: University of Tennessee Press, 2006.

Jones, Howard. *Blue and Gray Diplomacy.* Chapel Hill: University of North Carolina Press, 2010.

Jones, Virgil Carrington. *The Civil War at Sea.* 3 vols. New York: Holt, Rinehart, Winston, 1960–62.

Jones, Wilbur D. *The Confederate Rams at Birkenhead: A Chapter in Anglo-American Relations.* Tuscaloosa, Ala.: Confederate Publishing, 1961.

Krein, David F. "Russell's Decision to Retain the Laird Rams." *Civil War History* 22 (1976): 158–63.

Lebergott, Stanley. "Through the Blockade: The Profitability and Extent of Cotton Smuggling, 1861–1865." *Journal of Economic History* 41 (1981): 867–88.

Lonn, Ella. "The Extent and Importance of Federal Naval Raids on Salt-Making in Florida, 1862–1865." *Florida Historical Society Quarterly* 10 (1932): 167–84.

———. *Salt as a Factor in the Confederacy.* New York: W. Neale, 1933.

Luraghi, Raimondo. *A History of the Confederate Navy.* Translated by Paolo E. Coletta. Annapolis: Naval Institute Press, 1996.

Mahan, Alfred T. *Campaigns of the Civil War: The Gulf and Inland Waters.* New York: Scribner, 1883.

Marvel, William. *The* Alabama *and the* Kearsarge: *The Sailors' Civil War.* Chapel Hill: University of North Carolina Press, 1996.

McCaslin, Richard B. *The Last Stronghold: The Campaign for Fort Fisher.* Abilene, Tex.: McWhiney Foundation Press, 2003.

McPherson, James M. *Crossroads of Freedom: Antietam.* New York: Oxford University Press, 2002.

Melton, Maurice. *The Confederate Ironclads.* New York: Thomas Yoseloff, 1968.

Merli, Frank J. *The* Alabama, *British Neutrality, and the American Civil War.* Bloomington: Indiana University Press, 2004.

———. *Great Britain and the Confederate Navy, 1861–1865.* Bloomington: Indiana University Press, 1970.

Merrill, James M. *Battle Flags South: The Story of Civil War Navies on the Western Waters.* Rutherford, N.J.: Fairleigh Dickinson University Press, 1970.

———. *The Rebel Shore: The Story of Union Sea Power in the Civil War.* Boston: Little, Brown, 1957.

Miller, Francis Trevelyan, ed. *The Photographic History of the Civil War*. 10 vols. New York: Thomas Yoseloff, 1957.

Milligan, John D. *Gunboats down the Mississippi*. Annapolis: Naval Institute Press, 1965.

Milton, David Hepburn. *Lincoln's Spymaster: Thomas Haines Dudley and the Liverpool Network*. Mechanicsburg, Pa.: Stackpole Books, 2003.

Mindell, David A. *War, Technology, and Experience aboard the USS* Monitor. Baltimore: Johns Hopkins University Press, 2000.

Musicant, Ivan. *Divided Waters: The Naval History of the Civil War*. New York: HarperCollins, 1995.

Nash, Howard P., Jr. *A Naval History of the Civil War*. New York: A. S. Barnes & Co., 1972.

Nelson, James L. *Reign of Iron: The Story of the First Battling Ironclads, the* Monitor *and the* Merrimack. New York: William Morrow, 2004.

Nevins, Allan. *The War for the Union*. 4 vols. Charles Scribner's Sons, 1959–71.

Owsley, Frank L., Jr. *The C.S.S.* Florida: *Her Building and Operation*. Philadelphia: University of Pennsylvania Press, 1965.

Owsley, Frank L., Sr. *King Cotton Diplomacy: Foreign Relations of the Confederate States of America*. Chicago: University of Chicago Press, 1931.

———. *King Cotton Diplomacy: Foreign Relations of the Confederate States of America*. 2nd ed. Revised by Harriet C. Owsley. Chicago: University of Chicago Press, 1959.

Page, Dave. *Ships versus Shore: Civil War Engagements along Southern Shores*. Nashville, Tenn.: Rutledge Hill, 1994.

Perry, Milton F. *Infernal Machines: The Story of Confederate Submarines and Mine Warfare*. Baton Rouge: Louisiana State University Press, 1961.

Pierson, Michael D. *Mutiny at Fort Jackson: The Untold Story of the Fall of New Orleans*. Chapel Hill: University of North Carolina Press, 2008.

Porter, David Dixon. *Naval History of the Civil War*. Reprint edition, New York: Dover, 1998.

Quarles, Benjamin. *The Negro in the Civil War*. Boston: Little, Brown and Co., 1953.

Ragan, Mark K. *Union and Confederate Submarine Warfare in the Civil War*. Mason City, Iowa: Savas Pub. Co., 1999.

Ramold, Steven J. *Slaves, Sailors, Citizens: African Americans in the Union Navy*. De Kalb, Ill.: Northern Illinois University Press, 2002.

Randall, James G. *Constitutional Problems under Lincoln*. Revised edition. Urbana, Ill.: University of Illinois Press, 1951.

Reed, Rowena. *Combined Operations in the Civil War*. Annapolis: Naval Institute Press, 1978.

Ringle, Dennis J. *Life in Mr. Lincoln's Navy*. Annapolis: Naval Institute Press, 1998.

Ripley, Warren. *Artillery and Ammunition of the Civil War*. New York: Van Nostrand Reinhold, 1970.

Roberts, William B. "James D. Bulloch and the Confederate Navy." *North Carolina Historical Review* 24 (1947): 315–66.

Roberts, William H. *Civil War Ironclads: The U.S. Navy and Industrial Mobilization*. Baltimore: Johns Hopkins University Press, 2002.

———. *New Ironsides in the Civil War*. Annapolis: Naval Institute Press, 1999.

———. *Now for the Contest: Coastal and Naval Operations in the Civil War*. Lincoln: University of Nebraska Press, 2004.

Robinson, Charles M., III. *Hurricane of Fire: The Union Assault on Fort Fisher*. Annapolis: Naval Institute Press, 1998.

———. *Shark of the Confederacy: The Story of the CSS* Alabama. Naval Institute Press, 1995.

Robinson, William J., Jr. *The Confederate Privateers*. New Haven: Yale University Press, 1928. Reprint, Columbia: University of South Carolina Press, 1980.

Scharf, J. Thomas. *History of the Confederate States Navy*. New York: Rogers Y. Sherwood, 1887. Reprint, New York: Random House, 1996.

Schooler, Lynn. *The Last Shot: The Incredible Story of the CSS* Shenandoah *and the True Conclusion of the American Civil War*. New York: HarperCollins, 2005.

Shaw, David W. *Sea Wolf of the Confederacy: The Daring Civil War Raids of Naval Lt. Charles W. Read*. New York: Free Press, 2004.

Shea, William L., and Terrence J. Winschel. *Vicksburg Is the Key: The Struggle for the Mississippi River*. Lincoln: University of Nebraska Press, 2003.

Silverstone, Paul H. *Warships of the Civil War Navies*. Annapolis: Naval Institute Press, 1989.

Simson, Jay W. *Naval Strategies of the Civil War: Confederate Innovations and Federal Opportunism*. Nashville: Cumberland House, 2001.

Smith, Myron J. *The CSS* Arkansas*: A Confederate Ironclad on Western Waters*. Jefferson, N.C.: McFarland, 2011.

———. *The Timberclads in the Civil War: The* Lexington, Conestoga, *and* Tyler *on the Western Waters*. Jefferson, N.C.: McFarland, 2008.

———. *Tinclads in the Civil War: Union Light-Draught Gunboat Operations on Western Waters, 1862–1865*. Jefferson, N.C.: McFarland, 2010.

Soley, James Russell. *Campaigns of the Civil War: The Blockade and the Cruisers*. New York: Scribner, 1883.

Songini, Marc. *The Lost Fleet: A Yankee Whaler's Struggle with the Confederate Navy and Arctic Disaster*. New York: St. Martin's Press, 2007.

Spencer, Warren F. *The Confederate Navy in Europe*. Tuscaloosa: University of Alabama Press, 1983.

Stern, Philip Van Doren. *The Confederate Navy: A Pictorial History*. Garden City, N.Y.: Doubleday, 1962.

Still, William N., Jr. *Confederate Shipbuilding*. Columbia: University of South Carolina Press, 1987.

———. *Iron Afloat: The Story of the Confederate Armorclads*. Nashville, Tenn.: Vanderbilt University Press, 1971.

———, ed. *The Confederate Navy: The Ships, Men, and Organization, 1861–1865*. Annapolis: Naval Institute Press, 1997.

Strong, Thomas Buckley, and Annetta St. Clair. "The Odyssey of C.S.S. *Stonewall*, 1864–1865." *Civil War History* 30 (1984): 305–23.

Summersell, Charles G. *The Cruise of the C.S.S.* Sumter. Tuscaloosa, Ala.: Confederate
     Publishing Co., 1965.
————. *CSS* Alabama: *Builder, Captain, and Plans*. University, Ala.: University of
     Alabama Press, 1985.
Surdam, David G. *Northern Naval Superiority and the Economics of the American
     Civil War*. Columbia: University of South Carolina Press, 2001.
Symonds, Craig L. *The Civil War at Sea*. Santa Barbara, Calif.: Praeger, 2009.
————. *Historical Atlas of the U.S. Navy*. Annapolis: Naval Institute Press, 1995.
————. *Lincoln and His Admirals*. New York: Oxford University Press, 2008.
————, ed. *Union Combined Operations in the Civil War*. New York: Fordham
     University Press, 2010.
Taafe, Stephen R. *Commanding Lincoln's Navy: Union Naval Leadership during
     the Civil War*. Annapolis: Naval Institute Press, 2009.
Thomas, Mary Elizabeth. "The C.S.S. *Tallahassee*: A Factor in Anglo-American
     Relations." *Civil War History* 21 (1975): 148–59.
Thompson, Samuel B. *Confederate Purchasing Operations Abroad*. Chapel Hill:
     University of North Carolina Press, 1935.
Tomblin, Barbara Brooks. *Bluejackets and Contrabands: African Americans and the
     Union Navy*. Lexington: The University Press of Kentucky, 2009.
Tucker, Spencer C. *Arming the Fleet: U.S. Naval Ordnance in the Muzzle-Loading
     Era*. Annapolis: Naval Institute Press, 1989.
————. *Blue and Gray Navies: The Civil War Afloat*. Annapolis: Naval Institute
     Press, 2006.
————. *A Short History of the Civil War at Sea*. Wilmington, Del.: Scholarly
     Resources, 2002.
————, ed. *The Civil War Naval Encyclopedia*. 2 vols. Santa Barbara, Calif.: ABC-
     Clio, 2011.
Underwood, Rodman L. *Waters of Discord: The Union Blockade of Texas during the
     Civil War*. Jefferson, N.C.: McFarland, 2003.
U.S. Navy Department, Naval History Division. *Civil War Naval Chronology, 1861–
     1865*. 6 vols. in one. Washington, D.C.: Government Printing Office, 1971.
Valusak, David L. *The African American in the Union Navy, 1861–1865*. New York:
     Garland, 1993.
Ward, Andrew. *River Run Red: The Fort Pillow Massacre in the Civil War*. New York:
     Viking, 2005.
Weddle, Kevin J. "The Blockade Board of 1861 and Union Naval Strategy." *Civil War
     History* 48 (2002): 123–42.
Wells, Tom H. *The Confederate Navy: A Study in Organization*. University, Ala.:
     University of Alabama Press, 1971.
West, Richard S. *Mr. Lincoln's Navy*. New York: Longmans, Green, 1957.
Wise, Stephen R. *Gate of Hell: Campaign for Charleston Harbor, 1863*. Columbia:
     University of South Carolina Press, 1994.
————. *Lifeline of the Confederacy: Blockade Running during the Civil War*.
     Columbia: University of South Carolina Press, 1988.

Symonds, Craig L. *Confederate Admiral: The Life and Wars of Franklin Buchanan*. Annapolis: Naval Institute Press, 1999.

Roske, Ralph J., and Charles Van Doren. *Lincoln's Commando: The Biography of Commander W. B. Cushing*. New York: Harper & Brothers, 1957.

Schneller, Robert J. *Cushing: Civil War SEAL*. Washington, D.C.: Brasseys, 2004.

Schneller, Robert J., Jr. *A Quest for Glory: A Biography of Rear Admiral John A. Dahlgren*. Annapolis: Naval Institute Press, 1996.

Weddle, Kevin J. *Lincoln's Tragic Admiral: The Life of Samuel Francis Du Pont*. Charlottesville: University of Virginia Press, 2005.

Duffy, James P. *Lincoln's Admiral: The Civil War Campaigns of David Farragut*. New York: John Wiley, 1997.

Hearn, Chester G. *Admiral David Glasgow Farragut: The Civil War Years*. Annapolis: Naval Institute Press, 1998.

Martin, Christopher. *Damn the Torpedoes: The Story of America's First Admiral, David Glasgow Farragut*. New York: Abelard Schuman, 1970.

Smith, Myron J. *Le Roy Fitch: The Civil War Career of a Union River Gunboat Commander*. Jefferson, N.C.: McFarland, 2007.

Tucker, Spencer C. *Andrew Foote: Civil War Admiral on the Western Waters*. Annapolis: Naval Institute Press, 2000.

Hoogenboom, Ari. *Gustavus Vasa Fox of the Union Navy: A Biography*. Johns Hopkins University Press, 2008.

Cornish, Dudley Taylor, and Virginia Jeans Laas. *Lincoln's Lee: The Life of Samuel Phillips Lee, U.S. Navy, 1812–1897*. Lawrence: University Press of Kansas, 1986.

Shingleton, Royce. *High Seas Confederate: The Life and Times of John Newland Maffitt*. Columbia: University of South Carolina Press, 1994.

Durkin, Joseph T. *Stephen R. Mallory: Confederate Navy Chief*. Chapel Hill: University of North Carolina Press, 1954.

Underwood, Rodman L. *Stephen Russell Mallory: A Biography*. Jefferson, N.C.: McFarland, 2005.

Williams, Frances Leigh. *Matthew Fontaine Maury: Scientist of the Sea*. New Brunswick, N.J.: Rutgers University Press, 1963.

Slagle, Jay. *Ironclad Captain: Seth Ledyard Phelps and the U.S. Navy, 1841–1864*. Kent, Ohio: Kent State University Press, 1996.

Hearn, Chester G. *Admiral David Dixon Porter: The Civil War Years*. Annapolis: Naval Institute Press, 1996.

West, Richard S., Jr. *The Second Admiral: A Life of David Dixon Porter*. New York: Coward McCann, 1937.

Johnson, Robert Erwin. *Rear Admiral John Rodgers, 1812–1882*. Annapolis: U.S. Naval Institute, 1967.

Taylor, John M. *Confederate Raider: Raphael Semmes of the* Alabama. Washington, D.C.: Brassey's, 1984.

Tucker, Spencer C. *Raphael Semmes and the* Alabama. Abilene, Tex.: McWhiney Foundation Press, 1996.

McKay, Gary. *The Sea King: The Life of James Iredell Waddell*. Edinburgh: Birlinn, 2009.

Niven, John. *Gideon Welles: Lincoln's Secretary of the Navy*. New York: Oxford University Press, 1973.

West, Richard S., Jr. *Gideon Welles: Lincoln's Navy Department*. Indianapolis: Bobbs-Merrill, 1943.

Shingleton, Royce C. *John Taylor Wood: Sea Ghost of the Confederacy*. Athens: University of Georgia Press, 1979.

Index

201–3; efforts to acquire ships in France, 203–4; buys *Shenandoah* and *Stonewall*, 222

Burnside, Ambrose E., 105; and capture of Roanoke Island, 2–3, 34, 50–51; capture of New Bern and Fort Macon, 53–54; operations in east Tennessee, 189

Bushnell, Cornelius, 98–99

Butler, Benjamin: and Fort Fisher, 8, 214–15; capture of Hatteras Inlet, 33; and New Orleans Campaign, 50, 57, 58, 65–66, 67; relieved by Banks, 126; and contrabands, 136; operations on James River, 198, 200; removed from command, 217

Cable, George Washington, 66

Cairo, USS, 5, 132

Caldwell, Charles H. B., 58–59

Canby, Edward, 207, 213

Carondelet, USS, 81, 92

Casco class of shallow-draft monitors, failure of, 206

Catskill, USS, 173

Cayuga, USS, 60–62, 65

Charleston, S.C.: failure of attack on, 5, 6, 146–48; plans to attack, 133, 134, 135, 138–45; Dahlgren's campaign against, 150, 172–81

Chase, Salmon P., 108

Chickasaw, USS, 207, 210–12

Chickasaw Bluffs, attack on, 132–33, 156

Cincinnati, USS, 85, 167

Collins, Napoleon, 205–6

Conestoga, USS, 70, 74

Congress, USS, 100–101, 103

"Contrabands," and Union navy, 135–39

Craven, Thomas T., 64, 223

Cumberland, USS, 29, 33, 86, 100

Cushing, William Barker, 185–86, 219

Dahlgren, John A.: campaign against Charleston, 6, 173–78; and Dahlgren gun, 42; promoted to rear

admiral, 149; named commander of South Atlantic Squadron, 150; on Lincoln and Vicksburg, 165; on the *H. L. Hunley*, 179; and Confederate torpedoes, 180–81

David, CSS, 178–79

Davis, Charles H., 136; secretary of Blockade Board, 35; and Port Royal Campaign, 38–39; and "stone fleet," 48; commands Western Flotilla, 69, 84; at Fort Pillow, 85; and Ellet's ram fleet, 86–88; Battle of Memphis, 88–89; at Vicksburg, 92; reluctant to attack CSS *Arkansas*, 93–94; withdraws from Vicksburg, 94–95, 154; skeptical of *Monitor*, 98–99

Davis, Henry Winter, 142

Davis, Jefferson, 1; orders firing on Fort Sumter, 19; offers letters of marque to privateers, 20; threatens retaliation for executed privateers, 21; denounces blockade, 47, 49; capture of, 221

Dewey, George, 64

Drayton, Percival: Unionism of, 13–14; and Port Royal Campaign, 38, 41, 42, 135; and attack on Charleston, 145, 148; at Battle of Mobile Bay, 210

Drayton, Thomas, 13, 41

Drewry's Bluff, and repulse of Union fleet, 4, 109–10, 141

Dudley, Thomas H., 113, 114, 202–3

Duncan, Johnston K., 58

Du Pont, Samuel Francis, 12, 84; and Battle of Port Royal, 2, 13, 37–42, 136; loyalty of, 11, 15; praises Gustavus Fox, 20; chairs Blockade Board, 35; commands South Atlantic Blockading Squadron, 35–36; occupies South Atlantic ports and estuaries, 42–44, 50; on problems and effectiveness of blockade, 47–49, 120, 122–23, 125; on Confederate commerce raiders, 116; and plans for attack on Charleston, 133, 135, 139–45; on slavery and freed slaves, 137–38; failure

Fort Fisher Campaign, 8, 213–19; commands *Powhatan*, 18, 24; and New Orleans Campaign, 56, 58, 61–62, 65, 66–67; and attack on Vicksburg in 1862, 89; criticizes Charles Davis, 95; commander of Mississippi Squadron, 131; and attack on Chickasaw Bluffs, 131–33; recruits black sailors, 136–37; antiguerrilla efforts of, 154–55, 187; capture of Arkansas Post, 156–57; and 1863 Vicksburg Campaign, 158–60, 163–69; and trade restrictions in Mississippi valley, 191–92

Porter, John L., 17

Porter, William D., 94

Port Hudson: campaign and capture of, 5, 157–58, 167, 169; Confederates fortify, 95; Farragut runs past, 160–63

Port Royal, campaign and battle of, 2, 13, 37–42, 135–36

Preble, Edward, 113

Preble, George H., 113–14

Powhatan, USS, 18–19

Privateers and privateering, 20–22

Queen of the West, USS: at Fort Pillow, 87; and Battle of Memphis, 88; fights with CSS *Arkansas*, 92, 94; captured by Confederates, 158–59; sunk by Union gunboat, 162–63

Read, Charles W., 152–53

Red River Campaign, 6, 187, 192–97, 207

Renshaw, William, 129

Rhind, Alexander, 214

Richmond, USS: attacked by CSS *Manassas*, 55–56, 96; and capture of New Orleans, 65–66; at Vicksburg, 92; attempt to pass Port Hudson, 160, 162

Ripley, Roswell, 137

River Defense Fleet (Confederate): attacks Union fleet at Fort Pillow, 82, 85; destroyed at Memphis, 88–89

Roanoke Island, Battle of, 3, 51, 75

Rodgers, John, 70–71, 109, 148

Roe, Francis, 60, 62

Rosecrans, William S., 187, 189

Rowan, Stephen C., and victories in North Carolina, 50–54

Ruffin, Edmund, 67

Russell, Lord John: on blockade, 26, 48–49; and *Trent* affair, 45; and escape of *Alabama*, 114; detention of *Alexandra*, 202

Sabine Pass, Battle of, 171–72

St. Louis, USS, 71, 77

Salt: Union navy destroys saltworks, 182–83

San Jacinto, USS, 44

Scott, Winfield, 5

Secessionville, Battle of, 139

Selfridge, Thomas, 132, 193

Semmes, Raphael: cruise of the *Sumter*, 22–24; cruise of the *Alabama*, 115–17; sinking of the USS *Hatteras*, 130; battle with *Kearsarge*, 204–5; commands James River Fleet, 220

Seward, William H., 33; writes naval orders, 16–17; directs *Powhatan* to Fort Pickens, 18; on blockade, 31; and *Trent* affair, 45–46; and Charles Wilkes, 111, 152; wants invasion of Texas, 170

Shenandoah, CSS, 222–23

Sherman, Thomas West, 38–39, 50

Sherman, William T., 1, 6; attacks Chickasaw Bluffs, 131–33, 163; capture of Arkansas Post, 156–57; and 1863 Vicksburg Campaign, 164–66; troops convoyed by navy, 190; and Red River Campaign, 192, 196; capture of Atlanta, 212; and fall of Charleston, 219

Shiloh, Battle of, 82

Ship Island, Union seizure of, 35, 36

Sinclair, George T., 104, 105

Slidell, John: and *Trent* affair, 44–46, 111; on Union blockade, 49; efforts to acquire ships in Europe, 204

discourages attack on Mobile in 1863, 126; doctrine of continuous transportation, 127–28; wants army to occupy Brownsville, 129; creates Mississippi Squadron, 131; and recruiting of black sailors, 136, 175; and Du Pont's attack on Charleston, 142, 144–46, 148–49; and promotion of Dahlgren, 149–50; relieves Du Pont and Wilkes, 152; on Farragut's passage of Port Hudson, 162; urges Porter to cooperate with Grant at Vicksburg, 165; and capture of Vicksburg, 169; and Sabine Pass, 171; on "Du Pont clique," 178; orders cessation of Charleston attacks, 180; orders S. P. Lee to Beaufort, 200; names Porter to lead Fort Fisher attack, 213–14, 220; orders alert for escape of Jefferson Davis, 221; and court-martial of Craven, 223; ability of, 224

Western Flotilla, 69; and capture of Fort Henry, 2; and Island No. 10, 3, 82; at Fort Pillow, 87; upgraded to Mississippi Squadron, 131

Wheeler, Joseph, 189

Whiting, William H. C., 201, 217, 219

Wilkes, Charles: seizure of Mason and Slidell, 44–46; commands James River Flotilla, 110–11; command of "flying squadron," 111–12; captures *Peterhoff*, 128; relieved of command, 152

Williamson, William P., 97

Wilmington, N.C.: proposals to attack, 133, 213; importance as blockade-running port, 181–82; capture of, 219

Winslow, John A., 204–5

Wool, John, 108, 109

Worden, John: commands *Monitor*, 99; wounded, 104, 107; commands *Montauk*, 144